Unequal Laws Unto a Savage Race:
EUROPEAN LEGAL TRADITIONS
IN ARKANSAS, 1686–1836

It little profits that an idle king,
By this still hearth, among these barren crags,
Match'd with an aged wife, I mete and dole
Unequal laws unto a savage race,
That hoard and sleep, and feed, and know not me.

TENNYSON, *Ulysses*

Unequal Laws Unto a

Morris S. Arnold

Savage Race: EUROPEAN LEGAL TRADITIONS IN ARKANSAS, 1686–1836

The University of Arkansas Press
Fayetteville
1985

The paper used in this publication meets the minimum requirements of the
American National Standard for Permanence of Paper for Printed Library
Materials Z39.48-1984. ∞™

Library of Congress Cataloging-in-Publication Data

Arnold, Morris S.
   Unequal laws unto a savage race.

   Includes index.
   1. Law—Arkansas—History and criticism.   I. Title.
KFA 3678.A76   1985   349.767'09   84-168
ISBN 0-938626-33-7   347.67009
ISBN 0-938626-76-0 (PBK.)

For Robert A. Leflar, teacher and friend

On the Akansa River there live, under the name of hunters, some men of whose pernicious customs I must give your Lordship a brief account. . . . [M]ost of those who live there have either deserted from the troops and ships of the most Christian King or have committed robberies, rape, or homicide, that river being the asylum of the most wicked persons, without doubt, in all the Indies. . . . In view of this I earnestly beg your Lordship please to order that this race, through despairing of all supplies, may be forced to abandon the river on which they reside.

Athanase de Mézières, Lieutenant Governor
of Louisiana, to Luis de Unzaga y Amezaga,
Governor of Louisiana, 1770

After having ascended forty miles [from the mouth of the Arkansas] I found the *Village des Arkansas* advantageously situated on the left bank. The *habitants*, nearly all originally French emigrants from Canada, are hunters by profession, and grow only corn for the nourishment of their horses and of a small number of oxen employed in plowing. More than half the year one finds in this village only women, children, and old people. The men go hunting . . . On their return home, they pass their time playing games, dancing, drinking, or doing nothing, similar in this as in other things to the savage peoples with whom they pass the greater part of their lives, whose habits and customs they acquire.

Perrin du Lac, 1802

Contents

List of Illustrations

Preface

I did not set out to write this book. Very soon after I
returned to Arkansas almost four years ago I visited the
Arkansas History Commission, curious about a phenome-
non of which I was then only dimly aware, namely the
legal transformation that occurred as the result of the Louisiana Purchase. Though not a civilian by training, I knew
that Arkansas, having been part of Louisiana, had therefore been at least nominally a civil-law jurisdiction; and
since receptions have long presented legal historians with
paradigms, it seemed natural to inquire what had happened to European legal traditions following the American
takeover of Arkansas in 1804. Frankly, however, the work
that culminated in this book began as an act of piety by a
native son who was motivated more by an antiquarian interest than by a serious and fully-formed scholarly intent.
But, after I availed myself of the historical materials surviving in Arkansas, my curiosity took me to St. Louis,
New Orleans, Paris, Seville, and London, and to half a
dozen places whose names most people would not recognize; and I hope that the facts exposed to view here carry a
lesson sufficiently transcendent to make this book count as
one that will help its readers understand how the broader
world works. For while Arkansas was the remotest part of
what was anyway a small European colony, the reception

there turns out to be in some respects as interesting as the one that occurred centuries earlier in northern Italy; and it possesses the immediacy that only a backyard can provide. With William Blake, we can look into a grain of sand and sometimes find the world.

Over the years many people have aided me in my search for sources and in my attempt to fashion a framework for understanding and organizing what I eventually found. Russell P. Baker at the Arkansas History Commission in Little Rock; Deborah Bolas of the Missouri Historical Society Library in St. Louis; Gary W. Beahan, the State Archivist of Missouri; Dr. Glen Conrad of the University of Southwestern Louisiana in Lafayette, Louisiana; and Dr. Steven Reinhardt of the Library of the Louisiana History Center of the Louisiana State Museum in New Orleans all gave an importuning neophyte the help he very much required. Sra. Rosario Parra, Director of the Archivo General de Indias in Seville, sent me photostats and transparencies with a promptness entirely unexpected, and her staff was equally attentive when I visited the Archive itself. For their friendly and efficient help I am also obliged to staff members at the Archives Nationales in Paris, the Archives Nationales, Section Outre-Mer in Paris, the Service Historique de la Marine in Paris, and the Institute of Advanced Legal Studies in London. Thanks are also due to Ellen Shipley at the Mullins Library in Fayetteville, Arkansas; Irene Moran at the Bancroft Library in Berkeley; Harriet McLoone at the Huntington Library in San Marino, California; and the staffs of the National Archives and the Library of Congress for supplying copies of documents and granting permission to use them. I have bored more scholars with questions about eighteenth-century Louisiana than there is space here to record, but special mention needs to be made of Professors Hans Baade, A. P. Nasatir, Marcel Giraud, Gilbert Din, Lawrence Kinnaird, Allan J. Kuethe, and Mr. Robert W. Dhonau, all of whom gave needed assistance. Caldwell Delancy provided a photograph of the seventeenth-century portrait of Henry de Tonti at the Museum of the History of Mobile; and Mr. and Mrs. Howard Stebbins of Little Rock have allowed me to reproduce their portraits of Captains Josef Vallière and Carlos de Villemont. Mrs. Dorothy Jones Core of Almyra, Arkansas, very generously spent many days educating me on the eighteenth- and nineteenth-century population of Arkansas. She is a learned woman and a good friend. Doug Inglis and Dianne Epstein helped me with the translation of some Spanish documents, and Missy Anderson, Jenelle Arnold, Louisa Barker, John Barker, Linda Oakley, and Professor W. A. J. Watson read and criticized the typescript. I have lately had the help of Samuel D. Dickinson, and he has saved me many errors.

Part of the material that appears in this book has been published previously. Chapter I appeared more or less in its present form in Arnold, *The Arkansas Colonial Legal System, 1686–1766*, 7 U. ARK. LITTLE ROCK L. J. 391 (1984); part of Chapter II was published in Arnold, *The Relocation of Arkansas Post to* Écores Rouges *in 1779*, 42 AHQ 317 (1983); and Appendix V appeared as Arnold, *An Early Opinion of an Arkansas Trial Court*, 5 U.A.L.R. LAW JOURNAL 397 (1982). My thanks to the Arkansas Historical Association and the U.A.L.R. Law Journal for permission to incorporate these articles into the present work.

This book proved expensive to write and to publish. The University of Arkansas at Little Rock, the Ben J. Altheimer Foundation, the Arkansas Endowment for the Humanities, the National Endowment for the Humanities, and the American Bar Foundation provided funds in very generous amounts to support my research. The Arkansas Endowment for the Humanities, the National Endowment for the Humanities, the Donaghey Foundation, and the Arkansas Bar Foundation subvened the costs of publication. I cannot adequately express my thanks to these foundations and institutions which, like me, thought that colonial Arkansas deserved at last to be outfitted with something like a reliable history.

Little Rock, Arkansas
July 25, 1984

List of Abbreviations

AGI, PC *Archivo General de Indias*, Seville. *Papeles Procedentes de Cuba*. Various *legajos* (bundles, abbreviated *leg.*) are cited.

AHQ ARKANSAS HISTORICAL QUARTERLY.

ANC, C¹³ᴬ *Archives Nationales*, Paris. *Archives Coloniales, Sous-série* (sub-series) C¹³ᴬ Various other sub-series are cited.

GPHSB GRAND PRAIRIE HISTORICAL SOCIETY BULLETIN.

LHQ LOUISIANA HISTORICAL QUARTERLY.

Prologue

Except for the silence of its final letter, there is nothing nowadays very French about Arkansas. Yet before the American takeover in 1804 the great majority of the European inhabitants of the area presently occupied by the state were of French origin. There is some visible proof of this in the names, many now mangled beyond easy recognition, which eighteenth-century *voyageurs* and *coureurs de bois* gave to a good many Arkansas places and streams;[1] and there are, as well, a number of Arkansas townships which bear the names of their early French *habitants*.[2]

1. *See generally*, Branner, *Some Old French Place Names in the State of Arkansas*, 19 AHQ 191 (1960). The etymology of some of these names is difficult and interesting. Who would guess very quickly, for instance, that Smackover in Union County is *Chemin Couvert* (covered way) in disguise? *See id.* at 206. Tchemanihaut Creek (pronounced "Shamanahaw") in Ashley County is a good deal easier: *Chemin à haut* (high road or upper road) must have been its original name. Its initial letter, one local historian has plausibly suggested, is probably attributable to "a misguided attempt to derive the name from the Indian language." Y. ETHERIDGE, HISTORY OF ASHLEY COUNTY, ARKANSAS 17, 18 (1959). Other names should on sight be instantly intelligible to a modern Parisian, though their current pronunciation might cause him consternation: Examples are the *Terre Rouge* (red earth) Creek in Nevada County, the *Terre Noir* (black earth) Creek in Clark County, the *L'Anguille* (eel) River in northeast Arkansas, and *La Grue* (crane) township in Arkansas County.

2. Vaugine and Bogy Townships in Jefferson County, Darysaw (Desruisseaux) Township in Grant County, and Fourche La Fave (Lefevre) Township in Perry County are good examples.

While these faint traces of a remote European past survive, absolutely nothing remains of the laws and customs which the ancient residents of Arkansas observed. This is no accident; it was Jefferson's desire to introduce the common law of England into the vast Louisiana Territory as quickly as he could. In the lower territory he waited too late. New Orleans had had a large French population and a somewhat professionalized legal system for some time, and the civilian opposition, given time, proved to have sufficient muscle to win a partial victory.[3] As a result, in regard to substantive civil matters, the state of Louisiana is today a thoroughly civilian jurisdiction. In the upper territory, however, by a piecemeal process beginning in 1804, the English common law was insinuated into the legal system until 1816, when it was at last adopted virtually wholesale by the General Assembly of the Missouri Territory.[4] This book tells the story of how the legal transformation in Upper Louisiana occurred and deals especially with its effects in Arkansas. So far as I know, it is the only full-length study which attempts to describe and interpret the clash of legal traditions in the northern reaches of Jefferson's Louisiana. No doubt its shortcomings are many and its failings serious, but it seemed to me that a pioneer effort was worth making. It is, at the least, an entertaining story: A cultural conflict of this sort could not fail to provide one.

3. *See generally*, G. DARGO, JEFFERSON'S LOUISIANA: POLITICS AND THE CLASH OF LEGAL TRADITIONS (1975).

4. 1 LAWS OF A PUBLIC AND GENERAL NATURE, OF THE DISTRICT OF LOUISIANA, OF THE TERRITORY OF LOUISIANA, OF THE TERRITORY OF MISSOURI, AND OF THE STATE OF MISSOURI, UP TO THE YEAR 1824 ch. 154 (1842).

I
French Legal Foundations
1686–1766

At ten o'clock on the morning of March 12, 1682, Robert Cavalier, Sieur de La Salle, having been commissioned four years earlier by Louis XIV of France to explore and take possession of the Mississippi and its tributaries, drew near the Quapaw village of Kappa. The village was located on the west bank of the Mississippi River about twenty miles north of the mouth of the Arkansas. From the war chants emanating from the Indian town La Salle judged that he was in for a hostile reception; so he hastily constructed a fort on an island opposite the village and awaited developments. Soon, however, the Quapaw chief sent the calumet of peace, and La Salle and his men went to Kappa where they were received with every possible demonstration of affection both public and private. Asked by the Quapaws for help against their enemies, La Salle promised that they could thenceforth look for protection to the greatest prince of the world, in whose behalf he had come to them and to all the other nations who lived along and around the river. In return, La Salle said, the Quapaws had to consent to the erection in their village of a column on which His Majesty's arms were to be painted, symbolizing their recognition that he was the master of their lands.

The Indians agreed and Henry de Tonti, La Salle's lieutenant and commandant of one of the two brigades in the

1. Henry de Tonti, lieutenant of La Salle. He founded Arkansas Post in 1686 and in the late seventeenth century styled himself *seigneur de ville de Tonti*. He was the first European to possess judicial authority in Arkansas. (*Courtesy of the Museum of the History of Mobile.*)

company, had the column made immediately. A cross and the arms of France were painted on it, and it bore these words: "Louis the Great, King of France and of Navarre, rules. 13th of March, 1682."

Tonti then conducted the column with all the French men-at-arms to the plaza of the village. With La Salle at the head of his brigade and Tonti at the head of his, the Reverend Father Zénobe Membré sang the hymn *O crux, ave, spes unica.* The company then went three times around the plaza, each time singing the psalm *Exaudiat te Dominus* and shouting *vive le roy* to the discharge of their muskets. They planted the column while repeating the cries of *vive le roy,* and La Salle, standing near the column and holding the king's commission in his hand, spoke in a loud voice the following words in French: "On behalf of the very high, very invincible, and victorious prince Louis the Great, by the grace of God, King of France and of Navarre, the fourteenth of this name, today, the 13th of March, 1682, with the consent of the nation of the Arkansas assembled at the village of Kappa and present at this place, in the name of the king and his allies, I, by virtue of the commission of His Majesty of which I am bearer and which I hold presently in my hand. . . , have taken possession in the name of His Majesty, his heirs, and the successors to his crown, of the country of Louisiana and of all the nations, mines, minerals, ports, harbors, seas, straits, and roadsteads, and of everything contained within the same. . . ."

After more musket-firing and the giving of presents the Indians celebrated their new alliance throughout the night, pressing their hands to the column and then rubbing their bodies in testimony to the joy which they felt in having made so advantageous a connection. Thus did France gain ownership of and sovereignty over Arkansas.

We know all these details and more about La Salle's activities in Arkansas because Jacques de La Metairie, the notary of Fort Frontenac who was in La Salle's company, produced a lengthy *procès-verbal* describing the events at Kappa and officially attesting their occurrence.[1] This was Arkansas's first exposure to civilian legal processes. It

---

1. 2 P. Margry, Découvertes et établissements des français dans l'ouest et dans le sud de l'Amérique septentrionale, 1614–1754, 181 (1881).

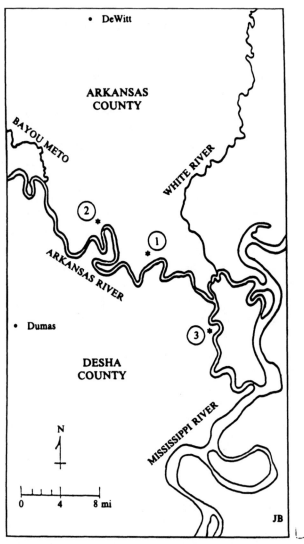

2. Locations of Arkansas Post, 1686–1985. (See Appendix II.)
   1. 1686–1699; 1721–1749.   2. 1749–1756; 1779–1985.
   3. 1756–1779.

(Based on a map drawn by John Baldwin which appeared in Arnold's, *The Relocation of Arkansas Post to* Écores Rouges *in 1779*, 42 AHQ 317 (1983). Used with permission of the Arkansas Historical Association.)

would be almost 150 years before the influence of the civil law ceased to make itself felt there.

I

Arkansas Post was the first European establishment in the lower Mississippi valley. It was first located about twenty-seven miles by river from the mouth of the Arkansas on the edge of Little Prairie at what is now called the Menard Site. Settled in 1686 by six tenants of Henry de Tonti to whom La Salle had granted the lower Arkansas as a seignory in 1682,[2] it was to serve as an Indian trading post and as an intermediate station between the Illinois country and the Gulf of Mexico.[3] Tonti's plans for the place had been large. In 1689 he promised the Jesuits that he would build a house and chapel at the Arkansas and grant a resident priest a sizeable amount of land; while there, Tonti confidently asserted, the priest could "come and say mass in the French quarter near our fort."[4]

However, no priest established himself during Tonti's ownership of the Arkansas and his French quarter and fort never materialized. When in an undated grant of land to Jacques Cardinal, one of his men at the Post, Tonti styled himself *seigneur de ville de Tonti* (lord of the town of Tonti),[5] he was in the grip of an excessive enthusiasm. There is no

2. See Faye, *The Arkansas Post of Louisiana: French Domination*, 26 LHQ 633 at 635–36 (1943).

3. Such was the view of Father Douay, a Jesuit who described Tonti's post in 1687. *See* M. Thomas, "The Arkansas Post of Louisiana, 1682–1783" (M.A. Thesis, University of California, 1948).

4. Tonti's grant to the Jesuits is quoted in 1 M. GIRAUD, HISTOIRE DE LA LOUISIANE FRANÇAISE 8, (J. LAMBERT trans., 1974).

5. The grant is translated in THE FRENCH FOUNDATIONS 396, (T. PEASE & R. WERNER, eds., 1934).

evidence that the European population of the place ever exceeded six. In fact, when Joutel arrived there in 1687 there were only two Frenchmen remaining in residence;[6] and the single log house he described is apparently the only structure ever erected at Tonti's Post. Joutel remarked of Tonti's two traders that "if I was joyous to find them, they participated in the joy since we left them the wherewithal to maintain themselves for some time." Indeed, he said, "they were almost as much in need of our help as we of theirs." He ridiculed the whole idea of a post at that location. "The said house," Joutel noted sarcastically, "was to serve as an *entrepôt* [way-station] for the French who travelled in these parts, but we were the only ones whom it so served."[7]

Short of supplies and virtually inaccessible, the tiny outpost never prospered. The war with the Iroquois closed the route to Canada and made trade to and from Arkansas impossible much of the time until 1693.[8] By 1696, Jean Couture, Tonti's lieutenant and commandant at the Post, had deserted to the English,[9] and in 1699 Jesuit missionaries to the Quapaws found no trace of a French settlement.[10] By then the French had evidently abandoned the Arkansas, though there may have remained behind a "few white savages thereabouts as wild as red savages."[11]

6. Faye, *supra* note 2, at 735.

7. JOUTEL, REMARQUES SUR L'OUVRAGE DE TONTI RELATIF À LA LOUISIANE (1703), Archives Service Hydrographique (Paris), vol. 115–9, no. 12 (Transcript in Little Rock Public Library). The translation in the text is mine.

8. Faye, *supra* note 2, at 638.

9. IBERVILLE'S GULF JOURNALS 144 at n. 98 (R. McWILLIAMS ed., 1950).

10. 18 COLLECTIONS OF THE WISCONSIN HISTORICAL SOCIETY 427 at n. 37 (1908).

11. Faye, *supra* note 2, at 646. *See also* 1 M. GIRAUD, *supra* note 4, at 8: "When d'Iberville reached the Mississippi [1699] the post had been abandoned." Some writers are reluctant to say that the Arkansas was

However grandiose and ambitious had been the schemes of Tonti, they would soon come to seem tame. In 1717 the *Mercure de France*, a Paris newspaper, began advertising the riches of Louisiana to its readers: Gold and silver could be mined there "with almost no labor." The mountains situated on the Arkansas River would be explored, and there, one correspondent exuded, "we shall gather, believe me, specimens from silver mines, since others already have gathered such there without trouble." When Cadillac sensibly protested that "the mines of the Arkansas were a dream" he was promptly committed to the Bastille "on suspicion of having spoken with scant propriety against the Government of France."[12]

The man behind the propaganda campaign was John Law, a Scot who owned a bank in Paris and who in 1717 had succeeded in securing for his *Compagnie d'Occident* a monopoly on Louisiana trade. Law's company recruited thousands of colonists to settle in Louisiana and the king gave it authority to grant land from the Royal domain. Since the interior of Louisiana was not well known, proprietors (*concessionaires*) of the company's land grants were given considerable latitude in choosing the spots for their settlements. They therefore exercised much discretion in locating their colonists on arrival.[13] The company had,

---

completely devoid of Europeans at this time. *See, e.g.*, P. HOLDER, ARCHAEOLOGICAL FIELD RESEARCH ON THE PROBLEM OF THE LOCATIONS OF ARKANSAS POST ARKANSAS 4 (1957): "The French occupation of the general area along the lower courses of the Arkansas and White Rivers was virtually continuous from the 1680's onward." The truth is that the sources simply fail to mention any Europeans in Arkansas, except Jesuit missionaries, between 1699 and 1721. It is, however, hard to resist believing that a few hunters and trappers ventured from time to time into the area and established temporary camps there, though almost certainly no real settlement existed.

12. Faye, *supra* note 2, at 653.

13. 4 M. GIRAUD, HISTOIRE DE LA LOUISIANE FRANÇAISE 198 (1974).

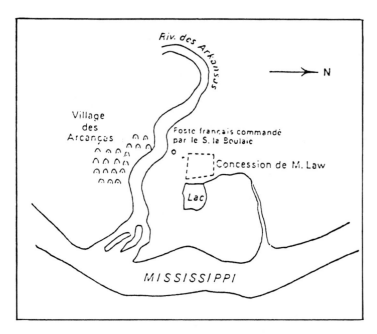

3. Sketch of the location of Law's colony by Dumont de Montigny, *Archives Nationales*, Paris, 6 JJ-75, Pièce 254.

however, recognized the Arkansas River as an important spot, since it was thought that it might well be the best route to the Spanish mines of Mexico. Thus, it specifically directed where the Arkansas concession should be located and ordered that it be the first occupied.[14] The company granted this concession to Law himself.

In August of 1721, a group of Law's French *engagés* (perhaps as many as eighty) took possession of land on Little Prairie at or near the site of Tonti's abandoned trading post.[15] Although Law was by then bankrupt and had fled France, the news did not reach Louisiana until after Jacques Levens, Law's director in Louisiana, had established the Arkansas colony under the command of some of his subordinates.[16] By December of that year Bertrand Dufresne.

14. *Id.*
15. *Id.*
16. *Id.* at 199.

Sieur du Demaine, replaced Levens as director for Arkansas and in March of 1722 he took possession of the concession and began an inventory of its effects and papers.[17] On his arrival he found only twenty cabins and three arpents (about 2.5 acres) of cleared ground. He reported a total of about fifty men and women resident,[18] *tristes débris*, Father Charlevoix called them,[19] of Law's concession. They had produced an insignificant harvest. Lieutenant La Boulaye was nearby with a military detachment of seventeen men.[20] Despite the existence of a company store at the Arkansas concession, both the colony and the military establishment were in considerable difficulty.[21] Dufresne therefore immediately released twenty of the *engagés* from service and gave them lots to cultivate in the hopes of a better harvest of corn and wheat in 1722. In February of the following year there were only forty-one colonists remaining, divided into two small farming communities: Fourteen men and one woman at Law's concession under Dufresne, and sixteen men, some with families, two leagues up the river with the troops. Among this latter group there lived six black slaves.[22] Bénard de La Harpe, while exploring the river in 1721, had predicted, or at least hoped for, a turn in the fortunes of the struggling colony, but that hope proved false and in 1727 Father Paul Du Poisson, the Jesuit missionary to the Arkansas, reported that only about thirty Frenchmen remained behind.[23] The military post had been

17. *Id.* at 271.
18. *Id.* at 272.
19. 6 P. DE CHARLEVOIX, JOURNAL D'UN VOYAGE FAIT PAR ORDRE DU ROI DANS L'AMÉRIQUE SEPTENTRIONALE 164 (1744).
20. 4 M. GIRAUD, *supra* note 13, at 273.
21. Based on *id.* at 273–74.
22. *Recensement General des Habitans Establys à Sotehouy Arkansas et des Ouvriers de la Concession cy devant Apartenant à M. Law,* 18 February, 1723. (Transcript at Louisiana History Center, Louisiana State Museum, New Orleans.)
23. Du Poisson to Father ———, translated in Falconer, *Arkansas and*

abandoned two years previous.[24]

This seems worth recounting in some detail because for generations Arkansas historians have believed that a colony of Germans once occupied their river. Law did recruit many Germans for settlement in Louisiana, and they were destined for the Arkansas, but as soon as the news of Law's bankruptcy reached the colony in June 1721, the *Compagnie des Indies* took over the direction of his concession;[25] and when the time arrived to transport the German immigrants to Arkansas, the company, in an economy move, decided instead to send them to Delaire's grant in Lower Louisiana.[26] In short, none of Law's Germans ever reached Arkansas. This is a pity, as the prospect of discussing, or at least imagining, a group of German immigrants living under French law on the Arkansas River is an intriguing one—one of which the facts have now unfortunately deprived us.

II

Before 1712, the colony of Louisiana, with a population of only a few hundred, had been entirely under military rule. On September 19, 1712, the Crown granted a trade monopoly to Antoine Crozat, but he was given no governmental authority: As Henry Dart noted, the charter was "only an operating contract with the duties of government retained in the Crown."[27] However, the charter did

---

the Jesuits in 1727—A Translation, 4 PUBLICATIONS ARK. HIST. ASSOC. 352 at 375 (1917).

24. Faye, *supra* note 2, at 670.
25. 4 M. GIRAUD, *supra* note 13, at 216.
26. *Id.* at 248.
27. Dart, *The Legal Institutions of Louisiana*, 3 SOUTHERN LAW QUAR-

adopt as law for the colony "*nos Edits, Ordonnances Et Coutumes Et les usages de la Prevosté Et Vicomté de Paris*" ("our edicts, ordinances, and customs, and the usages of the Provostry and Viscounty of Paris").[28] The *Coutume*, despite its name, was actually a small code of some 362 titles first reduced to writing in 1510,[29] and treating both substantive and adjective law. It was itself terse, indeed epigrammatic; but by the time of its adoption in Louisiana the commentary on it was voluminous.[30] Annotated versions of the *Coutume* were therefore very popular in France and in time they found their way to Louisiana.[31]

Also in 1712, by a separate instrument, a new and important institution was created for the colony, the Superior Council of Louisiana.[32] Modelled on the governmental arrangements already in place in other French colonies, the Council had original and exclusive jurisdiction to decide disputes arising anywhere in Louisiana. This council consisted of the Lieutenant General of New France, the Intendant of the same, the Governor of Louisiana, a first councilor of the king, two other councilors, the attorney general, and a clerk. Judgments in civil cases required the

TERLY 247 (1918). This article also appears in 2 LHQ 72 (1919).

28. The charter is printed in 4 PUBLICATIONS LA. HIST. SOC. 13 at 17 (1908).

29. For a *précis* of its provisions, title by title, *See* Schmidt, *History of the Jurisprudence of Louisiana*, 1 LA. LAW JOURNAL, no. 1, 1 (1841).

30. The most useful eighteenth-century commentary is C. FERRIÈRE, COMMENTAIRE SUR LA COUTUME DE LA PREVOTÉ ET VICOMTÉ DE PARIS. It is available in several editions.

31. Dart, *The Law Library of a Louisiana Lawyer in the 18th Century*, 25 REPORTS OF THE LOUISIANA BAR ASSOCIATION 12 at 22 *et seqq.* (1924).

32. *See* Dart, *supra* note 27, at 249 *et seq. See also*, for some discussion of the work of this body, Hardy, *The Superior Council in Colonial Louisiana*, in FRENCHMEN AND FRENCH WAYS IN THE MISSISSIPPI VALLEY 87 (J. MCDERMOTT ed., 1969); Micelle, *From Law Court to Local Government: Metamorphosis of the Superior Council of French Louisiana*, 9 LA. HIST. 85 (1968).

concurrence of at least three members, and in criminal cases of at least five. The Council was originally created to exist for three years, but on September 7, 1716, it became by virtue of a Royal Edict a permanent institution.[33] In 1717 a fundamental change occurred in the government of Louisiana. In that year Crozat, having lost an enormous sum under his operating charter, surrendered it, and John Law's *Compagnie d'Occident* was given a monopoly over trade in the colony. Unlike Crozat's company, the *Compagnie d'Occident* was granted extensive governmental authority: It had the power to appoint the Superior Council, to name governors and military commandants, and to appoint and remove all judges. The charter also provided that "*Seront tous les juges Etablis en tous les d. Lieux tenus de juger suivant les Loix Et ordonnances du Royaume Et se Conformer a la Coutume de la Prevosté Et Vicomté de Paris*" ("all the judges established in all the said places shall be bound to judge according to the laws and ordinances of the realm, and [shall also be bound] to conform to the customs of the Provostry and Viscounty of Paris").[34] This portion of the charter obviously provided for the reception of general French legislation and the *Coutume de Paris*. In addition, it has been shown that subsequent French legislation, as soon as it was registered in the colony, and the legislation of the Superior Council itself, formed part of the body of colonial Louisiana law.[35] The subsequent French legislation was of three distinct sorts: General legislation, special colonial legislation, and colonial legislation passed specifically for Louisiana.[36]

33. The edict is printed in 4 PUBLICATIONS LA. HIST. SOC. 21–23 (1908).
34. *Id.* at 48.
35. Baade, *Marriage Contracts in French and Spanish Louisiana: A study in "Notarial" Jurisprudence,* 53 TULANE L. REV. 1 at 9 (1978).
36. *Id.*

Two years later inferior courts for outlying portions of the colony are mentioned for the first time. On September 12, 1719, the king noted the need to appoint persons to act as judges "to facilitate the administration of justice in places distant from the place where the Superior Council holds its sessions."[37] The "heads or directors" of concessions along with "other of our subjects, capable and of probity" were to "exercise both civil and criminal justice." The edict went on to provide that, even in these inferior courts, "three judges shall sit in civil matters and in criminal matters five judges. . . ." The plan, evidently, was to have a kind of provincial council at each settlement. The king further provided that an appeal from these local tribunals would lie in all cases to the Superior Council.[38] All this was being done, of course, to make ready the way for Law's colonizing schemes.

In 1720 or 1721 Louisiana was divided for the first time into districts (or counties). Arkansas was one of the nine districts originally created, and a local "commandant and judge" were assigned to each "to put justice with greater ease in reach of the colonists."[39] Presumably, and understandably, the plan to establish local councils outside New Orleans was abandoned at this time. The sources simply fail to say whether more than one person was expected to sit on local courts, but it could not have proved workable

---

37. The edict is printed in 4 PUBLICATIONS LA. HIST. SOC. 63 (1908).
38. The translation in the text is mine. The entire edict is translated and discussed in Dart, *supra* note 27, at 261 *et seqq.* Further discussion of this edict can be found in Dart, *The Colonial Legal Systems of Arkansas, Louisiana, and Texas*, 27 REPORTS OF THE LOUISIANA BAR ASSOCIATION 43 at 52 (1926).
39. *Id.* at 267. The other districts were New Orleans, Biloxi, Mobile, Alibamous, Natchez, Yazoo, Natchitoches, and the Illinois. It is not clear whether the commandant and the judge were to be the same person.

in remote places like Arkansas to assemble a multi-member judicial body.

In May of 1722 the Regent issued an order creating a provincial council for Illinois, the jurisdiction of which supposedly extended from "all places on and above the Arkansas River. . . to the boundaries of the Wabash River." The commandant of the Illinois, Lieutenant De Boisbriant, was to serve as "chief and judge" of this council, and three other persons were assigned to sit on it.[40] It thus seems to have been the plan to abolish the Arkansas district and annex its territory to its nearest northern neighbor; and the Illinois provincial council was directed "to hold its sessions at the places where the principal factories of the company shall be established."[41] This language could have been construed to require the Illinois council to sit at the Arkansas. It is, however, very much to be doubted that such a session was ever held, and certainly it is not believable that in 1722 anyone would repair from Arkansas to Illinois to settle a grievance.

It seems probable, then, that whatever judicial functions were exercised at the Arkansas were entrusted to its resident directors even after the supposed creation of the council of the Illinois. The only resident director that the Arkansas ever had was Bertrand Dufresne, Sieur du Demaine, who arrived at the Post on March 22, 1722, and he was evidently the judge from that time on. Prior to that, Jacques Levens had been director, but as he never took up residence in Arkansas, we have to presume that if judicial functions were undertaken by anyone, it was by one or more of the three subordinates to whom Levens had en-

40. Translated extracts from this order appear in 2 J. WHITE, A NEW COLLECTION OF LAWS, CHARTERS, AND LOCAL ORDINANCES OF THE GOVERNMENTS OF GREAT BRITAIN, FRANCE, AND SPAIN, RELATING TO THE CONCESSION OF LAND IN THEIR RESPECTIVE COLONIES 439–40 (1837).

41. *Id.* at 440.

trusted the management of the struggling colony: Jean-Baptiste Ménard, Martin Merrick, and Labro.[42] When Dufresne left the Arkansas around 1726, it is hard to guess the means resorted to for the settlement of disputes. Probably Father Paul du Poisson, the Jesuit missionary resident from 1727 to 1729, used his good offices to maintain order among the approximately thirty Frenchmen who had remained behind.[43]

It seems probable, therefore, that Arkansas's first sustained exposure to European legal proceedings and principles occurred in the period during which Law's company held sway in Louisiana. Tonti's seventeenth-century feudal seignory no doubt carried with it the right to render justice. Though his charter from La Salle has not as yet come to light,[44] other conveyances of La Salle's are extant; and in them he gave his grantees judicial power over small cases (this is called "low justice") while specifically reserving important cases ("high justice") to himself. (Cases of the latter type he directed to be heard by the judge "who shall be established at Fort St. Louis.")[45] We do not know whether Tonti's charter contained identical provisions, but it certainly would have contained similar ones. During the fifteen years or so that Tonti held the right to dispose of cer-

42. 4 M Giraud, *supra* note 13, at 272. Menard left the Arkansas in 1722 (*id*. at 275) and was in New Orleans in 1720. *Index to the Records of the Superior Council of Louisiana*, 4 LHQ 349 (1921).

43. Dufresne appears in the Arkansas census of January 1, 1726; but on October 21, 1726, he is described as a "settler in Arkansas, but now domiciled with Mr. Traguidy [in New Orleans]." *Index to the Records of Superior Council in New Orleans*, 3 LHQ 420 (1920). In 1727 there was no director at the Arkansas, as Father Du Poisson tells us that he took up residence in "the India Company's house, which is also that of the commandants when there are any here. . . ." *See* Falconer, *supra* note 23, at 371.

44. For a charter from Tonti to Jacques Cardinal, one of his men at the Arkansas, *see* THE FRENCH FOUNDATIONS, *supra* note 5, at 396.

45. Concession in fee by La Salle to Pierre Prudhomme, in *id*. at 32.

tain cases arising in his seignory, however, it hardly seems credible that he or his deputies ever held anything resembling a court, or even executed many instruments or documents.[46]

III

In 1731 the *Compagnie d'Occident* surrendered its charter to Louis XV, and for the rest of the period of French dominion Louisiana was a Crown Colony. Late that same year a military garrison was re-established in Arkansas; it consisted of twelve men commanded by First Ensign De Coulange and was located again on the edge of Little Prairie.[47] (*See* Illustration 2.) It was apparently during the reorganization of the colony in 1731 that civil and military authority at the outposts of Louisiana were combined in the commandant of the garrison—an arrangement that would survive into the Spanish period and even for a short time during the American regime.

46. When Tonti petitioned for confirmation of his charter, he was evidently refused. The petition is printed in E. MURPHEY, HENRY DE TONTI, FUR TRADER OF THE MISSISSIPPI 119 (1941). It is possible that La Salle did not have the power to make permanent grants and that may be the reason that Tonti needed confirmation. The Letters Patent of May 12, 1678, giving La Salle the right to explore "the western part of New France" in the king's behalf, also gave him the power to build forts wherever he deemed them necessary; and he was "to hold them on the same terms and conditions as Fort Frontenac." *See* T. FALCONER, ON THE DISCOVERY OF THE MISSISSIPPI 19 (1844). La Salle said expressly in 1683 that this allowed him to "divide with the French and the Indians both the lands and the commerce of said country until it may please his majesty to command otherwise. . . ." *See* THE FRENCH FOUNDATIONS, *supra* note 5, at 43. The language is ambiguous, but on one permissible reading it indicates a specifically reserved power in the king to revoke grants made by La Salle.

47. Faye, *supra* note 2, at 673.

Part of a post commandant's civil authority was to act as notary and judge. The exact scope of his judicial jurisdiction during the French period is obscure, there apparently being no document that describes it specifically. Parkman, writing of conditions in the Illinois in 1764, says that the "military commandant whose station was at Fort Chartres on the Mississippi, ruled the Colony with a sway as absolute as that of the Pasha of Egypt, and judged civil and criminal cases without right of appeal."[48] Captain Philip Pittman, an English engineer and Mississippi explorer who wrote about 1765, gives a slightly different version. According to him, the Illinois commandant "was absolute in authority, except in matters of life and death; capital offences were tried by the council at New Orleans."[49] Of course, the Arkansas commandant's judicial jurisdiction was not necessarily as extensive as that possessed by the commandant of the Illinois. He may very well have been subordinate to the Illinois commandant during most of the French period.

Some fitful light is thrown on the judicial authority of the Arkansas commandant by an interesting proceeding which took place at the Post in 1743.[50] In October of that year, Anne Catherine Chenalenne, the widow of Jean François Lepine, petitioned Lieutenant Jean-François Tisserant de Montcharvaux, whom she styled "Commandant for the King at the Fort of Arkansas," asking him to cause an inventory and appraisal to be made of the community property in her possession. The widow wished to make a distribution to her son-in-law and daughter who had lost all their goods the previous May when attacked by Chickasaws on the Mississippi not far below the mouth of the

---

48. Quoted in Dart, *supra* note 27, at 249.

49. P. PITTMAN, THE PRESENT STATE OF THE EUROPEAN SETTLEMENT ON THE MISSISSIPPI 53 (1770) (Reprinted with intro. by R. REA 1973).

50. The relevant documents are translated in Core, *Arkansas through the Looking Glass of 1743 Documents*, 22 GPHSB 16 (1979).

Arkansas. They had narrowly escaped with their lives.[51] Widow Lepine had decided to make a distribution to "her poor children, at least to those who have run so much risk among the savages." She was preparing to marry Charles Lincto, a well-to-do resident of the Post, and she wished to dissolve the old community which by custom had continued in her and her children after her husband's death.

The commandant informed Madame Lepine that on October 26, 1743, he would inventory the "real and personal property derived from the marital community" and would bring with him two persons to look after the widow's interest and two to represent the children. The idea was that each party in interest should have independent appraisers present to insure the impartiality of the inventory and evaluation. De Montcharvaux in the presence of these and other witnesses made the inventory on the appointed day. The estate was fairly sizeable, being valued at 14,530 *livres* and 10 *sols*. It contained a great deal of personalty (movables), including four slaves, a number of animals, 1600 pounds of tobacco, and notes and accounts receivable; the realty (immovables) noted was "an old house" with three small outbuildings. Interestingly, no land was mentioned.

There are two possible explanations for the absence of land in the inventory. One is that land may not have been actually granted to Arkansas settlers but only given over temporarily to their use. The other possibility is that the land on which the house was built had belonged to Lepine before the marriage and had remained his separate property under his marriage contract or under the general provisions of the *Coutume de Paris*. The *Coutume*, which was in force in French Louisiana, provided that all movables belonging to a husband or wife, whenever acquired, became part of the community; but only certain immovables

51. This incident is reported and discussed in Faye, *supra* note 2, at 677–78.

acquired after the marriage were so treated.[52] This rule could be altered by contract, but in Louisiana, as in France, the *Coutume* was often specifically incorporated into marriage contracts by future spouses in defining the regime that would rule their property;[53] if there was no contract provision creating a property regime, the *Coutume* automatically applied.

The inventory is said to have been made "*Pardevant nous Jean Francois Tisserant Ecuyer Sieur Demoncharvaus Commandant pour le Roy au Fort des Arkansas.*" The formula *pardevant nous* ("before us") is Parisian notarial boiler-plate and indicates that the commandant was acting in his surrogate notarial capacity. To an American common lawyer, the notary is not a member of the legal profession, not even a paralegal. But in seventeenth- and eighteenth-century France he enjoyed a much more elevated status, as indeed he still does in that country. Originally an official of the medieval European ecclesiastical courts, the notary developed into a noncontentious secular legal professional in France. In England, partly because the canon and secular laws were not on speaking terms, "the notarial system never took deep root."[54] For one thing, an important aspect of the notary's duties, his authority to "authenticate" documents, was of little use to the English. The whole notion of a state-sanctioned authenticator of private acts was entirely foreign to English common law; whereas in France we see notaries "making" and "passing" contracts, the common law left that to the parties. The state was very much in the background in England, and was called upon only to enforce obligations that arose by force of nature. The other aspects of the French notary's duties—the

52. *See* Baade, *supra* note 35, at 7, 8.
53. Id. at 25.
54. 1 F. POLLOCK & F. MAITLAND, A HISTORY OF ENGLISH LAW 218 (2nd ed., reissued with intro. by S. MILSOM 1968).

drafting of instruments, conveyancing, and the giving of legal advice—came to be performed by the regular legal profession in England. In sixteenth-century London a scriveners' company was organized and it was granted a charter in the reign of James I.[55] Members were empowered to draft legal documents, especially obligations (or bonds), and they gave a certain amount of low-level legal advice, particularly in commercial and banking matters.[56] The few secular notaries who practiced in London at that time concerned themselves mainly with drafting documents relevant to international trade, and they were members of this company.[57] But in the eighteenth century the company lost its effort to keep common-law attorneys from competing and in 1804 parliament made conveyancing the monopoly of the regular legal profession.[58] In contrast, the eighteenth-century French notary's duties had come to include not only the familiar ones of administering oaths, taking acknowledgments, and giving "authenticity" to "acts" of private persons by attesting them officially, but they also ran generally to the drafting of documents, conveyancing, and the giving of practical legal advice.[59] It is not surprising, therefore, that notaries would make an appearance in eighteenth-century Louisiana. In New Or-

---

55. *See* 12 W. HOLDSWORTH, A HISTORY OF ENGLISH LAW 70 (1938). *See generally*, on the notary in England, Gutteridge, *The Origin and Development of the Profession of Notaries Public in England*, in CAMBRIDGE LEGAL ESSAYS 12 (1926).

56. 12 W. HOLDSWORTH, *supra* note 55, at *id.*

57. 5 *id.* at 115 (3d ed. 1945).

58. 12 *id.* at 71–72 (1938); T. PLUCKNETT, A CONCISE HISTORY OF THE COMMON LAW 227–28 (5th ed. 1956).

59. As draftman of wills, marriage contracts, and conveyances, *Mons. le Notaire* has survived in France as a much respected person, especially in the country villages. He is a general non-forensic legal practitioner, his part in the legal scheme "being confined to voluntary as distinct from contentious jurisdiction." Brown, *The office of Notary in France*, 2 INTERNATIONAL COMPARATIVE LAW QUARTERLY 60 at 64 (1953).

leans, of course, there was much work for them, but there were also provincial notaries operating in Biloxi, Mobile, Natchitoches, Pointe Coupée, and Kaskaskia.[60] Since De Montcharvaux acted as notary for the Lepine inventory, it is reasonably clear that there was no provincial notary resident at the Arkansas at that time. This comes as no surprise since in 1746 there were at the Post only twelve *habitant* families, ten slaves, and twenty men in the garrison,[61] hardly a sufficient population to require or at-

Indeed, the French notary is close to the equivalent of the English solicitor, except for the latter's participation in litigation. Thus one modern-day commentator opined that "a solicitor would feel much at home in the *étude* of the French notary, though he would be surprised, and perhaps disappointed, by the cordiality of the morning post." *Id.* at 71.

Today in Louisiana as well the notary enjoys considerable powers. *See* Burke & Fox, *The Notaire in North America: A Short Study of the Adaptation of a Civil Law Institution*, 50 TULANE L. REV. 318 at 328–32 (1975); Brosman, *Louisiana—An Accidental Experiment in Fusion*, 24 TULANE L. REV. 95, 98–99 (1949). The Louisiana notary has the power "to make inventories, appraisements, and petitions; to receive wills, make protests, matrimonial contracts, conveyances, and generally, all contracts and instruments of writing; to hold family meetings and meetings of creditors; . . . to affix the seals upon the effects of deceased persons and to raise the same." LA. STAT. ANN. § 35:2 (1964). When the Louisiana legislature defined the practice of law, and prohibited all but licensed attorneys from engaging in it, it therefore remembered to except acts performed by the notary which were "necessary or incidental to the exercise of the powers and functions of [his] office." LA. STAT. ANN. § 37:212(B)(1974). A walk through modern-day New Orleans will reveal a number of signs proclaiming the existence of "Law and Notarial Offices," a combination having an odd ring in the ears of an American common lawyer. The Louisiana notary is simply "a different and more important official person than is the notary public in other jurisdictions of the United States." Brosman, *supra*, at 98.

60. *See* Baade, *supra* note 35, at 12.

61. *Mémoire sur l'État de la Colonie de la Louisiane en 1746.* ANC, C[13A] 30:242–281, at 249 (Transcript in Little Rock Public Library). As the average family size in Arkansas in the middle of the eighteenth century was about four, this would put the number of habitant whites at the

tract a law-trained scrivener. When it was time to have
their marriage contract made, the widow Chenalenne and
her future spouse executed it in New Orleans. No doubt
legal advice on which they might more comfortably rely
was available there.[62] Besides, at that time there was no
resident priest at the Post to perform the marriage.

IV

On May 10, 1749, an event occurred that considerably
reduced the European population of Arkansas and also
made it difficult to attract settlers there for some time. On
that day, the Post was attacked by a group of about 150
Chickasaw and Abeka warriors. Their coming was un-
detected[63] and thus they caught the small *habitant* population altogether unaware. They burned the settlement, killed
six male settlers, and took eight women and children as
slaves.[64] The census taken later that year shows, not surprisingly, that the population had decreased since the previous census. Seven men, eight women, eight boys, and
eight girls remained, a total of only thirty-one white *habi-*

Post at about forty-eight.

62. For an abstract of this marriage contract, *see Records of the Superior Council of Louisiana*, 13 LHQ 129 (1944).

63. However, the *habitants* may have had a warning that something
was afoot, for on May 1 François Sarrazin had written from Arkansas
that "two savages have killed a man and a woman and burnt a man
in the frame." *Records of the Superior Council of Louisiana*, 20 LHQ 505
(1937). This incident may have been connected with the attack nine days
later.

64. Vaudreuil to Rouille, September 22, 1749, calendared in THE
VAUDREUIL PAPERS 59–60 (B. BARRON ed., 1975). *See also*, Faye, *supra*
note 2, at 684 *et seqq*. W. BAIRD, THE QUAPAW INDIANS: A HISTORY OF
THE DOWNSTREAM PEOPLE 34 (1980) gives the number taken as slaves as
thirteen.

tants at the *Poste des Akansa.*[65] Nor did all this mark an end to serious trouble. When in June of 1751 First Ensign Louis-Xavier-Martin Delinó de Chalmette, the commandant of the Post, went uninvited to New Orleans to consult with the governor, his entire garrison of six men took the opportunity to desert.[66] Things were obviously at a critical juncture.

When later in 1751 Lieutenant Paul Augustin le Pelletier de La Houssaye took command at Arkansas he found there a post recently rebuilt by its *habitants* and *voyageurs* and probably already relocated to a spot ten or twelve miles upriver at the edge of the Grand Prairie. It is clear that Governor Vaudreuil had determined to hold the Arkansas even if the cost proved high, for he assigned to La Houssaye a large company of forty-five men.[67] The lieutenant was also authorized to build a new fort; government funds being lacking, he undertook the construction at his own expense in return for a five-year Indian trade monopoly.[68]

This new beginning could, in the nature of things, have given only a slight lift to the prospects for sustained settlement in the Arkansas country. Late in 1752 Governor Vaudreuil was informed that the Osages had attempted an attack on Arkansas Post but had failed.[69] While this indicates a stability of sorts for the Post, thanks no doubt to the size of the new garrison, still the perceived danger must have been so high as to discourage all but the most intrepid from taking up residence at the Arkansas. Mentions of

65. Arkansas Post Census, 1749. Loudon Papers 200, Huntington Library. There were also fourteen slaves resident at the post and sixteen *voyageurs* who had returned after their winter's work. There were five hunters on the White River and four on the St. Francis. Thirty-five hunters had failed to return from the Arkansas River.

66. Faye, *supra* note 2, at 708.

67. *Id.* at 211.

68. *Id.*

69. THE VAUDREUIL PAPERS, *supra* note 64, at 136.

Arkansas in the legal records tend to emphasize the dangerousness of the place. For instance, a Pointe Coupée couple, on the verge of leaving for a hunting trip to the White River country, thought it best to deed their property to a relative, with the stipulation that the deed was to be void if they returned.[70] It is not surprising, therefore, that even as late as 1766, the last year of French dominion, only eight *habitant* families, consisting in all of forty white persons, were resident at Arkansas Post.[71]

All of these difficulties, and others, made for a place in which it might be regarded as too polite to expect the presence of much which corresponds to a legal system. In addition, political exigencies sometimes interfered to such an extent that the application of even-handed legal principle became inexpedient and thus entirely impracticable. For instance, the continued existence of the Arkansas settlement depended heavily on the loyalty of the Quapaws and their wishes were therefore relevant to any important decision made there. Their influence could extend even to the operation of the legal system as the following incident demonstrates.

On September 12, 1756, a meeting was held in the Government House in New Orleans to hear an extraordinary request from Guedetonguay, the Medal Chief of the Quapaws.[72] His tribe had captured four deserters from the Arkansas garrison and had returned them; but the chief had come on behalf of his nation to ask Governor Kerlérec to pardon the soldiers. In addition to having deserted, one

70. *Index to the Records of the Superior Council of Louisiana*, 24 LHQ 75 (1941).

71. *See* Din, *Arkansas Post in the American Revolution*, 40 AHQ 3, at 4 (1980).

72. What follows is based on a memorandum entitled "*Harangues faites dans l'assemblée tenue à l'hôtel du gouvernment cejourdhui, 20 Juin 1756*," found in ANC, C¹³ᴬ 39:177–180 (Transcript in Little Rock Public Library). The translations are mine.

of those captured, Jean Baptiste Bernard, had killed his corporal Jean Nicolet within the precincts of the fort. The chief, obviously a great orator, said that he had come a long distance to plead for the soldiers' lives despite the heat and the demands of the harvest; and in his peroration he said that his head hung low, his eyes were fixed to the ground, and his heart wept for these men. He knew, he explained, that if he had not come they would have been executed, and this was intolerable to him because he regarded them as his own children. He recited many friendly acts of the Quapaws to prove the fidelity of his people to the French. Among them was the release of six slaves (perhaps Chickasaws captured by the Quapaws) "who would have been burned" otherwise, and the recent capture of five Choctaws and two trespassing Englishmen. He himself, he noted, had recently lost one son and had had another wounded in the war against the Chickasaws; and he counted this "a mark of affection for the French." In recompense he asked for the pardon of the soldiers. The chief added that this was the only such pardon his nation had thus far requested, and he promised never to ask again. He did not doubt that Kerlérec, "the great chief of the French, father of the red men," charged to govern them on behalf of the "great chief of all the French who lived in the great town on the other side of the great lake," would listen and do the just thing.

Guedetonguay left his best argument for last. He maintained vigorously that, under his law, any criminal who managed to reach the refuge of the *Cabanne de Valeur* where the Quapaws practiced their religious rites was regarded as having been absolved of his crime. It was their custom everywhere that the chief of the *Cabanne de Valeur* "would sooner lose his life than suffer the refugee to undergo punishment for his crime." Evidently the soldiers were claiming this right; and Ouyayonsas, the chief of the *Cabanne de Valeur*, was there to back them up. This last argument was an excellent one because it called upon the French to recognize an established Indian usage not dissimilar from the European custom of sanctuary. And the argument carried with it a threat of violent reaction if the custom were not allowed.

Kerlérec answered the chief that he was not unmindful of the past services of the Quapaws, nor was he ungrateful for them. "But," he said, "I cannot change the words declared by the great chief of all the French against such crimes, and . . . it would be a great abuse for the future" to pardon the soldiers. "So," he continued, "despite all the friendship that the French have for you and your nation, these men deserve death."

The great chief stood for a long time with his head down and finally answered ominously that he could not be responsible for the revolutions which the chief of the privileged house might stir up—revolutions which he said "would not fail to occur." The argument continued and the governor offered to grant the chief "anything else except these four pardons." But Guedetonguay stubbornly maintained that "the sole purpose of his journey was to obtain the pardon of the four men." In the end the Governor extracted from the Quapaw chiefs "publicly and formally their word . . . that they would in the future deliver up all deserting soldiers as malefactors or other guilty persons without any restriction or condition whatsoever, and that . . . pardons would be accorded at the sole discretion of the French."

No immediate decision was reached by the Governor, but later that day some of his advisors, having reflected on what they had heard, reckoned "that a refusal of the obstinate demands of these chiefs . . . the faithful allies of the French would only involve the colony in troublesome upheavals on the part of the said nations who have otherwise up to the present served very faithfully." They concluded that "saving a better idea by Monsieur le Gouverneur it would be dangerous, under all the present circumstances, not to satisfy the Indians with the pardons which they demanded." The governor took the advice but evidently did not write of the event to Berryer, the French Minister of the Marine, for some time. From the comfort of Versailles it was easy for Berryer to pick at Kerlérec's decision.[73] In responding to Kerlérec, Berryer first made the point that Bernard's case was different from that of the other captured soldiers since he was accused of homicide in addition to desertion. Then, too, the minister had a lot of questions. Couldn't the difference in Bernard's case have been urged on the Arkansas chiefs to get them to relent in his case? Where was the record of the legal proceedings which should have been conducted relative to the killing? If this was a wilfull murder, the pardon had been conceded too easily. "It would be dangerous," the minister warned, "to leave such a subject in the colony, not only because he would be an example of impunity, but also because of new crimes that he might commit." (The arguments of general and specific deterrence are not very recent inventions.) Finally, the governor was sternly admonished "not to surrender easily to demands of this sort on the part of the savages . . . If on the one hand it is necessary, considering all the present circumstances, to humor the savages, it is also necessary to be careful of letting them set a tone that accords neither with the king's authority nor the good of the colony."

Nevertheless, the minister talked to the king and he ratified the governor's decision. Writs of pardon were therefore issued under the king's name for each of the Arkansas soldiers. Because the homicide committed by Bernard was not a military crime and was cognizable there-

73. What follows is based on Berryer's letter to Kerlérec and Bobé Descloseaux dated July 14, 1769. ANC, B 109:487–88 (Transcript in Little Rock Public Library). The translation is mine.

fore by the Superior Council of Louisiana, his pardon was directed to the Council. Interestingly, though Berryer admitted knowing nothing of the circumstances surrounding the killing, the pardon recited that a quarrel had arisen between Bernard and Nicolet, that they had beaten each other, that Bernard "had had the misfortune to kill the said Nicolet," and that the death "had occurred without premeditated murder."[74] Thus Louis XV pardoned Jean Baptiste Bernard for killing by mischance when there was no evidence adduced as to the facts resulting in Nicolet's death. The decision was generated simply by a desire to accommodate an important ally. Faithful adherence to legal principle sometimes had to take a back seat to the more compelling demands of politics.

V

Father Louis Carette, the Jesuit missionary who came to the Post of Arkansas in 1750, attempted to bring some order to the legal affairs of the place. As he noted in a *procuration* (power of attorney), dated at Arkansas in 1753, he was "authorized by the king to make in every post where there is not a Notary Royal all contracts and acts. . . ."[75] There is no evidence that he had any formal legal training, but he was a Jesuit, and thus a learned man, one of a handful of such who made their residence in eighteenth-century Arkansas.

The 1753 *procuration* is itself of some interest, as it sheds light on how litigants whose cases were technically beyond

74. The pardon (*brevet de grâce*) was enclosed in the letter and is ANC, B 109:489 (Transcript in Little Rock Public Library). The translation is mine.

75. *Index to the Records of the Superior Council of Louisiana*, 22 LHQ 255 (1939).

the jurisdiction exercised by the Arkansas commandant (whatever that was) might have had their cases heard if they wanted to resort to regular methods of dispute settlement. As incredible as it seems, it is probable that the only court of general jurisdiction in the entire colony was the Superior Council of Louisiana. In 1769 La Harpe said that it was a two-week boat trip from the Arkansas to New Orleans, and six to eight weeks back.[76] Obviously, the *procuration* was an important device for people in remote posts like Arkansas, for it enabled them through their attorneys, in the language of the document under discussion, "to act . . . as though they were personally present."[77] Convoys or individual vessels travelled down the Mississippi frequently enough to make this means of tending to legal affairs more tolerable than it might otherwise have been. In this case, the attorney chosen was Commandant La Houssaye, who was deputed to act in a probate matter at Pointe Coupée for Étienne de Vaugine de Nuysement and his wife Antoinette Pélagie Petit de Divilliers. An interesting feature of *procurations* which increased their utility and flexibility was that they were assignable. This feature came in handy in this instance since La Houssaye, having been detained at the Arkansas due to illness, simply transferred the power of attorney to a member of the Superior Council "to act in my place as myself."[78]

Perhaps one of the reasons that Carette had acted as notary in this instance was that the commandant, the only other person in the little community so authorized, was a party to the instrument. But in the French period priests were given general notarial powers and could act even when circumstances prevented the commandant from doing so. For instance, Carette acted as notary, and thus

76. La Harpe to Choiseul, August 8, 1763 (Transcript in Little Rock Public Library).

77. *Records, supra* note 75, at *id.*

78. *Id.*

probably draftsman, for a marriage contract in which the commandant was not interested—the marriage contract of François Sarrazin and Françoise Lepine, executed at Arkansas Post on January 6, 1752.

Marriage contracts have no exact parallel in common-law practice, and thus it seems worthwhile to devote some time to their explanation and description before discussing the particulars of the Sarrazin-Lepine contract. In a recent seminal study, Professor Hans Baade outlined the provisions typically found in marriage contracts executed in accordance with eighteenth-century Parisian notarial practice.[79] The first and invariable undertaking by the future spouses was a promise to celebrate their marriage *in facie ecclesiae*. The parties would then choose the regime which would govern their property during the marriage. Next would come a declaration that the ante-nuptial debts of the parties were to remain their separate obligations; this was followed by a disclosure of the parties' assets, a requirement for the validity of the provision regarding debts. The dowry brought to the marriage by the wife was recited; and delineating *préciput*, the right of the spouse to specific property in the event of dissolution of the community, frequently followed. Finally came the donation clause, usually a reciprocal grant of all or part of the predeceasing spouse's estate. In order to be valid in Louisiana, this donation had to be registered with the Superior Council in New Orleans.

An inspection of the Sarrazin-Lepine marriage contract reveals that it very clearly drew on these French notarial precedents, and it reflects, moreover, an awareness of the practical requirements of the Louisiana registration provisions. It contained clauses regarding the celebration of the marriage in regular fashion, the creation of a community property regime, the amount of the wife's dowry, a mutual

---

79. What follows is taken from Baade, *supra* note 35, at 15–18.

donation to the survivor of all property owned at death, and an undertaking to have the contract registered in New Orleans.[80] While there was no clause dealing with antenuptial debts and no mention of *préciput*, it is quite obvious that the good Jesuit knew more than a little about French notarial practice, and may well have had at his disposal a form book on which he could draw. For all practical purposes, he was for a time the "lawyer" of the post as well as its *curé*.

There is an aspect of this interesting document which bears detailed attention. The property regime chosen by the parties included in the community "all property, movable and immovable,"[81] as common lawyers would say, all property, both personal and real. In this respect the contract departs from the *Coutume de Paris* which included in the community all movables but only certain immovables (*conquêts*) acquired after marriage.[82] Parties were allowed in Louisiana to contract almost any property arrangement they wanted,[83] and Sarrazin and Lepine had elected a somewhat unusual variety of community. Curiously, however, the contract reckoned that this regime was "in accordance with the custom received in the colony of Louisiana."

A few months after the execution of this contract Commandant La Houssaye wrote the governor that Monsieur Étienne Vaugine, a French officer, was of a mind to marry Madame De Gouyon, the commandant's sister-in-law, and he sent along "the proposed conditions for the contract of marriage."[84] This was a draft of the contract, as La Houssaye asked the governor to pass "*l'exemplair du contrat*"

80. *Records of the Superior Council of Louisiana*, 25 LHQ 856–57 (1942).
81. *Id.* at 856.
82. Baade, *supra* note 35, at 15.
83. *Id.*
84. La Houssaye to Vaudreuil, Dec. 1, 1752, LO 410, Huntington Library, San Marino, CA.

along to the New Orleans notary Chantaloux if the governor decided to give his permission for the marriage. Chantaloux was "to make it as it should be."[85] Three weeks later
the governor wrote to say that the contract would be sent
back soon and that Chantaloux had left it intact except for
one reasonably minor alteration.[86]

In 1758 Father Carette, dismayed by the irreligious inclination of his flock, left the Arkansas and no replacement
was sent. In 1764, after Madame Sarrazin found herself
widowed, Captain Pierre Marie Cabaret Detrépi, commandant at the Arkansas, passed a second marriage contract for her which was extremely unsophisticated and
rudimentary.[87] It contained only a promise to marry regularly and a mutual donation. Perhaps the good widow had
tired of long-winded formalities. Just as likely, the Post
was feeling the absence of Carette's drafting skills.

VI

As tiny, remote, and inconsequential as the Arkansas
settlement was, then, it is nevertheless clear that at least
some of its people were part of the time adherents to
French legal culture. Of course, almost everyone who
lived at the Post during the period of French domination
was either a native of France or French Canadian; and by
the end of the French period a substantial number of native
Louisianians were there. It is most interesting to find the
survival of civilian legal form in so remote an outpost of
empire. Obviously, not all of Arkansas's residents lapsed
into a kind of legal barbarism.

85. *Id.*
86. THE VAUDREUIL PAPERS, *supra* note 64, at 152.
87. Records of the Superior Council of Louisiana, Feb. 11, 1764,
Louisiana History Center, Louisiana State Museum, New Orleans.

There were, however, circumstances at work which would make it impossible for some time to establish a community that could be expected to value the observance of legal niceties very highly. As we have already seen, the Post could not have been very attractive to the more civilized settler owing to its dangerous location. Arkansas Post, moreover, experienced an extreme physical instability over the years, since it was necessary to relocate it several times due partly to flooding. (*See* Illustration 2.) The Arkansas River was in the eighteenth century "a turbulent, silt-laden stream, subject to frequent floods which were disastrous along its lower course."[88] This proved to be a considerable disincentive to settlement. Add to that the enormous expanse occupied by the alluvial plain of the Mississippi and the difficulty becomes plain.

Almost any site within thirty miles of the mouth of the Arkansas carried with it a considerable risk of floods. Law's colony on the Arkansas, twenty-seven miles or so from its mouth, was said in 1721 to be "in a fertile sector but subject to floods."[89] The success of the Chickasaw attack in 1749, when the Post was at the same location, was made possible by the absence of the Quapaws from the neighborhood: Because of recent floods they had abandoned their old fields for a more promising place upstream.[90] This place, called *Écores Rouges* (Red Bluffs) by the French, was about thirty-six miles from the mouth of the Arkansas and was at the present location of the Arkansas Post Memorial.[91] After the attack, the Post was moved to join the Indians at *Écores Rouges* so as to provide for mutual protection.[92]

The new spot was free from floods but proved un-

88. P. HOLDER, *supra* note 11, at 152.
89. 4 M. GIRAUD, *supra* note 13, at 273 (1974).
90. Faye, *supra* note 2, at 717–19.
91. See *infra*, p.
92. For details, *see* Appendix II.

satisfactory from a strategic standpoint because of its distance from the Mississippi. The location delayed convoys and Governor Vaudreuil expressed the view that "a post on the Mississippi would be more practical."[93] Therefore in 1756 the Post was moved back downriver to about ten miles above the mouth. But the inevitable soon occurred. In 1758 severe flooding, graphically described in a letter of Étienne Maurafet Layssard, the *garde magasin* (storekeeper) of the Post, caused heavy damage, almost undoing the work of builders and architects who had been at work for the better part of a year. The houses were saved by virtue of being raised on stakes against such a day as this; but the *habitants'* fields, everything but Layssard's garden for which he had providently provided a levee, were entirely inundated.[94]

It was in fact a small enough loss. From the beginning, and understandably, the attempt to make a stable agricultural community of the Arkansas had failed miserably. There is no doubt that the European population of Arkansas during the French period consisted almost entirely of hunters and Indian traders. In 1726 the reporter of the Louisiana census remarked of the Arkansas that "all the *habitants* were poor and lived only from the Indians' hunting."[95] A 1746 report said of the twelve Arkansas *habitant* families that "their principal occupation is hunting, curing meat, and commerce in tallow and bear oil." As for cultivating the soil, the same source reported that the *habitants* grew

93. The Vaudreuil Papers, *supra* note 64, at 118.

94. Faye, *supra* note 2, at 718–19. A detailed description of the repairs made in the summer of 1758, evidently necessitated by these floods, is in ANC, C¹ᴶᴬ 40:349–50 (Transcript in Little Rock Public Library). In addition to making repairs, the builders constructed a house 26 feet long and 19 wide just outside the fort for the Indians who came there on business. It was of *poteaux en terre* construction, was covered with shingles, and was enclosed with stakes. The report is signed by Devergés, chief engineer of the Province of Louisiana.

95. ANC, G¹, 464 (Transcript in Little Rock Public Library).

"some tobacco for their own use and for that of the savages and *voyageurs*."[96] In 1765 Captain Phillip Pittman, an Englishman, said that there were eight families living outside the fort who had cleared the land about nine hundred yards in depth. But, according to him, "on account of the sandiness of the soil, and the lowness of the situation, which makes it subject to be overflowed," their harvest was not enough even to supply them with their necessary provisions. Pittman noted that "when the Mississippi is at its utmost height the Lands are overflow'd upwards of five feet; for this reason all the buildings are rais'd six feet from the ground." Thus the residents of the Arkansas, he said, subsisted mainly by hunting and every season sent to New Orleans "great quantities of bear's oil, tallow, salted buffalo meat, and a few skins."[97]

Both Layssard[98] and Father Watrin[99] hint that the discouragement produced by the frequent flooding contributed to Father Carette's decision to leave. However that may be, it must be clear that during the period of French dominion the Post did not provide fertile soil for either crops or religion. Would regular *bourgeois* legal procedures have generally been afforded a more cordial acceptance? Even without direct evidence, this would seem most unlikely. Unsafe, unstable, and uncomfortable, the Arkansas Post of Louisiana during the period of French dominion

96. *Mémoire, supra* note 61 (Transcript in Little Rock Public Library).
97. P. PITTMAN, *supra* note 49, at xliv, 40–41.
98. *See* ANC, C¹³ᴬ 40:357 (Transcript in Little Rock Public Library). Layssard there remarks that the inhabitants at Arkansas were too poor to build a levee, and that "the Father would rather leave than go to such an expense. He is very poor."
99. *See* J. DELANGLEZ, THE FRENCH JESUITS IN LOWER LOUISIANA 444 (1935), where Watrin is quoted as saying that, despite there being little hope for conversion of the Quapaws, Father Carette "nevertheless followed both the French and the savages in their various changes of place, occasioned by the overflowing of the Mississippi near which the post is situated."

must surely also have been largely unmindful of *bourgeois* legal values.

It is true, as we have seen, that some of the Post's residents tried to maintain a connection between their remote outpost and European legal culture. But the few legal records that chance has allowed to come down to us from the French period are remarkable not only for their small number, but also for the social and economic characteristics they reveal of the people who figured in them. They were an elite, related by marriage and blood, struggling under the difficult circumstances of their situation to participate in regular legal processes. The probate proceeding of 1743 was instituted by one of the most well-to-do residents of Arkansas in the person of Anne Catherine Chenalenne, widow of Jean François Lepine. The community property inventoried included four slaves.[100] Her future husband Charles Lincto became the most substantial civilian resident of the Post. The 1749 census, if one excludes from it for the moment the commandant and his household, reveals that Lincto's household accounted for eight of the twenty-nine white *habitants* and seven of the eleven slaves at the Arkansas.[101] Étienne de Vaugine de Nuysement, who executed the *procuration* of 1753, was a member of one of the most distinguished French families of Louisiana;[102] and he granted the power to Commandant La Houssaye, soon to become a Major of New Orleans and a Knight of the Royal and Military Order of St. Louis.[103] Vaugine and La Houssaye married sisters. The marriage

100. For a translation of this inventory, *see* Core, *supra* note 50, at 22.

101. *Resancement General des habitants, voyageurs, femmes, enfans, esclaves, chevaus, beufs, vaches, cochons etc. de Poste des Akansa, 1749.* Lo. 200, Huntington Library, San Marino, CA.

102. On the Arkansas Vaugines, see Core, *The Vaugine Arkansas Connection*, 20 GPHSB 6 (1978).

103. Faye, *supra* note 2, at 709.

contract executed at the Arkansas in 1752 was entered into by the Post's *garde magasin* and Françoise Lepine, a daughter of Anne Catherine Chenalenne, the petitioner in the probate proceeding of 1743; the bride's dowry had resulted from the dissolution of the community which had been the aim of that proceeding. Finally, Françoise Lepine's second marriage contract, passed by Detépi in 1764, was prelude to her marriage to Jean Baptiste Tisserant de Montcharvaux, officer and interpreter at the Post and son of the commandant who executed the 1743 inventory. We are dealing with a propertied and interconnected gentry here, a tiny portion of what was anyway a very small population.

How the other, the major part of the Arkansas populace regulated their lives during the French period will, in the nature of things, be difficult to document. But there is some evidence on this point and it indicates that there was a good deal of lawlessness on the Arkansas. According to Athanase de Mézières, the Lieutenant Governor at Natchitoches, the Arkansas River above the Post was inhabited largely by outlaws. "Most of those who live there," he claimed, "have either deserted from the troops and ships of the most Christian King or have committed robberies, rape, or homicide, that river being the asylum of the most wicked persons, without doubt, in all the Indies." [104] On another occasion, De Mézières singled out as a particularly heinous offender an Arkansas denizen nicknamed Brindamúr, a man "of gigantic frame and extraordinary strength." Brindamúr, De Mézières complained, "has made himself a petty king over those brigands and highwaymen, who, with contempt for law and subordination with equal insult to Christians, and the shame of the very heathen, up to now have maintained themselves on that river." [105] Brindamúr had been resident on the Arkansas for a long time.

104. 1 ATHANASE DE MÉZIÈRES AND THE LOUISIANA–TEXAS FRONTIER, 1768–1780, 166 (H. BOLTON ed., 1914).
105. *Id.* at 168–69.

as his name appears in the census of 1749. Interestingly, it is placed at the very head of a considerable list of "*voyageurs* who have remained up the rivers despite the orders given them."[106] All persons hunting on the rivers were supposed to return every year as passports were not issued for longer periods. But there were large numbers of hunters who lived for twenty years or more in their camps without ever reporting to the Post. They constituted a large proportion, indeed sometimes a majority, of the European population in Arkansas during the French period. The 1749 census, for instance, lists a *habitant* population of only thirty-one, including the commandant and his wife. But there were forty hunters on the Arkansas River whose passports had expired, and nine on the White and St. Francis rivers. Sixteen hunters were said to be at the Post being outfitted to return to the hunt.

Brindamúr, the bandit king, was murdered by one of his men after the end of the French period, "though tardily" De Mézières reckoned, and "by divine justice."[107] In the Spanish period, as we shall see, an effort was made to rid the river of these malefactors.

VII

Since no records of litigation initiated at the Arkansas during the French period have survived, if indeed any were ever kept, little can be said directly on how lawsuits were conducted there. However, in 1747 François Jahan initiated a suit in the Superior Council in New Orleans against one Clermont, a resident of Arkansas Post, claiming damages for the conversion of a cask of rum at Arkansas.[108] The Su-

---

106. *Resancement, supra* note 101.
107. H. BOLTON, *supra* note 104, at 167.
108. *Index to the Records of the Superior Council of Louisiana,* 17 LHQ

perior Council had jurisdiction throughout Louisiana, and this case reveals how it was exercised against a defendant in the hinterlands. The summons was served on the Attorney General of Louisiana; thus, as Henry Dart pointed out, "it would seem . . . that a resident of the Post of Arkansas could be sued in New Orleans by serving the citation on the Procureur [Attorney] General."[109] How the case would have proceeded from there in the ordinary instance is difficult to say. Probably the Arkansas commandant would have been asked to act as a master to gather facts and to report to the Superior Council. But it seems that the commandant had already ruled independently on the matter. Commandant De Montcharvaux's statement on this case, which is entered in the record a few days after the suit was initiated, indicates that he had held a hearing on the matter at the Arkansas, had taken testimony as to the rum, and had "sentenced Clermont to pay for it."[110] Apparently he had kept no record of the proceeding, as none was offered: The good lieutenant bore his own record. It is interesting to note, however, that this case was evidently not brought to enforce the commandant's judgment but was an independent action.

How did the justice provided by the Post commandant during the French period measure up? In the absence of litigation records, this is the hardest kind of question to answer. However, whatever jurisdiction was exercisable by the commandant, he acted alone, without official advisors and without, of course, a jury. To say that rule is autocratic is not to say necessarily that it is bad. But the possibilities for arbitrary action are large in such circumstances and much depends on the personality and character of the autocrat.

569 (1934).
    109. Id.
    110. Id. at 571.

Parkman claimed that the Illinois commandant exercised his considerable power "in a patriarchal spirit and . . . usually commanded the respect and confidence of the people."[111] But for the most part the eighteenth-century French commandants in Louisiana had a reputation for arbitrariness. Captain Phillip Pittman had a low opinion of them, and accused the commandants in Illinois of extortion in matters of trade.[112] He once remarked generally on "the tyranny, which has been always exerted by officers of that nation commanding outposts."[113] Another commentator has written of the French post commandants as "small tyrants who were oppressing all those living under their jurisdiction."[114] At least one eighteenth-century Arkansan would have agreed with these assessments. That was Étienne Layssard, the previously mentioned storekeeper at the Post; except for Father Carette and the various commandants already alluded to, he was the most visible member of the Arkansas settlement in the 1750s. He wrote long and rambling letters about conditions at the Post and complained constantly of his poverty and of his difficulties with his commandant, Captain De Gamon de La Rochette. In November of 1758 he wrote his superior in New Orleans that De Gamon claimed to be "sole master of all the commerce, of the garrison, as well as the *voyageurs*, and is paid preferentially by virtue of his office, saying that if anything is left over the others can have it." He went on to say that "not knowing any law which establishes such authority, . . . I believe that when the commandant sells to a private person he is a merchant like me and ought to collect only his proportionate share."[115] On another occasion,

111. Quoted in Dart, *supra* note 27, at 279.
112. *See* P. PITTMAN, *supra* note 49, at 53.
113. *Id.* at 36.
114. J. DELANGLEZ, *supra* note 99, at 445.
115. ANC, C[13A] 40:328–29 (Calendar at Arkansas History Commission, Little Rock).

according to Layssard, De Gamon had said that "no one had a right to go the [Quapaw] village to trade but him . . . and that the trade belonged to him." Layssard complained bitterly that this deprived him of a living and he described his desperate circumstances: "My wife and I, four children, five slaves, a dog, a cat, and chickens live in a small house 25 feet long and 10 feet wide, with one little chimney to warm us all . . ."[116] While there is reason to think that Layssard was cranky and litigious (he once wrote to New Orleans demanding the prosecution of the Post surgeon for an unnamed offense),[117] there is no good reason to question his claims about the commandant's behavior. These incidents are good examples of the possibilities for the abuse of power when civilian and military authority are combined. When Layssard wrote his letters in 1758 Arkansas Post was virtually a garrison state. There were only six houses and thus a total resident white civilian population that could not have much exceeded thirty-five.[118] On the other hand, there was a permanent garrison of fifty soldiers which was temporarily reinforced in 1756 by an additional force of sixty men because of the difficulty with the Quapaws discussed above.[119] As we noted, in August of 1758 Father Carette, discouraged by the irredeemably bad character of the Post population, gave up his post.[120] The commandant would thereafter have no one with whom to share his authority and no near equal to challenge it.

Of the ten military officers who exercised judicial au-

116. ANC, C[13A] 40:306–12 (Calendar at Arkansas History Commission, Little Rock). The translation is mine and is made from a transcript in the Little Rock Public Library.

117. ANC, C[13A] 40:323–26 (Calendar at Arkansas History Commission, Little Rock).

118. Faye, *supra* note 2, at 716.

119. *Id.* at 715.

120. J. DELANGLEZ, *supra* note 99, at 445.

thority in Arkansas during French rule we know precious little of relevance.[121] Only La Houssaye, the commandant from 1751 to 1753, has come down to us outfitted with any kind of clear indication of character, and he does not appear to have possessed much of a judicial temperament. Governor De Vaudreuil said that he had found it necessary to relieve La Houssaye of his position at the Alibamous Post because of "his passion for drink . . . after giving him several charitable warnings on the subject, but without effect." The governor then delivered this ominous *coup de grâce*: "In addition, his character could not be worse or more dangerous."[122]

121. For a list of these and the dates during which they commanded at the Arkansas, *see* Appendix III.

122. Faye, *supra* note 2, at 709.

II
The Civil Law in Spanish Arkansas
1766–1804

By a secret covenant of November 3, 1762, France ceded the whole of Louisiana to Spain, but plans for transferring possession of the colony were held in abeyance for a considerable time. It was not until almost two years had elapsed that word of the agreement even reached Louisiana. Two more years passed before Antonio de Ulloa, the first Spanish governor, arrived on March 5, 1766.

Not surprisingly, the treaty between France and Spain by which the sovereignty over Louisiana was transferred made no mention of what legal system was to be in effect under the new regime. However, the Royal Letter of April 21, 1764, by which Louis XV notified the Louisiana governor of the cession, expressed the hope that the king of Spain would order that the *"juges ordinaires continuent, ainsi que le conseil supérieur, a rendre la justice suivant les lois, formes et usages de la colonie"*—(that the "judges ordinary and the Superior Council continue to render justice according to the laws, forms, and usages of the colony").[1] In fact, it seems to have been the original Spanish plan not to replace French law with Spanish, at least not immediately,[2] but in the event that was done.

---

1. Royal Letter of April 21, 1764, quoted in Baade, *Marriage Contracts in French and Spanish Louisiana: A Study in "Notarial" Jurisprudence,* 53 Tulane L. Rev. 1 at 31, n. 159 (1978).

2. For the details, see *id.* at 31–33.

44
Unequal Laws Unto a Savage Race

Ulloa ran into considerable difficulty when he attempted
to establish his authority in the province and was expelled
from it late in 1768.³ It was nine months before General
Alexandro O'Reilly resumed Spanish control. When he
did, he did so swiftly, firmly, and (some say) cruelly. Within
two months of his arrival he had held treason trials resulting in the execution of five of the principal participants in
the bloodless revolution against Ulloa. Significantly, the
judgment in the case recited that the Spanish court had
proceeded "*según nuestras leyes*" ("according to our laws").⁴
It was a portent of things to come.

On November 25, 1769, O'Reilly abolished the Superior Council and issued two documents known today as
"O'Reilly's Laws." One of these documents consisted of
ordinances creating the *Ayuntamiento* or Secular Cabildo of
New Orleans as a replacement for the Superior Council.
These ordinances also regulated the Cabildo's judicial func-
tions.⁵ The other document was a set of *Instructions* containing rules of civil and criminal procedure, the substantive law of crimes, and provisions for testate and intestate
succession.⁶ These two instruments left no doubt as to the
sources employed to produce them, for annotations to two
Spanish digests, the *Recopilación de las Indias* and the *Nueva
Recopilación de Castilla*, were provided by the draftsmen.
The first work is a digest of Spanish ultramarine law before 1680 that deals mainly with public-law matters; the
second is a digest of Castilian law and concerns itself with
private-law matters.⁷ Professional lawyers were at work:
The preamble to these *Instructions* stated that they were di-

3. *Id.* at 33.
4. *Id.* at 36.
5. Translations are available in 1 La. Law Journal no. 2, 1 (1841); 1
·Spain in the Mississippi Valley 108 (L. Kinnaird ed. 1949); 1 American State Papers, Misc., 350 (1834).
6. There is a translation in 1 La. Law Journal, no. 2, 27 (1841).
7. *See* Baade, *supra* note 1, at 40.

gested and arranged "by the Doctor Don Manuel Joseph de Urrustia and the counsellor Don Felix Rey."

Because the *Instructions* did not cover every substantive legal area, and because their preamble contained a somewhat tentative declaration that they were to serve "until a more extensive information upon those laws [*i.e.*, Spanish law in general] may be acquired," it used to be a question much mooted whether Spanish law ever completely superseded French law in Louisiana. It is now established beyond cavil that O'Reilly introduced Spanish law wholesale, that he deliberately annihilated French law, and that he had had royal authority to do so in advance and royal approbation afterwards.[8]

Ensign Le Gros de Grandcour, the Arkansas commandant at the end of the French era, stayed on as commandant under the Spanish and was not replaced until February of 1768 when Governor Ulloa chose Captain Alexandre de Clouet for the post.[9] The change to Spanish sovereignty caused a considerable nervousness at the Arkansas that manifested itself in a number of ways. For instance, when the news of Ulloa's expulsion reached Arkansas, one of the Post's merchants refused, "on account of the revolution," to take the script money offered him in payment for the soldiers' food. De Clouet wrote that "I had to show my teeth to this man" to get him to relent.[10] The establishment of Spanish control caused, moreover, some anxiety among the Indians, especially when they found out about O'Reilly's executions. Early in 1770, when Captain François Demasellière had been commandant at Arkansas

---

8. *Id.* at 35–36, 43, 89; Batiza, *The Unity of Private Law in Louisiana Under Spanish Rule*, 4 INTER-AMERICAN LAW REVIEW 139 (1962).

9. Faye, *The Arkansas Post of Louisiana: Spanish Domination*, 27 LHQ 629, 632 (1944).

10. De Clouet to Commandant, Feb. 14, 1769, AGI, PC, *leg.* 107.

about a month, he told the Quapaws a stupid lie that they could not have believed. The excuse he offered for the five executions, he wrote O'Reilly, was "that this had been done at the request of the French, since these five people had lost their minds."[11] Whatever misgivings the French settlers at Arkansas Post had about the change in regime, they evidently quietly submitted to the oath of allegiance to the Spanish king which the commandant required them all to take in the summer of 1769. The Arkansas commandant wrote the governor to report that he had administered the oath; everything had gone well enough, he said, except that he was not sure that he had done it correctly since the law governing this kind of activity was unknown to him.[12]

Confusion about what country's law was in effect, and ignorance of its substance, caused other problems at Arkansas Post. While, as we have seen, O'Reilly formally replaced French law with Spanish in 1769, he seems not to have relayed that message to the posts, at least not to the Arkansas. In July of 1770, Commandant Demasellière said that he had a case pending against a Lieutenant Orieta (with whom he was having all kinds of altercations) and that one of the charges was based on the fact that a search of Orieta's house had turned up firearms. The commandant, apparently believing that French law still prevailed, said that this was "against the French law which forbids anyone to have arms without the post commandant's permission." Orieta, a Spaniard, claimed not to know these laws and asked to be sent back home.[13] Yet on the other hand, an unnamed French soldier, accused of complaining overmuch about the abjectly miserable conditions at the

---

11. Demasellière to O'Reilly, Jan. 15, 1770, AGI, PC, *leg.* 107.
12. De Clouet to General, Aug. 14, 1769, AGI, PC, *leg.* 107.
13. Demasellière to General, July 15, 1770, AGI, PC, *leg.* 107.

Post, had sought to escape punishment four months earlier
because "he did not know well the laws and customs of the
Spanish army."[14] In another unspecified matter, the commandant was ambiguously instructed in August of 1770
that "the Ordinances of the kings of France and Spain must
be adhered to."[15]

By the autumn of 1770, however, some order was beginning to emerge from the confusion. In a letter from
Arkansas dated October 4, the "Penal Code" is mentioned,[16] an obvious reference to the substantive criminal
provisions of O'Reilly's *Instructions* of November 25, 1769.

On November 7, 1770, someone, probably the Governor,
wrote from New Orleans to Lieutenant Orieta (who had
taken over at the Arkansas) and commended him for asking for "a printed copy of the Penal Code." The writer
then admonished Orieta: "You must give the example of
behavior. The traders must be held in check so as not to
alienate the Indians' affection from your country."[17] Interestingly, it appears from this letter that the remote and inconsequential post of *Los Arcos*, as the Spaniards called the
Arkansas settlement, had not been sent a copy of these
laws when they were sent to the other forest posts; and it
had taken a letter to New Orleans to correct the bureau-
cracy's forgetfulness.

II

Probably at the same time that the Penal Code was sent
to Arkansas, O'Reilly also sent along a printed document

14. Demasellière to Governor(?), March 4, 1770, AGI, PC, *leg.* 107.
15. ? to Demasellière, Aug. 10, 1770, AGI, PC, *leg.* 107.
16. De Virzaga to Governor, October 4, 1770, AGI, PC, *leg.* 107.
17. Governor (?) to Orieta, Nov. 7, 1770, AGI, PC, *leg.* 107.

4. Captain Josef Vallière, Commandant of Arkansas Post from 1787 to 1790. From 1731 to 1804 judicial authority at the Arkansas was exercised by the French and Spanish officers in charge of the garrison there. (*Courtesy of Mr. and Mrs. Howard Stebbins, Little Rock.*)

dated February 12, 1770. It was styled "Instructions to which *lieutenants particuliers* [*i.e.*, post commandants] ought to conform . . . in all that belongs to the police and the administration of justice, civil as well as criminal."[18]

Under these provisions, every post commandant was given civil jurisdiction to judge "verbally" demands which did not exceed twenty *piastres*; cases exceeding this sum were reserved to the court of the Governor General in New Orleans.[19] Each commandant was also given a probate jurisdiction. In the case of a testate succession, the goods of the deceased were to be delivered for administration to his widow or, if none, to his heirs; if there were no widow or heirs, the administration was to be entrusted to some other suitable person.[20] If the value of the estate was less than 100 *piastres*, the commandant could immediately liquidate it; having assembled the interested parties in his house, he was then to make distribution of the proceeds to the widow and heirs, "having regard to the widow's rights to nuptial gains." If there were minor heirs, the commandant was to appoint a guardian for them. Larger estates required a formal inventory, appraisal, and public auction before distribution.[21] The fees the commandant could charge for supervising successions were set by the *Instructions*.[22] An appeal could be made to the Governor's court in New Orleans in probate matters,[23] but not in other civil causes.

In criminal matters the commandant had a vague and in-

---

18. For the posts to which these Instructions were first sent, *see* Baade, *supra* note 1, at 37–8. Arkansas Post was not among them. Professor Baade very kindly supplied me with a copy of this document which he found in AGI, PC, *leg.* 188A. There is another copy in the Missouri Historical Society at St. Louis which I have also consulted. It will be cited hereafter as *Instructions*.

  19. *Instructions*, § 1.
  20. *Id.*, § 2.
  21. *Id.*, § 4.
  22. *Id.*, § 2.
  23. *Id.*, § 5.

consequential authority. He could proceed to judgment only "if the criminal cause was quite light."[24] No precise jurisdictional boundary was defined, and perhaps in the nature of things that was not possible. The draftsman of the *Instructions* resorted instead to examples: "A quarrel, or injurious words of little consequence," were the kinds of criminal cases within the commandant's judicial competence. Even then he was not specifically allowed to punish anyone; he was supposed to call the parties before him, reprimand the offender, and try to establish peace between them.[25] Obviously, no appeal could lie from such a "judgment." In serious criminal matters (again only examples are given: Killing, wounding, theft) the commandant was to take the depositions of witnesses and send a report (*information*) to the governor, keeping the prisoner under guard until the governor decided what to do.[26] In this procedure, as in others, the commandant acted as a surrogate notary in which capacity he was assisted by two witnesses who were to be present throughout the entire proceeding.[27]

In French Louisiana, as we have seen, there had been a number of provincial notaries in some of the remote outposts. The Spanish, however, very severely limited the number of notaries and none was allowed outside New Orleans.[28] Therefore, the post commandants were given surrogate notarial responsibilities in places beyond the city. "Since there are no longer any notaries [*écrivains*] established . . . who can draft and authenticate the acts and contracts of the *habitants*," the *Instructions* noted, the commandants were authorized to make *procurations*, and to sign all other necessary acts, with the assistance of two witnesses.

24. *Id.*, § 8.
25. *Id.*
26. *Id.*, § 6.
27. *Id.*, § 7.
28. Baade, *supra* note 1, at 39.

In addition, three other witnesses were required.[29] Any instrument that created a mortgage, as, typically, a marriage contract did, was supposed to be reported to the government notary at the Cabildo in New Orleans; the date and all the particulars should be sent so that the notary could make a public note of them.[30]

The commandant's police duties also found a place in this document. A commandant was to allow no one to settle in his bailiwick who did not have the written permission of the governor.[31] Only two "cabarets" were to be allowed in each jurisdiction, and only *habitants* of good repute and conduct should be licensed. The commandant was to instruct licensees expressly not to sell any strong drink to slaves unless they had with them the written permission of a master whose signature was known. Selling anything under any other circumstances to slaves would bring a fine of ten *piastres* (to be given to the church) and permanent revocation of the seller's license.[32] There was a bounty on deserters for which the commandant was eligible,[33] and he was to make sure that no one without a passport journeyed into his jurisdiction.[34] As though all this were not enough, he was to keep his *habitants* from trafficking with the English on the boats that travelled the Mississippi and in the English posts established on that river's left bank.[35] It also fell to him to oversee the building and repair of roads and enclosures (levees); they were to be built and maintained at the expense of the *habitants*.[36]

A very interesting duty of the commandant of a judicial

29. *Instructions*, § 9.
30. *Id.*, § 10.
31. *Id.*, § 14.
32. *Id.*, § 15.
33. *Id.*, § 17.
34. *Id.*
35. *Id.*, § 19.
36. *Id.*, § 20.

or administrative sort deserves separate mention. In the event a runaway slave was captured and it was determined that his master was a local resident, the slave was to be interrogated to discover his reason for fleeing. If he had run away because he had not proper food or shelter, the commandant was to proceed against the master, collect costs, and impose a fine of ten *piastres* to be given to the church.[37]

Another important document of relevance, dated January 26, 1770, contained instructions which O'Reilly sent to his lieutenant governors at Natchitoches and St. Louis defining their police duties and judicial jurisdiction.[38] Their authority in civil matters extended to cases in which the demand did not exceed 100 *piastres*.[39] In larger civil cases, the lieutenant governors were authorized to proceed up to the judgment stage, at which point the file was to be sent to the governor for his determination.[40] In all civil cases the rules of civil procedure formulated in 1769 were to be adhered to. In serious criminal matters, the lieutenant governors were empowered to proceed up to the judgment stage, following the rules of criminal procedure promulgated in 1769, and they were then to pass the matter to the governor for decision.[41]

If the Arkansas commandant had followed his instructions, his jurisdiction would have been rather restricted. His criminal judicial jurisdiction was clearly trivial, al-

---

37. *Id.*, § 18.

38. *Instruccion a que se arreglarian los Tenientes de Governador . . . .* New Orleans, January 26, 1770 [cited hereinafter as *Instruccion.*] Unlike the *Instructions* to the post commandants, this document was not printed. A copy from AGI, PC, *leg.* 2357 was very kindly provided me by Professor Baade. I also made use of this document at the Archivo General de Indias in Seville.

39. *Instruccion*, § 1.

40. *Id.*, § 2.

41. *Id.*, § 3.

though his police and investigative duties were quite considerable. Civil cases in which the demand did not exceed twenty *piastres*—a very small amount—could not have been of much importance. It follows that the people of the Arkansas who were of a mind to resort to a technically competent governmental authority for the settlement of their disputes would often have had to go elsewhere.

Even if it had occurred to some eighteenth-century Arkansan to apply to the lieutenant governor at Natchitoches for relief, that avenue was specifically closed by the *Instructions* to post commandants. Section One of those instructions provided that "as to cases which exceed that sum [twenty *piastres*], they shall be judged by the Governor General, to which tribunal the parties shall repair either in person or by someone charged with their powers. . . ."[42] Incredibly, then, in nontrivial civil matters persons who followed these rules were expected, either personally or through an attorney, to make the trek to New Orleans for an adjudication of their difficulties. According to La Harpe, the mouth of the Arkansas was forty or fifty days by river from New Orleans, and the return trip consumed twelve to fifteen days.[43] The river, moreover, was not open all year: Ice in the winter and, occasionally, low water in the summer made reliable travel a seasonal affair. Even though the use of attorneys was specifically authorized, resort to regular governmental tribunals for sorting out disputes would have been very difficult at the least. At times, and for some Arkansans most of the time, it would have been next to impossible.

Nevertheless, the meager record evidence that survives reveals a process of practical adaptation that made the system more tolerable. As noted above, post commandants were given authority to adjudicate "verbally" the civil

42. *Instructions*, § 1.
43. Bénard de La Harpe to the Duc de Choiseul, Minister of the Ma-

matters within their competence. This evidently meant that there was no need for written pleadings, the taking of depositions, or even (until some time later) a written judgment. The rules of civil procedure of 1769 did sometimes require written pleadings and depositions, but they applied only in the governor's court and the courts of the lieutenant governors. In the nature of things, then, the cases in which commandants had the power to proceed to judgment would leave no trace on the records. These cases were no doubt handled as part of the administrative routine of the post, and with respect to them the commandant was the final arbiter. Since there was no appeal from the commandant's judgment, and no trace in the Spanish judicial records of anything like a writ of prohibition, there is reason to believe that a commandant who wished to could exceed his jurisdiction without much fear of interference from the central authority. Even in the absence of record evidence, it would be a reasonable guess that this often happened at Arkansas Post.

Indeed, occasional glimpses of litigation at the Arkansas positively show that the Spanish government winked at the exercise of unauthorized judicial power by the commandant and that the hardship which strict adherence to the rules would have produced was thus obviated in actual practice. For example, in 1770 a merchant named Tounoir took a great deal of bear oil from the boat of Francoeur, a hunter who had come in from the White River. Lambert, an *engagé* of Francoeur, petitioned the commandant in writing to order Tounoir to replace the oil; Francoeur owed him wages, he said, and he claimed preference to Tounoir because his claim was "due for hard work." Captain Demasellière, the commandant, thereupon ordered Tounoir to return the oil. When Tounoir refused, the com-

---

rine, August 8, 1763 (Transcript in Little Rock Public Library).

mandant was obliged to send his sergeant to execute his order.

At this point, Francoeur asked to have set off a debt of 944 *pesos* owed him by Tounoir; the note evidencing this debt, unfortunately, was in New Orleans in the hands of De Clouet the former commandant. Demasellière wrote to the governor to ask that he order this note paid since Francoeur had nothing but his gun. The commandant then ordered Tounoir to pay court costs—that is, the sergeant's fee for taking the oil back; when Tounoir refused, Demasellière had him jailed. A short time thereafter the commandant ordered Tounoir to leave, but before doing so, Tounoir got Francoeur to sign some sort of "certificate," probably a release of Tounoir's note; and, to insult the commandant and literally as a parting shot, as he was leaving he and his company fired a volley of thirty shots at high noon. Francoeur thereafter signed an affidavit that the release to Tounoir was executed "when I was drunk and thus is of no value."[44]

This case, involving a great deal more than twenty *piastres*, obviously did not fall within the commandant's jurisdictional limits. Yet it seems reasonably clear that Demasellière found it impossible to do nothing, so he did his best to resolve the dispute. In fact, the governor was of the view that the commandant, far from having exceeded his jurisdiction, had been too timid. When the governor received the commandant's request to collect the note from Tounoir to Francoeur, he wrote him that he should have handled the matter himself: The proper procedure, the governor scolded, was to "hear both sides, taking the testi-

---

44. Lambert to Demasellière, June 1, 1770, AGI, PC, *leg.* 107; Franceour to Demasellière, June 16, 1770, AGI, PC, *leg.* 107; Demasellière to O'Reilly, June 28, 1770, AGI, PC, *leg.* 107; Demasellière to O'Reilly, July 15, 1770, AGI, PC, *leg.* 107; Demasellière to ?, July 15, 1770, AGI, PC, *leg.* 107.

mony of reputable witnesses on both sides, and then give me the arguments on both sides."[45]

In fairness to the commandant, there was no way that he could have known from the *Instructions* (assuming they had arrived by then, which as we saw is doubtful) that this was the proper procedure. The whole conflict was beyond his cognizance. What O'Reilly suggested the commandant should have done corresponds with the *Instruccion* to the lieutenant governors, not with the *Instructions* to the commandants. That in fact was the only practicable way to govern a remote and mobile population like that at the Arkansas. Besides, it would make no sense whatsoever to compel the commencement of the suit in New Orleans when the first act of the court there would be to order the Arkansas commandant to take the depositions of witnesses at or in the environs of his post. The commandant was not infrequently asked by the New Orleans court to act as a master to gather facts for the settlement of disputes involving Arkansas facts.

No judgment was rendered in this case. For our immediate purposes, however, the lesson is plain enough. Despite what the *Instructions* had said, when the Arkansas commandant was faced with a case which was beyond his power to adjudicate, he was expected to act as a master, gather facts, and send the file to New Orleans for decision. The procedure involved was more a matter of common administrative sense than of adherence to formal rules and was at least partly shaped by practical difficulties created by geography.

Nor did matters become more formalized very soon. A good example of the informality of legal procedure at the Arkansas in later times occurred in May of 1780.[46] At

45. Governor(?) to Demasellière, July 20, 1770, AGI, PC, *leg.* 107.
46. What follows is taken from 1 L. KINNAIRD, *supra* note 5, at 377–82.

that time, François Menard, a well-to-do merchant at the Arkansas, filed a written reply to a written petition which had been directed to Captain Balthazar de Villiers, commandant at the Post. The petition, signed by Zabulon Matheo, an Anglo-American, stated that Menard had taken seven hundred pounds of tallow from the plaintiff's partners. By way of defense, Menard claimed that one of the plaintiff's partners had delivered the tallow to him as payment for drinking debts; and he said that the plaintiff's complaint should therefore have been directed against the plaintiff's partner. Menard had settled this debt out of the hunters' catch before they had returned to the Post from upriver; according to his account, he had taken this precaution because the merchants had been unable to realize anything from the hunters' catches for the last three years. Menard's answer was quite chatty, more an irate letter than a pleading. He excoriated the plaintiff for using the phrase "make restitution" in his complaint. He did not explain why this phrase was so offensive, but he maintained that "the style of the Englishman's secretary might have been more polite"; and he opined that "only a vulgar person uses these expressions."

De Villiers, in passing the case on to New Orleans for judgment, told Governor Gálvez that it was a rule at the Arkansas "that the last person to equip a hunter should, upon the latter's return, have first claim on him for repayment." Menard had short-circuited the equipper's lien by getting the hunters to pay him first, and De Villiers therefore caused the tallow to be withdrawn from Menard's stores "in favor of the persons to whom the hunters are indebted." He asked the governor to approve his view that Menard had to pay the debt owed by the petitioner's partner out of the tallow. Interestingly, De Villiers went on to say that he believed himself "authorized to do this by virtue of an ordinance, the articles of which I have sent you . . ." and he said that "the said Menard himself invoked [the ordinance] when it was favorable to him." This ordinance, passed at the Post in 1778, established the rule that the last equipper of a hunter had a first lien on the hunter's catch and voided conveyances of the catch that were in fraud of creditors.[47] Though the pleadings had been in writing in this case, the good captain did not bother to take testimony in a formal way or provide a record of the proceedings. He simply reported facts that he had gathered informally. He told the governor casually that he "had first started legal proceedings in connection with what I mentioned in this letter, but I felt that in miserable posts like this one it was better to avoid pettifogging as much as possible." In other words, legal formality was an inefficient complication wholly unsuited to places like Arkansas Post.

That was not all. The commandant went on to paint the blackest possible picture of Menard's character. "[T]he duplicity of this man is remarkable in that he knows how to claim the protection of the laws or ignore them according to his interest." He claimed that Menard had been at odds with previous commandants and "through illegal trading had acquired some property and become arrogant. . . ." According to the captain, Menard made a habit of receiving preferential payments "by causing the hunters to get drunk, making them gamble, and by this means getting hold of their cargos. . . ." De Villiers then stated: "He supports at his house most of the time a band of vagabonds and people of his ilk who protect him by testifying to his directions. His conversation is always evil and he disregards my orders to such an extent that last month he went so far as to induce some people who were living with him to refuse to march with a detachment that I had ordered them to join. If I am to be blamed, Sir, it is for not

____

47. A partial copy of this ordinance has survived in AGI, PC, *leg.* 191.

having sent him to you then. I fined him last year for giving brandy to the savages, and he should have been fined a hundred times."

Clearly, the commandant saw the real dispute as being between Menard and himself. The informality of the proceedings is underscored by the fact that the "judgment" recommended to the governor was not in favor of either of the real parties: De Villiers's view was that the tallow should have been awarded to those who had equipped the plaintiff and his partner.

In the same year, however, De Villiers proceeded in a much more regular fashion in another case involving the same ordinance. Louis Boulard, André Lopez, and François Menard complained in writing about several hunters who were about to take their catch to town without paying their creditors, presumably the merchants who equipped them. They prayed that the hunters be deposed and that the commandant then "do right to whomever it belongs." De Villiers took the depositions and wrote on the bottom of the petition his judgment decreeing that the boats be unloaded.[48] The proceeding seems altogether remarkably craftsmanlike and professional.

Towards the end of the Spanish period, at the time that Arkansas Post was becoming a stable settlement, an extremely interesting criminal proceeding took place there.[49] In 1791, Francisco Lecler was wounded with a hatchet by Anselmo Lachenese at the Post. On his way to New Orleans to seek medical attention, Lecler stopped at the Royal Hospital at Natchez where he expressed a desire to initiate criminal charges against Lachenese. Gayoso de Lemos, the lieutenant governor at Natchez, took his sworn

48. De Villiers to Gálvez, Feb. 23, 1780, AGI, PC, *leg.* 193A.

49. What follows is taken from *Declaraciónes tomadas sobre el herido qe vaso de Arkanzas nombrado Francisco le Cler*, Aug. 19, 1791. Judicial Records of Spanish Louisiana, Louisiana History Center, Louisiana State Museum, New Orleans.

deposition and a physician provided him with a certificate describing his wounds. He continued his journey to New Orleans where he pressed his case at the Cabildo. Governor Miró then ordered Captain Juan Ignace Delinó de Chalmette, the Arkansas commandant, to take the sworn depositions of relevant witnesses and send them along with his recommendations on the case to New Orleans for final decision.

Delinó first deposed four witnesses: Pedro Jardela, Luis Jardela, Gayetano Bougine (Vaugine), and Pierre Lefevre. None of the men had seen the incident; but they all testified that they had found Lecler sitting on the floor in François Menard's house, wounded in the knee and in a great deal of pain. Lecler had said at that time that Lachenese had done it, but he had expressed no view on whether it had been done maliciously. The captain then deposed Lachenese who maintained steadfastly that he had been working at Menard's house with a hatchet and that he had accidentally struck Lecler.

After weighing the testimony, Delinó rendered a kind of interlocutory decision. He said that "according to the said depositions [declaraciónes] it does not seem that the said wound given by the accused Anselmo Lachenesis was effected with bad intentions." He therefore released Lachenese from the jail of the fort, but cautioned him to be available for the governor's questioning, should he request it. The depositions and the commandant's view of the case were sent to the governor in New Orleans. It was still pending in 1792 when the record ends.

This is the best example of a complete legal proceeding at the Arkansas in the entire eighteenth century. Delinó did an excellent job of questioning the witnesses, and the transcript of their testimony, covering about twenty pages, was nicely prepared. Second Sergeant Manuel Reyes acted as escribano. The depositions were written in Spanish, but the interrogation was done in French; and when the testimony was read back to the deponents for their signatures it was translated into French for them by Gayetano Vaugine. It can hardly be coincidental that this professional piece of administrative work occurred just as Arkansas Post was beginning to achieve some respectability.

III

Residents of Arkansas who were temporarily in New Orleans or who had removed there could, of course, take advantage of the general, province-wide jurisdiction of the Cabildo to sue an Arkansas resident. On April 8, 1771, for instance, Santiago Jacquelin and his wife Maria Montcharvaux sued François Menard, who was then in Arkansas, for an accounting.[50] The claim was that Menard had agreed to act as agent for Madame Montcharvaux, and a list of notes and personal belongings of hers was attached to the complaint. With the advice of his assessor, a law-trained advisor, the governor sent a dispatch to Fernando de Leyba, commandant at Arkansas, directing him to summon Menard and to take his deposition in order to learn what he had done with Madame Montcharvaux's effects. Having received the order, Leyba first summoned his sergeant and swore him in to act as *escribano pro tempore* (*ad hoc* notary). He then summoned Menard, had him sworn in, and questioned him as to the affairs entrusted to him by the plaintiff. Menard admitted that he was supposed to collect Doña Maria's notes and personal effects and account for

50. What follows is taken from *Index to the Spanish Judicial Records*, 8 LHQ 314–16 (1925). I have also examined the original papers in Montcharvaux vs. Fransisco Menar(d), April 18, 1771. Judicial Records of Spanish Louisiana, Louisiana History Center, Louisiana State Museum, New Orleans. This Maria Montcharvaux is the same person as Françoise Lepine who figured in the marriage contracts discussed *supra* p. 30.

them. He accounted for the notes, but in some of the personal effects he claimed property by virtue of a gift. All of this was transmitted to New Orleans for "His Lordship to determine what he may find suitable." This case shows that the local Arkansas commandant acted as an examining magistrate or master for cases in which Post residents were sued in New Orleans. The flexibility made possible by the civilian habit of relying on depositions taken outside the presence of the parties is exposed to view here. Had *viva voce* testimony in open court in front of the parties been required, as it usually was in common-law courts, the province-wide jurisdiction of the governor's court would not have been nearly so useful. It would not very often have been reasonable to expect witnesses and parties to travel from the forest settlements to attend hearings and give testimony. The centralized authority of the governor's court in New Orleans made it possible to collect evidence from the remotest posts and bring it together in a central point for evaluation and eventually for rendering judgment.

Once judgment was rendered against an Arkansas resident in a suit initiated in New Orleans, the Arkansas commandant was expected to execute it. For instance, in 1787 François Menard sued Anselm Billet, a resident of the Post who had acted as surety on a note executed by De Villiers for the purchase price of a slave. De Villiers had died in 1782 and his estate was insolvent; thus a cause of action had accrued against Billet. Menard prayed judgment on the strength of the note and asked that a writ of execution against Billet issue to the Commandant of *Los Arcos*. The court complied with the request.[51] In 1791, Santiago Gaignard sued a resident of Arkansas Post, Juan Bautista Saussié, for contribution. Gaignard claimed that he had

51. Francisco Menard vs. Anselme Billet, Aug. 29, 1787. Judicial Records of Spanish Louisiana, Louisiana History Center, Louisiana State Museum, New Orleans.

paid a note owed by both him and the defendant which had been endorsed by the original payee to De Villiers's widow; and he presented her receipt as evidence of the payment. He asked for summary judgment, as a common lawyer would say, and for a writ of execution to the commandant of Arkansas Post.[52]

IV

Another class of case which bears on Arkansas legal history is the sort which involves occurrences at Arkansas but does not involve Arkansas residents. These might be expected to have arisen fairly frequently in an *entrepôt* like the Post. An extremely interesting example is to be found in the case of *Poureé vs. Chouteau*.[53]

In March of 1782 Eugene Pourée outfitted a *bateau* in New Orleans in which he received freight "subject to the ordinary conditions of carriage by water." One of his shippers was Auguste Chouteau, a well-known St. Louis merchant. On reaching the Yazoo River, Pourée's *bateau* was attacked by a party of Englishmen, and it was consequently compelled to descend to Natchez. After joining a convoy there for safety, the boat resumed its voyage. On reaching the St. Francis River, Pourée encountered a *bateau* belonging to a Mr. Lebaddie and, having been informed by its crew that they had been attacked and pillaged by English brigands at what is now Memphis, Pourée decided to retreat to Arkansas Post until conditions improved. After a

52. Santiago Gaignard vs. Juan Batista Saussié, Jan. 25, 1791. Judicial Records of Spanish Louisiana, Louisiana History Center, Louisiana State Museum, New Orleans.

53. The records of this case are transcribed and translated in *The Case of Pourée against Chouteau*, 2 PUBLICATIONS OF THE MISSOURI HISTORICAL SOCIETY 68 (1900).

stay of some length there, he learned that the Englishmen had retired inland and he set off again, arriving safely at St. Louis after a considerable delay. Pourée wanted to recover from his shippers the extra expenses occasioned by the delays. These included: 1. Payments to Choctaw Indians for reconnoitering for the preservation of the *bateau*; 2. Payments to Quapaw Indians who accompanied Pourée to the St. Francis River; 3. Rent for a house at Arkansas Post in which the cargo was stored; 4. Payment for 150 trips of a cart for loading and unloading the *bateau* at Arkansas Post; 5. Wages of a crew sent down from St. Louis to man the vessel when it resumed its trip; 6. Payment of men at Arkansas Post for outfitting the *bateau*; 7. Payment for 1700 lbs. of biscuits bought at the Arkansas and 800 lbs. of bacon; and 8. The cost of powder and balls.

When Chouteau refused Pourée's demand, Pourée sued him in the court of the lieutenant governor in St. Louis. He recited the facts and closed his petition by noting his surprise that Mr. Chouteau would not pay his proportionate share of the increased expenses and by making known his view of the substantive law applicable to the case. He claimed that had the voyage not been completed due to *force majeur*, the law was that the shipper would not have been entitled to a refund; likewise, "if the master makes a second equipment, the shippers are obliged to pay expenses." Pourée's complaint, in other words, doubled as a "brief" for his view of the relevant legal principles.[54] Mr. Chouteau answered simply that he had paid in advance and he added his own view of the applicable rule: ". . . it would be a great wrong to shippers to have to pay a second time the freight upon a venture embarked in a *bateau*, upon which the freight had already been paid before it left port."[55]

---

54. Pourée's petition appears in *id.* at 69–71.
55. Chouteau's answer appears in *id.* at 72.

The lieutenant governor, rather than decide the case himself, referred it to arbitration: Each party named one arbitrator and these arbitrators elected a third. The record noted that "this tribunal shall finally decide and determine this cause according to the rights of each party." The arbitrators were all well-known and well-respected merchants of St. Louis. Though the record does not say so, the parties presumably agreed to this mode of settling their differences. The arbitrators decided that Chouteau was obligated to pay for some of the extra expenses occasioned by the layover at Arkansas Post, but not nearly as much as Pourée was claiming.

The use of expert arbitrators to settle lawsuits in St. Louis was, as we have seen, not authorized by the *Instruccion* of 1770. Nevertheless, this mode of dispute resolution was quite common there from the beginning of the Spanish period.[56] It was an extremely popular device, especially among the merchant class; and, by passing the duty to decide to others, it relieved the commandant of having to irritate one or the other of the parties.

The manner of proceeding in civil cases in the lieutenant governor's court in St. Louis, as at the Arkansas, was a model of simplicity. Some cases were heard on oral plaint. If written pleadings were used, an informal petition initiated the action. The petition told the plaintiff's story simply, reciting the facts in a straightforward, frequently discursive way. No particular form was prescribed; as in common-law bill procedure, all the plaintiff had to do was to set out the salient features of his case.[57] The defendant

56. For an early agreement to submit a lawsuit to arbitration in St. Louis, *see* F. BILLON, ANNALS OF ST. LOUIS IN ITS EARLY DAYS UNDER THE FRENCH AND SPANISH DOMINATIONS 919 (1886). The custom is alluded to in Douglas, *The Spanish Domination of Upper Louisiana*, PROCEEDINGS OF THE WISCONSIN HISTORICAL SOCIETY 74 at 83 (1914).

57. For examples of petitions in St. Louis civil litigation, see F. BILLON, *supra* note 56, at 131, 136, 151, 155, 162, 174, and 179. In Douglas,

then replied with his version of the facts. Occasionally a defendant replied with an answer containing a counterclaim to which the plaintiff answers; but only rarely will the plaintiff otherwise file a responsive pleading.

V

As was the case during the French period, one of the Arkansas commandant's chief duties during the Spanish regime was to attract and hold the loyalty of the Quapaw Indians. Very soon after Captain Alexandre de Clouet took command of the Post in 1768, he wrote that supplying the Indians with liquor was absolutely necessary to an amicable relationship with them. Otherwise, he claimed, they simply could not be relied on.[58] Besides, he said a few months later, they would get liquor whether the French supplied it or not: In 1768 the English had begun building a settlement called Concordia on the left bank of the Mississippi across from the mouth of the Arkansas, and the Quapaws were quite happy with this development "since it is to be expected that they will get more food and drink."[59] To make matters worse, De Clouet reported the same year that for the last four years "because of the fear of floods [the inhabitants] have not made any crop." As a result, the French were completely dependent on the Indians for food, and the Quapaws threatened that in the future they would take only liquor in exchange for their corn.[60]

---

supra note 56 at 83, the author notes of procedure in the lieutenant governor's court: "The proceedings were summary. The injured party addressed a petition to the governor setting forth the particulars of his complaint written in the French language."

58. De Clouet to General, March 21, 1768, AGI, PC, *leg.* 107.
59. *Id.* to *id.*, July 26, 1768, AGI, PC, *leg.* 107.
60. *Id.* to *id.*, Oct. 6, 1768, AGI, PC, *leg.* 107.

Despite De Clouet's animadversions, the governor chided the commandant for using liquor to buy the Indians' friendship. His duty, the governor said, was to keep the Quapaws away from the English "by persuasion."[61] Later he suggested to De Clouet that he call the Indians together and "make a speech to them on the evils of drinking." If that was done, it accomplished little: A year later a drunken Quapaw became so rowdy that the commandant was obliged to make an inquiry and confiscate the remaining stock of the person who had supplied it.[62] Again we see that the Arkansas commandants exercised judicial power beyond that technically delegated to them by their formal instructions.

The English continued to put pressure on the French by trading liquor to the Quapaws. De Clouet claimed in 1769 that "the English make canteens [saloons] for the red men out of their posts."[63] When Captain François Demasellière took command at the Post late in 1769 he said that the Quapaws complained to him of De Clouet's policy of not allowing them to trade for liquor. This caused them to take their corn to the English to trade. "What they miss is liquor," the Captain bluntly noted, "and I need more."[64] A few months later, the captain renewed his demand.[65] In 1770 a Quapaw chief named "Long Thin One" gave him a good deal of trouble because he was refused liquor and tried to strike the commandant in the head. "I threw him out of my house," Demasellière noted laconically, "and I told him I did not want to see him any more."[66]

In 1772 Captain Fernando de Leyba, the Arkansas commandant, was faced with a very alarming situation. Things

61. *Id.* to *id.*, March 21, 1768, AGI, PC, *leg.* 107.
62. *Id.* to *id.*, Aug. 1, 1769, AGI, PC, *leg*, 107.
63. *Id.* to *id.*, Aug. 14, 1769, AGI, PC, *leg.* 107.
64. Demasellière to General, Jan. 15, 1770, AGI, PC, *leg.* 107.
65. *Id.* to *id.*, March 4, 1770, AGI, PC, *leg.* 107.
66. *Id.* to *id.*, AGI, PC, *leg.* 107 (1770?).

had been simmering for some time. The Quapaw head chief had flatly told General O'Reilly that he believed Leyba did not like the Quapaws,[67] and he wanted him replaced. Part of the difficulty was that the Spanish were not paying the Indians as well as the French had for their goods;[68] part of the difficulty was that Leyba was a Spaniard. The Quapaws quite frankly expressed their preference for a Frenchman,[69] and Leyba could not even speak French.[70]

On June 13, 1772, Leyba arrested Nicholas Labussière, the trader stationed among the Quapaws, for selling liquor to the Indians and other trade violations. This so enraged the Quapaws that one of their chiefs threatened to raze the Post and kill all the civilians there unless Labussière was released. Some time was bought for sixty *pesos*; but if the white man was not returned within three months, the Quapaw chief promised "to cut every throat on the post." Even after striking this bargain, the chief, according to Leyba, sent an Indian "back for a barrel of whiskey or my head."[71] A few days later representatives from the three villages came to humiliate the captain. They brought him a dead horse and demanded whiskey in exchange for it. They threatened to kill everyone unless they got it, and so menaced the women that the commandant's wife fainted and all the rest were crying.[72] The governor finally wrote the Quapaw chief demanding that he behave himself "or else."[73]

Shortly thereafter relations improved somewhat, aided

67. Leyba to Governor, June 24, 1772, AGI, PC, *leg.* 107.

68. Demasellière to General, Oct. 7, 1770, AGI, PC, *leg.* 107.

69. Leyba to ?, July 27, 1771, AGI, PC, *leg.* 107.

70. June 4, 1771, AGI, PC, *leg.* 107.

71. Leyba to Governor, June 15, 1772, AGI, PC, *leg.* 107.

72. *Id.* to *id.*, June 24, 1772, AGI, PC, *leg.* 107.

73. Governor to the General Chief of the Arkansas, June 30, 1772, AGI, PC, *leg.* 107.

greatly by the arrival of presents and medals for the Quapaw chiefs. On April 13, 1773, those tokens of affection were distributed and were so well received that one chief allowed that he was embarrassed by the commandant's largesse. Another said that Leyba was daily becoming better.[74] The next month, when the Great Chief Casanonpoint died and there was an attempt to make his eleven-year-old son his successor, the Captain intervened and got the Quapaws to elect someone who could personally govern. Clearly the commandant's influence was very much on the increase.[75] He nevertheless renewed his request to be relieved at the end of the year.

In the fall of 1773 he reported to Governor Unzaga that an Englishman was living among the Quapaws under the protection of a powerful member of the tribe. This man was associated with the English trading community across the Mississippi opposite the mouth of the Arkansas, and had married a well-connected Indian girl. He dressed in Indian fashion and in every way aped their manners. His mission was plainly to disaffect the Quapaws from the Spanish; and to this end he told the Indians that the Spaniards were tyrants who would never have any factories to provide them with clothing, that even if some day the Spanish had merchandise to sell it would have been bought from the English and resold at a profit, and that soon the English would oust the Spanish who were only temporarily in possession. He had, moreover, the audacity actually to set up a store in the Quapaw village and was actively engaged in trade. He was so arrogant that he dared to enter the commandant's room dressed and painted like an Indian.

Such was the smallness of his garrison (twelve to fifteen soldiers), and the ludicrous condition of his fort and its ordnance, that the commandant knew that he was in no

74. Leyba to Governor, April 30, 1773, AGI, PC, *leg.* 107.
75. *Id.* to *id.*, May 25, 1773, AGI, PC, *leg.* 107.

position to do anything about this interloper; and so he resigned himself to tolerating him. After some repairs were made in 1774, however, Leyba's successor Captain Josef Orieta called the Quapaws to his fort, showed them the renovations, and discharged his cannon and swivel guns. This demonstration greatly impressed the Indians, who said that the English had told lies when they had ridiculed the impotence of the Spanish. Whereupon the assembled Quapaws drank the health of the governor, the commandant ordered another volley discharged, and the Englishman and his party were expelled.[76]

The regulation of the liquor trade with the Indians remained of grave concern throughout the Spanish Period.[77] In 1779 De Villiers wrote to Governor Gálvez and said that when he arrived at the Post he had found a regulation in effect which he had followed since it seemed to him "wise and necessary." Under it, no one was to trade liquor to the Quapaws without a license from the commandant and sales had to be made at a place designated by custom. The Quapaw chiefs complained that every other sort of trade was free and that it was an irritating discrimination that the Indian liquor trade was not. De Villiers, who wrote eloquently on the virtues of, and his devotion to, the ideal of free trade, had decided to open the Indian liquor trade to anyone. The *habitants* and merchants reacted strongly to this deregulation. They wrote: "Today, the thirteenth of the month of September, 1779, we, the *habitants* and merchants of the Post of Arkansas, on the decision that Mons. De Villiers our commandant has told us was taken, that to content the savages he would permit them the full liberty to trade for *eau de vie* wherever they want, are assembled and of one common accord we declare that such a liberty

76. Leyba to Unzaga, Oct. 26, 1773, AGI, PC, *leg.* 107; Orieta to Unzaga, July 14, 1774, AGI, PC, *leg.* 107.

77. What follows is based on De Villiers to Gálvez, Sept. 15, 1779, AGI, PC, *leg.* 192.

would expose the *habitants* to the continual insults of the
said savages . . . [and we ask] whether the commandant
would not make a wiser decision than this, namely, that a
single place be established where drink would be distributed to them with order and propriety [*avec ordre et mes-
ure*]." De Villers evidently acceded to this request. He
could not very well have done otherwise.

It would not be long before the Indian chiefs' complaints
would be stood on their heads. In 1786 the three great
chiefs of the Quapaws asked the governor to forbid all liquor trade to the tribe because of widespread drunkenness
and addiction to alcohol among the members of the tribe.[78]
The governor did not do so immediately, and within the
first three months of Vallière's command five Quapaws
died in drunken brawls. Finally, after a minor Quapaw
chief had been murdered and his mutilated body thrown
into the river during a drunken altercation, Governor Miró
issued an order that the liquor trade to the Indians at Arkansas Post be entirely prohibited. Vallière published the
order at the Post on October 17, 1787.[79]

Throughout the Spanish period the tiny Arkansas settlement continued to experience difficulty with hostile Indians. In 1770 the Quapaws asked to be supplied with
powder and bullets as they had it on good authority that
the Choctaws were coming to attack. The settlers, or some
of the women at least, were brought into the fort where
they were billeted for a time; the memory of the 1749 raid
in which six settlers had been slain and eight captured and
enslaved while trying desperately to reach the safety of the
fort had probably not faded much.[80] Happily, this turned
out to be a false alarm, but the settlement remained anxious about its safety.

78. *See* Faye, *supra* note 9, at 693–94.
79. *Id.* at 694.
80. Demasellière to General, May 14, 1770, AGI, PC, *leg.* 107. What

Another considerable threat to European lives and property came from the Osages. The Quapaws had been urging the Arkansas commandant for some time to allow them to attack the Osages and drive them from the river; but Spanish officials in New Orleans were opposed to such efforts. They preferred to try to persuade the Osages to come to terms. Nevertheless, in the fall of 1770 two small war parties of Quapaws (one of six, the other of ten) struck out in search of the Osages.[81] Early the following year another party of Quapaws took to the warpath. Captain Josef Orieta, who had in December of 1770 taken command at Arkansas, wrote the governor that he "could not stop them."[82] They returned a week later without having encountered the enemy.[83] Meanwhile, the Osages continued their depredations on those hunters still venturing onto the river. Antoine Lepine arrived at the Post in January of 1771 "in very bad shape;"[84] he had been robbed of his hides, gunpowder, and weapons. Yet many hunters resolutely refused to abandon a life the risks of which they had long since come to accept.

Despite a pact to behave in more friendly fashion toward the hunters, the Osages resumed hostilities in the fall of 1771 and the fort at the Post became a refugee center for people often wholly deprived of clothing, tools, and weapons. Many others were reported to have been killed.[85] But the lure of the money to be made on the Arkansas kept a number of hunters stubbornly in place since that river was

---

follows is a synopsis of the main events which involved Spanish-Osage relations in late eighteenth-century Arkansas. For a full treatment of this subject, see G. DIN & A. NASATIR, THE IMPERIAL OSAGES, SPANISH-INDIAN DIPLOMACY IN THE MISSISSIPPI VALLEY (1983).

81. Demasellière to General, Oct. 17, 1770, AGI, PC, leg. 107.
82. Orieta to Governor, Jan. 28, 1771, AGI, PC, leg. 107.
83. Id. to id., Feb. 2, 1771, AGI, PC, leg. 107.
84. Id. to id., Sept. 11, 1771, AGI, PC, leg. 107.
85. Id.

ten times as lucrative as either the White or the St. Francis. Early the next year, full of apprehension, Captain Fernando de Leyba wrote to the governor. Two hunters had fallen victim to the Osages the day after Christmas the preceding year, and just now a Mr. Castelin had come from the river to report that a Mr. Doget, his wife, and some of his children had been killed by a war party of forty Osages. They were only sixty leagues away and heading toward the fort. As the Quapaw warriors were forty leagues away hunting on the White River they could be of no help. Arkansas Post was "the weakest in the colony," the commandant lamented, and the Osages may see the opportunity to destroy it. The cannon were so old and there was so little ammunition that the garrison would doubtless find it necessary, he believed, to resort to hand-to-hand combat. "We can only die," he said, "while killing the Indians."[86] Fortunately this last necessity was averted when the Osages lost interest and pulled back upriver.[87] The governor could only comfort Leyba by holding out the hope that perhaps within two years he could relieve him of "this wretched fate." In the meantime, Leyba was directed to instruct the hunters "to meet force with force and to hunt in groups with a rallying point."[88]

In April of the following year a Quapaw war party brought back five Osage scalps and an Osage woman and child as prisoners. The chief made the commandant a present of two of the scalps to be transmitted to General O'Reilly in New Orleans. Leyba thus found himself in an increasingly impossible position. On the one hand, his instructions were to try to discourage this kind of thing. On the other hand, the French settlers were delighted with the activities of the Quapaws, calling them their protectors, and embracing them when they returned from raids on the

86. Leyba to Governor, Jan. 4, 1772, AGI, PC, leg. 107.
87. Id. to id., Jan. 25, 1772, AGI, PC, leg. 107.
88. Governor to Leyba, Jan. 26, 1772, AGI, PC, leg. 107.

Osages. When the commandant showed no enthusiasm for these adventures the Quapaws became infuriated "and say I seem to be glad," Leyba complained, "that the Osages kill the whites." The settlers and hunters formed cliques and when the commandant was out of earshot made fun of his efforts to persuade the Quapaws to be peaceful.[89]

The commandants' letters from Arkansas during the 1770s continue to reveal raids by the Osages on the hunters of the Arkansas River.[90] Likewise, the Quapaws persisted in sending out small war parties which met with occasional success.[91] In 1775 the Illinois Indians caught some Osages in the act of stealing horses and killed them. They gave one of the scalps thus procured to the Quapaw chief who promptly hung it on the main gate of the fort, as had become the custom.[92] All this seemed to have little enough impact on the Osages, who continued to harass, rob, and sometimes murder the French hunters, who in turn continued to risk their necks in pursuit of furs and skins.

The Osages were, for the most part, Missouri Indians, and they were supposed to be controlled by and receive their presents from the lieutenant governor at St. Louis.[93] This official had a great deal of authority over his territory, called simply "the Illinois" in the early Spanish period, and "Upper Louisiana" later. At first, the settlements in the northern reaches of the province were not considerable. Before the founding of St. Louis in 1764, the only right-bank European establishment was Ste. Genevieve which was settled around 1750. For a number of years, Ste. Genevieve, on the Mississippi about sixty miles south of

89. *Id.* to *id.*, April 20, 1773, AGI, PC, *leg.* 107.
90. *See, e.g.*, Orieta to Unzaga, July 19, 1774, AGI, PC, *leg.* 107; *id.* to *id.*, Oct. 30, 1774, AGI, PC, *leg.* 107.
91. *See, e.g.*, Orieta to Governor, May 1, 1775, AGI, PC, *leg.* 107.
92. *Id.*
93. For a list of the Indian tribes for which this lieutenant governor was responsible, see 1 L. KINNAIRD, *supra* note 5, at 155.

St. Louis, was as large as or larger than the latter city. However, St. Louis began early to generate smaller satellite villages: Carondolet in 1767, St. Charles in 1768, and St. Ferdinand in 1785 were the most important.[94] In 1789 New Madrid was founded; and though it was always quite small, it would figure prominently in Arkansas history. At almost exactly 250 miles by river (down the Arkansas and up the Mississippi) from the Post of Arkansas, it was the Post's nearest northern neighbor until the very end of the Spanish period. It also marked the southern boundary of Upper Louisiana until 1797 when a small garrison was placed at Esperanza, known today as West Memphis, Arkansas. Delassus, the last Spanish lieutenant governor of Upper Louisiana, in 1803 regarded Esperanza as the last settlement under his jurisdiction;[95] and Captain Amos Stoddard, who in 1804 became Delassus's counterpart under the American regime, remarked that the Spanish had considered the tiny encampment as the boundary.[96]

Lieutenant Governor Piernas was greatly agitated by the barbarous activities of the Osages and devoted much of his time to dealing with them. In 1772, he succeeded in having two boys who had been captured by the Osages on the Arkansas released and returned to their families at the Post.[97] The Osages had great affection for the English, who courted them constantly and had even given them a flag which they flew over one of their villages. In 1779, Gover-

94. J. PRIMM, LION OF THE VALLEY: ST. LOUIS, MISSOURI 64–6 (1981).

95. Delassus was instructed by the Spanish government to gather up the ordnance and other possessions of the king at the posts under his command and bring them to New Orleans. According to his journal, available at the Missouri Historical Society in St. Louis, Esperanza was the last settlement he visited for this purpose. The main features of Delassus's narrative are given in 2 L. HOUCK, A HISTORY OF MISSOURI 364–69 (1908).

96. A. STODDARD, SKETCHES, HISTORICAL AND DESCRIPTIVE, OF LOUISIANA 205 (1812).

97. 1 L. KINNAIRD, supra note 5, at 204–05.

nor Gálvez wrote to a new lieutenant governor in St. Louis that the Arkansas commandant (now Captain Balthazar de Villiers) was still complaining about the murders and robberies committed by the Osages on the Arkansas River; and he ordered him to consult secretly with the *habitants* of the Arkansas "as to the best means to prevent such atrocities."[98] However, the Osages continued to be a major impediment to the peaceful settlement of the Arkansas throughout the period of Spanish domination of Louisiana. In 1785, Governor Miró called the chiefs of the Arkansas Osages and the Caddos to New Orleans and arranged a treaty, but the peace was quickly broken by the Osages.[99]

Matters worsened. In 1787 the Arkansas commandant Josef Vallière wrote to the governor to report that a hunter just returned from the river said that he had found the bodies of two men and a woman killed by the Osages about 150 miles up the river. The Osages had also set fire to all the hunters' camps and the surrounding prairies.[100] In 1789 twenty "hunters and *habitants*" of the Arkansas Post petitioned Vallière to communicate to the governor their intention to go to war against the Osages. The petition stated that the signatories were in a "state of great poverty, for they are not able to support their families or pay their debts." The reason was graphically put: "We are robbed by the Osages not only of the products of the hunt but even of our shirts."[101]

The petition was not granted. But four years later what is surely one of the most remarkable documents in the entire legal history of Louisiana was written. On April 8, 1793, "the hunters of the dependencies of the Post of Arkansas, being in full agreement to go to war against

98. *Id.* at 321.
99. *Id.* at 173–75.
100. *Id.* at 200.
101. *Id.* at 273–74.

the Osage Indians" executed "the following articles" in French:[102]

1. As it is necessary for the good of humanity and our private interests to punish the Osages for their cruelty towards us, we are unanimously agreed to go to war against them on the first day of May of this year, and, if one of us at that time desires for some frivolous pretext to exempt himself from marching with us, we beg the government not to accord him the right to hunt in this district, for the reason that he did not want to contribute to the public peace.

2. With the consent of Monsieur Delino, our commandant, we name as our group leaders Michel Bonne, Baptiste Dardaine, and Louis Souligny, as being the most capable, and we obligate ourselves to obey their orders implicitly.

3. If one of us happens to lose one of his limbs during the expedition, each hunter agrees to give him two piastres a year to help him to live.

4. Everything which will be taken from the enemy shall be brought to this post, sold at public auction, and the sum divided equally between the members of the expedition.

And will it be believed that the commandant, Captain Juan Ignace Delinó de Chalmette, certified the execution of this contract as having taken place *pardevant nous* and two witnesses, and deposited the same in the archives of the Post?

102. 3 *id.* at 144–45.

VI

Though Indian relations demanded much of the Post commandants' attention, controlling the activities of the European hunters on the Arkansas and the other nearby rivers also gave them considerable grief. "[These hunters] lead a pretty fast life," Captain Josef Orieta complained; "They claim that, being on the river, they owe obeisance to no one."[103] They were thus self-proclaimed "outlaws" in the technical sense. To hear some tell it, many of them were also outlaws in the popular sense.

In 1770, as we noted before, Athanase de Mézières, the lieutenant governor at Natchitoches, wrote to Governor Unzaga about some of the hunters of Arkansas.[104] "On the Akansa River," he said, "there live, under the name of hunters, some men of whose pernicious customs I must give your Lordship a brief account." He painted these people with a broad brush: "Most of those who live there," he claimed, "have either deserted from the troops and ships of the most Christian King or have committed robberies, rape or homicide, that river being the asylum of the most wicked persons, without doubt, in all the Indies." He went on to assess their morality and, in particular, their attitude towards law: "They live so forgetful of the laws that it is easy to find persons who have not returned to Christian lands for ten, twenty, or thirty years, and who pass their scandalous lives in public concubinage with the captive Indian women whom for this purpose they purchase among the heathen, loaning those of whom they tire to others of less power, that they may labor in their service, giving them no other wage than the promise of quieting their lascivious passions; in short they have no other rule than their own caprice, and the respect which they pay the

103. Orieta to Governor, Feb. 2, 1771, AGI, PC, *leg.* 107.
104. ATHANASE DE MÉZIÈRES AND THE LOUISIANA-TEXAS FRONTIER, 1768–1780, 166–68 (H. BOLTON ed., 1913).

boldest and most daring, who control them." The out-
raged lieutenant governor went so far as to assert that these
hunters supplied the Osages with guns and ammunition
and encouraged them to attack the people in his district
and steal women, children, and horses. He suggested to
the governor that he "order that this race, through despairing of all supplies, may be forced to abandon the river on
which they reside." In this way, the lieutenant governor
hoped that the Osages would be deprived of a market
for their human contraband and would pull back farther
north. The same day that he suggested this plan to the governor, De Mézières wrote him to say that François Beau-
doin, "one of the hunters and magnates of the Arkansas
River," had arrived at Natchitoches with his family and a
captive Indian girl. The lieutenant governor had arrested
him immediately, he reported, and was sending him to
New Orleans.[105]

In another letter, De Mézières gives some information about an Arkansas denizen nicknamed Brindamúr, to
whom we alluded briefly before, "whose sole employment
was to roam the forests and entertain himself in hunting—
an occupation very conducive to laziness and to all other
vices as well."[106] It seems that this man had seduced a
married lady of Pointe Coupée and had taken her to his
camp in Arkansas. When Brindamúr and his paramour
learned of the death of the good lady's husband (which
De Mézières attributed to "the unexpected rashness of
his wife"), they descended the Arkansas River, "famous
aslyum of evildoers," to the Post where they got married.
The lieutenant governor continued his tale: "They then returned at once to their haunts, because the groom, who
was of gigantic frame and extraordinary strength, had
made himself a petty king over those vagabonds and highwaymen, who, with contempt for law and subordination,

105. *Id.* at 168-69.
106. *Id.* at 160-63.

with equal insult to Christians, and to the shame of the very heathen, up to now have maintained themselves on that river. But a short time after this new journey inland, it happened that one of his subjects, not only angered at the ill treatment which Brindamúr gave him, but frightened as well of the threats which he made that he would kill him (which he would have done on three different occasions had not the rest prevented it), killed Brindamúr, though tardily, by divine justice for the punishment of the misdeeds chargeable to the said Brindamúr."

It needs no saying after this that at least in Lower Louisiana the reputation of some of the Arkansas hunters could hardly be worse.

It seems likely that De Mézières's account of the Arkansas population alarmed Unzaga. Whether he thought the reports were completely accurate we cannot tell, but very soon we hear of a scheme aimed at civilizing the hunters of the various Arkansas rivers. In 1770 all the hunters were ordered to return to the Post "under penalty of having to pay all the damages caused by Indian raids."[107] Evidently it was thought, at the very least, that their presence on the rivers was aggravating the Osages and that their removal might relieve tensions some. Perhaps also the governor had believed De Mézières's claim that some of them were instigating the Osage attacks in his district.

In May of 1770, seven separate war parties of Osages ransacked many of the hunting camps along the Arkansas taking weapons and ammunition; the Arkansas commandant suspected the English, not any of the French hunters, of instigating the attacks.[108] A few days later a number of hunters sent word that they were returning to the fort with their families,[109] and some in fact soon began trickling in. The Francoeur brothers, for instance, arrived from the

107. Demasellière to General, no date, AGI, PC, *leg.* 107.
108. *Id.* to *id.*, May 14, June 2, and June 4, 1770, AGI, PC, *leg.* 107.
109. *Id.* to *id.*, June 6, 1770, AGI, PC, *leg.* 107.

White River in June of 1770 with women and children; the children did not even have shirts.[110] The Francoeurs had lived on the river for twenty-five years, had taken up with Indian women, and had had a large number of children by them.[111] A man named Sasemission also showed up soon with a family in the same general shape.[112] A month later, a hunter named Bartolmieu arrived with an Indian "wife" and six children. They were so ragged that the *habitants* had to take up a collection for them that brought sixty *piastres* worth of clothing.[113] The commandant's plan was to make all the hunters "go to town"—that is, to New Orleans—to get married and get their children baptized. Better yet, he suggested to the governor, why not send a priest or a monk to the Arkansas for a few days to take care of all of this at once?[114]

One of the reasons that some of the hunters had so readily complied with the order to come down to the Post was that, as we noted, they had been relieved of most of their guns and ammunition by the Osages. Demasellière had ordered the merchants of the Post not to resupply the hunters in order to force their obedience to his order, but this plan proved difficult to effect.[115] On July 15, 1770, the commandant wrote to O'Reilly that while some hunters had returned from the river, "others supplied by [the merchant] Tounoir, against my orders, have remained."[116] The scheme to clear the river of hunters nevertheless continued to meet with some success. The next month the commandant renewed his request for a priest as there had by now arrived

110. *Id.* to *id.*, June 16, 1770, AGI, PC, *leg.* 107.
111. Brothers Francoeur to Demasellière, June 17, 1770, AGI, PC, *leg.* 107.
112. Demasellière to General, June 16, 1770, AGI, PC, *leg.* 107.
113. *Id.* to *id.*, July 15, 1770, AGI, PC, *leg.* 107.
114. *Id.* to *id.*, June 16, 1770, AGI, PC, *leg.* 107.
115. *See id.*
116. Demasellière to ?, July 15, 1770, AGI, PC, *leg.* 107.

at the Post seventy children in need of baptism.[117] When some of the hunters requested permission to return to their camps for their things, Demasellière allowed them to do so but kept back all their women to ensure their return.[118]

By 1786 the general reputation of the Arkansas *coureurs de bois* had not markedly improved. In that year Jean Filhiol, commandant at Ouachita Post (modern-day Monroe, La.), wrote an extremely informative description of his baili-wick, much of which lay within the present-day boundaries of Arkansas.[119] The inhabitants of the Ouachita, like most of the Arkansas population, were subsistence hunters. "These men," Filhiol said, "are composed of the scum of all sorts of nations, several fugitives from their native countries, and who have become fixed here through their attachment to their idleness and their independence, perhaps even to escape from the pursuit of justice before there

117. *Id.* to General, Aug. 7, 1770, AGI, PC, *leg.* 107.

118. *Id.* to *id.*, Aug. 11, 1770, AGI, PC, *leg.* 107.

119. See Filhiol, *Description of the Ouachita in 1786*, 20 LHQ 476 (1937). Jean-Baptiste Filhiol arrived in the Ouachita country in April of 1782 and first settled at Écore à Fabri, the site of present-day Camden, Arkansas. E. WILLIAMS, FILHIOL AND THE FOUNDING OF THE SPANISH POSTE D'OUACHITA: THE OUACHITA VALLEY IN COLONIAL LOUISIANA, 1783–1804, 18 (1982). It is likely that he encountered opposition there from established traders and within a few weeks descended to the site of present-day Monroe, Louisiana, to establish his command. (*Id.*, Preface and 18.) He divided his district into two military units, one of which lay north of the confluence of the Ouachita and Saline Rivers and thus entirely in Arkansas; the unit was supposed to muster every six months at Écore à Fabri. E. WILLIAMS, THE MILITARY TRADITION OF FORT MIRO AND THE POSTE D'OUACHITA IN COLONIAL LOUISIANA, 1783–1804, 1 (1982). At the first muster of the Écore à Fabri unit, probably late in 1784, Filhiol auctioned off a tavern license to Pierre Cuvillier *dit* Champignolle. E. WILLIAMS, SPANISH LAW, JUSTICE, AND THE CHURCH IN THE COLONIAL OUACHITA VALLEY 26 (1983). Presumably the site was at or near Champagnolle in Union County. Filhiol abandoned the Écore à Fabri muster after three years. E. WILLIAMS, THE MILITARY TRADITION OF FORT MIRO AND THE POSTE D'OUACHITA IN COLONIAL LOUISIANA, 1783–1804, 2 (1982).

was a command."[120] As for their morals, Filhiol stated: "Hardly do they know whether they are Christians."[121] At the slightest provocation they would abandon any settlement as "their rifle and their powder horn comprise their entire property, and every country is good to them;" and "if they hunt a little," he said, "it is only to satisfy their first needs of nature."[122] Filhiol tried to coax them into forming an agricultural community, "hoping to have them close together to bring them more easily into social life by counsels and example." His attempt met with little success.[123]

VII

Whether the Spanish government grew bored with its efforts to rid the Arkansas of undesirables, or whether the task was simply beyond its power, it nevertheless is the case that hunters continued for a long time to compose the major portion of Arkansas's eighteenth-century population. The census of Arkansas Post for 1768 reported a total of twelve *habitant* families, including those of Commandant De Clouet and La Vigne the *garde magasin*. The total number of Europeans was seventy-eight, of whom fifty were children. There were thirty slaves living with them.[124] Two years later a census of the white population reported a total of seventy-five persons at the Arkansas.[125] The bulk of the residents at the Post were hunters or mer-

120. Filhiol, *supra.* note 119, at 483–84.
121. *Id.* at 484.
122. *Id.*
123. *Id.*
124. *Recensement des habitants, femmes, enfants, et esclaves du Poste des Arkansas,* AGI, PC, leg. 107.
125. *Estada presente de todo los inhabitantes del Puesto de los Arkancas* . . . , AGI, PC, leg. 107.

chants. *Habitants* of a more or less permanent sort with a stake in making a true and lasting settlement of the Post were extremely difficult to attract, because engaging in agriculture there was almost impossible.

Proof of this is provided by a lengthy and interesting report which Captain De Villiers submitted to the governor in August of 1777, in which he gave a short account of the history of the Post and recounted the extreme difficulties which the few *habitants* there had experienced.[126] "This settlement was moved about 1756," he said, "during the governorship of Kerlérec when Monsieur De Reggio was commandant, from the place called *Écore Rouge* [Red Bluff] to the place where it is presently situated, eleven leagues down the river [on the right bank in descending] and four leagues from its mouth." (*Écores Rouges* is what the French called the area where the Arkansas Post National Memorial is now located.) When the Post was moved, the commandant claimed, its new situation was flooded only every eight or nine years. "Today", however, he went on to say, "it is regularly underwater every year." De Villiers complained that the "water rises and destroys the fruits of the labor of the *habitants* and the savages, and they are all discouraged." He argued vigorously that the Post should be moved back to *Écores Rouges*. It was true that this might cause some inconvenience to the Illinois convoys. But river traffic was slight anyway: "The king no longer sends boats on his own account," he asserted, "and the four or five which ascend to the Illinois on behalf of private parties can just as well (and a good deal more securely) obtain supplies eleven leagues higher up the river where livestock and other produce could come without any obstacle." More importantly, he said, one could attract respectable

126. What follows is based on De Villiers to Gálvez, August 3, 1777, AGI, PC, *leg.* 190.

habitants to such a place.

As expected, De Villiers was much concerned about the character of the people who lived in Arkansas. More than once in his letters he referred to his desire to establish a "respectable settlement" on his river. The census included in his 1777 report had listed only seven *habitant* families of fifty whites and eleven slaves; and at least four of these families were headed by merchants. De Villiers described the Post as being "a place of residence for merchants and a supply point for the hunters who come here to equip themselves . . . paying their debts and then equipping themselves anew or taking their catch to town."[127] He regarded the hunters as altogether undesirable people. "You would not believe," he wrote the governor in January of 1777, "the brigandage, the insubordination, and the libertinage which have reigned for so long on this river."[128] In March of 1779 he was much more pointed: "The hunters [are] for the most part people of bad behavior who could soon be replaced by more useful colonists"[129] if only a more suitable settling place were provided. "Farmers without the embarrassment of the families of hunters" were what, in De Villiers's view, was needed; and that required moving the Post to a place where agriculture was possible.

The *habitants* were, however, quite skeptical about De Villiers's scheme. They were at first "all determined to descend to the coast of the colony rather than [move upriver and] expose themselves to the incursions of the savage Chickasaws."[130] Thus, not "being assured of being protected by a fort," and given the reluctance of his *habitants*, De Villiers for a time suspended his plan for removal. But

127. *Id.*
128. De Villiers to Gálvez, January 25, 1777, AGI, PC, *leg.* 190.
129. *Id.* to *id.*, March 2, 1779, AGI, PC, *leg.* 192.
130. *Id.*

the ravages of the spring flood of 1779 convinced the *habitants* that their position was no longer tenable. Even the most elevated houses faced ruin, almost all the livestock had drowned, the fort was open in several places, and the well had caved in.[131] Somehow the good captain convinced the *habitants* to make the twenty-seven mile journey up the river despite the lack of a fort there, rather than abandon the Arkansas entirely.

On March 2, the commandant wrote that in a few days he was going to lead a first contingent to the new establishment at *Écores Rouges*.[132] These were the families of some hunters from the St. Francis and the families of Anglo-American refugees that had been granted asylum the year before when they had found Concordia (British Ozark) deserted.[133] Their arrival had more than doubled the white population of Arkansas Post. They were to make some temporary cabins at the new site. "The savages," De Villiers claimed, "strongly approve the steps that I am taking, and so much the more since there are eight inches of water on the place where they planted their crops—the which are lost."[134]

Three weeks later De Villiers wrote that on March 16 he had removed to *Écores Rouges* with a part of his detachment.[135] The relocation of the Post, he said, was being made "with the unanimous consent of the *habitants* who could no longer stay at the old settlement, there being six

---

131. *Id.*

132. *Id.*

133. Their petition for asylum is in AGI, PC, *leg.* 191, as is a census of them taken Feb. 20, 1778.

134. De Villiers to Gálvez, March 2, 1779, AGI, PC, *leg.* 192.

135. What follows is based on De Villiers to Gálvez, March 22, 1779, AGI, PC, *leg.* 192.

inches of water in the most elevated house." *Les Écores Rouges*, De Villiers wrote, were on the left bank (north side) of the river and were a little over a mile long. They formed three hills. On the first hill in ascending some of the Quapaws from the three villages had camped; on the second the captain placed the Anglo-American refugee families; and on the third he situated the French *habitants* and projected a fort.

By April 10, the commandant could write that "the new post now contains all the *habitants* of the old one. Their houses are built or in preparation and the livestock that was saved [has also arrived]."[136] With this letter De Villiers sent a map of his new establishment, drawn to scale and giving an excellent picture of his circumstances. He had put the *habitants* on two streets. On the river front (the first row of houses) he had placed "the merchants and others who hardly ever bother to make a crop"; and on the back row he had placed "the farmers, to whom I shall give a depth which you judge to be appropriate and which is proportionate to the small frontage which they have." De Villiers explained that the *habitants'* lots were only twenty *toises* (about forty-four yards) wide "in order to put them as close to the fort as possible." This was a far cry from the usual width of a holding in a common field in Spanish Louisiana and was made necessary by the danger of Indian attack. The projected fort was to be built only about seventy yards from the cliff because the river had formed at this new location a *batture* (gravel beach) that "widens constantly and thus protects the bank from caving in." Though he was obviously quite pleased with his prospects, De Villiers again cautioned the governor that "to give any

136. What follows is based on De Villiers to Gálvez, April 10, 1779, AGI, PC, *leg.* 192.

1. Encampment of the detachment   2. Site of the fort   3. Glacis (slope)   4. *Habitants* of the 1st row
5. *Habitants* of the 2nd row   6. Streets   7. An American *habitant*   8. American settlement
9. Arkansas of the 3 villages   10. Low country flooded at high water   11. Bayou draining the prairies

5. Settlement of the Post of Arkansas at Red Bluffs (*Écores Rouges*) on March 17, 1779.

stability to this new settlement it is necessary to have farmers." Only a little more than two weeks later the commandant wrote proudly that "this new post finds itself completely established."[137] The captain now remembered to be concerned about the settlers' title to their land. "The *habitants* have built on the assurance which I have given them that you will not change anything in the dispositions which I have made in the arrangement of their lands," he wrote, and he asked the governor's approval of what he had done. "Please authorize me," he requested, "to guarantee them their property."

The governor replied that De Villiers should send the *habitants'* papers to him so that he could execute grants in proper form in order to avoid the titles being put in question in the future.[138] This was in accord with the regulations, promulgated in 1770 by General O'Reilly, which required all grants to be made by the Governor.[139] In fact, those same regulations required that the governor send a surveyor to fix the bounds of all grants in the presence of the commandant of the district and two adjoining landowners.[140] There is no indication that De Villiers ever provided the governor with the papers requested, and there is no evidence that any Spanish surveyor was at work in Arkansas until very late in the century.

In the same letter the captain identified another pressing need of his fledgling establishment, and in doing so divulged important information about the nature of his pop-

137. De Villiers to Gálvez, April 28, 1779, AGI, PC, *leg.* 192. The paragraph that follows is based on this letter.

138. Gálvez to De Villiers, no date, 1779, AGI, PC, *leg.* 192.

139. These regulations are translated several places. I have used the version which appears in 2 J. WHITE, A NEW COLLECTION OF LAWS, CHARTERS, AND LOCAL ORDINANCES . . . . 231–33 (1830). The relevant portion is § 13.

140. *Id.*

ulation. "The few *habitants* there are at this place, nearly all hunters and always outside, desire for their safety and that of their families to have a fort and a detachment capable of protecting them." He stressed that without these precautions there could never be "a respectable settlement" on the Arkansas. Doors, windows, and frames from the old fort could be used, leaving as the greatest expense a "palisaded fortification sufficient to repel the savages." Perhaps the *habitants* should be compelled to contribute, he opined, but since the fort was to be only about seventy-five or eighty yards square, it should not prove too expensive.

According to De Villiers's map, the new Post had thirty houses and perhaps ten acres of land devoted to agriculture, and was perched on a highland on a horseshoe bend of the Arkansas River. Seventeen of these houses, however, belonged to the American refugees and were only temporary. De Villiers calls them *cabans* in his letters. Of the other thirteen houses (called *maisons* by De Villiers, an indication of greater permanence), only four were on the back row which the commandant had reserved for farmers. De Villiers gave each American refugee only twenty feet of land on the river, and his map shows at the *Établissement Américain* no fields behind their cabins. In the spring of 1780 nine American agricultural families arrived from Illinois, as did a number of others from South Carolina.[141] Obviously, steps were being taken to encourage settlement and De Villiers must have felt himself on the verge of success in his effort to make a respectable village of Arkansas Post. In May De Villiers wrote excitedly that "an Ameri-

141. M. Thomas, "The Arkansas Post of Louisiana, 1682–1783" 75 (M.A. Thesis, Berkeley, 1948). In April of 1780 the commandant reported that "twenty American families coming from South Carolina have arrived at the mouth of this river; seven asked me for settlements in this post which I have given them awaiting your orders." De Villiers to Gálvez, April 27, 1780, AGI, PC, *leg.* 192.

can family composed of nine persons has arrived to stay. They came from Illinois and ought to be followed by several others, all farmers. This is going to give this Post a stability which it has never had. I am doing my best to encourage them."[142] That summer, the commandant formed the first militia company in Arkansas since the "habitants of this post have reached a sufficient number;" there were two units, one for the French and another for the Americans.[143] That fall, sixteen more American families arrived and the captain said that he was "going to give them settlements."[144]

However, in 1782 the commandant reported only fifteen habitant families at the Arkansas; and five of these abandoned the river later that year.[145] This loss of population is almost certainly attributable to the cataclysmic events which occurred at the Post in the 1780s. Only a very few months after the 1779 map was drawn, Spain sided with the American colonists and declared war on Great Britain.[146] Arkansas Post was the most vulnerable of all the Spanish forts in the Mississippi Valley because of its isolation and the smallness of its garrison. Until it was reinforced by twelve soldiers in 1781, the garrison at full strength boasted only a captain and twenty soldiers. The possibility of a British attack on the Post was therefore very much on the minds of its soldiers and habitants. In this tense atmosphere, two German soldiers (members of the Spanish detachment) and several American settlers at the Post were accused early in 1782 of plotting to betray it. They had planned to open the gates of the fort to British

142. De Villiers to Gálvez, May 15, 1780, AGI, PC, leg. 192.
143. Id. to id., July 18, 1780, AGI, PC, leg. 192.
144. Id. to id., October 16, 1780, AGI, PC, leg. 192.
145. Faye, The Arkansas Post of Louisiana: Spanish Domination, 27 LHQ 629 at 639 (1944).
146. What follows is based on Din, Arkansas Post in the American Revolution, 40 AHQ 3 at 4 et seqq. (1981).

sympathizers who would then butcher the garrison. De Villiers took depositions from various people, including those accused, and sent the record and the defendants to New Orleans where a special tribunal sentenced two of the Americans and the two German soldiers to death.[147]

Most unfortunately, the records of De Villiers's proceedings cannot be located. But when Governor Miró wrote to the captain general in Havana for confirmation of the sentence, though his letter was short, he revealed a great deal in it.[148] He described Arkansas Post as being very vulnerable since it was 250 leagues [sic] from its nearest northern neighbor. Arkansas was an immense country, he said, inhabited by innumerable Indians among whom lived many wandering Englishmen, the one group influencing the other, "and as hard to get rid of as a hydra-headed monster." The governor then went on sheepishly to admit that the record he was sending would reveal an error: The accused had not been confronted by the two witnesses against them. But since they had confessed and it would take too long to get the witnesses to New Orleans, Miró asked that the captain general overlook *esta pequeña falta* ("this small error"). Time was of the essence and Miró closed by saying that allowing such acts as these to go unpunished leads to occurances like the Natchez rebellion of the previous year—"fatal consequences" Miró termed them. The short reply from Cuba followed three and a half weeks later. The captain general let the conviction stand and the sentence was carried out.[149]

Under O'Reilly's Laws, no appeal was allowed in criminal cases; but it was provided that "if the judge shall have doubts, or from some difficulties on the trial he shall think it desirable, he can, if he likes, seek the counsel of a supe-

147. *Id.* at 13, n. 28; Faye, *supra* note 145, at 671.
148. For the following, *see* Miró to Cagigla, May 5, 1782, AGI, PC, *leg.* 1305.
149. Din, *supra* note 146, at *id.*

rior tribunal."[150] Here the governor had good reason to doubt the validity of the sentence, for under Spanish law there was no question that even a confessed traitor was entitled to be confronted by the witnesses against him.[151] Everyone involved knew this. This case is yet another example of legal norms yielding to political exigency and reveals again the highly subjective character of the process of adjudication in eighteenth-century Arkansas.

Suspected of treason, and many of them probably still segregated in hovels, the Americans remaining behind must have felt at the very least unwelcome and would have been justified in feeling apprehensive as to their safety. When De Villiers called up the militia a few months later, only five "honest" farmers among the Americans were included in the call; the rest, he said, remained suspect following the conspiracy.[152] It is no wonder that many American families emigrated late in 1782.

On April 17, 1783, at 2:30 a.m. a pro-British force of fewer than seventy men, mostly Chickasaws, led by the squawman James Colbert, struck the Arkansas Post. They had reached the settlement without alerting the patrol and killed two soldiers, wounded another, and captured an officer, six soldiers, and five *habitant* families. After a considerable battle during which the soldiers in the fort fired perhaps 300 cannon rounds, a daring sally from the fort by a force of ten soldiers and four Quapaws so unnerved Colbert's band that it beat an immediate retreat.[153] Only four years after having reestablished itself primarily for the purpose of attracting settlers, therefore, the hapless Arkansas settlement was in a shambles. Its little community rent by treason, executions, and warfare, it had once again es-

150. See *Instructions, supra*, note 6, at 41, 42.
151. Professor Allan J. Kuethe kindly corresponded with me concerning this matter.
152. Din, *supra* note 146, at 17.
153. *Id.* at 23–25.

tablished itself as a place to avoid. Arkansas Post long remained a place where it was well, whatever your nationality or status, to keep your opinions to yourself. In 1788 François Menard, by now surely the richest man at the Post, confided to the Abenaki medal chief that it would not be long until the Americans took over Louisiana, and that the tribe had better look to taking the right side in the event of a struggle.[154] So at least Joseph Tessié, in his deposition, accused Menard of saying; no one else heard it, but three sergeants of the garrison swore that they were in the same room where the words were alleged to have been spoken. Tessié had turned to them and repeated what he claimed Menard had said. Captain Josef Vallière sent the depositions and Menard to New Orleans. He apologized for not sending a pre-trial examination of the defendant, but the Post had no jail, a defect that he was hoping soon to supply.

VIII

In 1785, Captain Jacobo Dubreuil Saint-Cyr, commandant at the Post, wrote to Governor Miró in New Orleans.[155] Reports of recent Acadian arrivals in Louisiana had reached the Quapaws, Dubreuil said, and they had implored him to write to have some of the new immigrants establish at Arkansas. In an early example of Arkansas boosterism, the captain waxed eloquent about the "properties of this soil and of the flat, high land" which, he assured the governor, was "capable of supporting at least a thousand families." He sent a sample of the tobacco grown at the Post, for which he claimed "a better quality than that

154. What follows is based on Vallière to Miró, May 16, 1788, AGI, PC, *leg.* 140.
155. Dubreuil to Miró, Oct. 28, 1785, AGI, PC, *leg.* 107.

of Natchitoches." Nuts and acorns were so plentiful, he boasted, that the cows grew larger than New Orleans oxen. The governor, unimpressed, wrote back to say that although he knew the advantages of Arkansas Post, it was "necessary to populate Lower Louisiana before Upper."[156] Nevertheless, in time and in its new situation, Arkansas Post was able to attract a few agricultural families. By 1791, the census reveals twenty-seven households at *Poste des Arkansas*.[157] Almost all the people enumerated were French, mostly French Canadian and some native Louisianians. Desruisseaux, Soumande, Beauvay, Bougy, Placie, Racine, Pino, Menard, Billiet, Lefevre, Jardela, Vasseur, Duchassin, Levergne, Pitre, and Trudeau: All these families are known to be of French origin.[158] Martin Serrano, who had been in the garrison, having been captured by Colbert's raiders and later released, was the only Spaniard apparent among the inhabitants. A German-speaking community was beginning to appear: Michael Wolf, Leonard Keplar, George Leard, Francis Gimblet, and Pierre Christian belonged to it. They evidently had lived in the British colonies or the United States before migrating to the Post; but there is no one in the census who can be classified as Anglo-American. Even a conservative estimate puts the French proportion of the white population at upwards of eighty percent.

The occupations of thirty-six of the persons enumerated in this census are given. There is a carpenter, five merchants, two seamstresses (both of mixed French and Indian blood), one laborer, a craftsman (*menuisier*), and twenty-six who claimed to be farmers (*cultivateurs*). However, there are only sixteen farmer households (many of those

156. Miró to Dubreuil, Dec. 23, 1785, AGI, PC, *leg*. 107.

157. *Rescencement du Poste des Arkansas de l'Anné 1791*, AGI, PC, *leg*. 2365.

158. Mrs. Dorothy Jones Core very kindly assisted me in identifying the nationality of the people in the 1791 census.

called *cultivateurs* were sons of heads of households), and their entire product for the year was 126 barrels of wheat and 1,815 barrels of corn. With eight slaves and three sons, the good widow Desruisseaux had produced six barrels of wheat and 200 of corn; Antoine Beauvay, with a wife, five sons, a daughter, and six slaves, had produced ten barrels of wheat and 200 of corn; and Joseph Bougy, with a wife, three sons, two daughters, and seven slaves, had produced twelve barrels of wheat and 180 of corn. Together these three families owned twenty-one of the thirty-seven slaves at the Post and produced about thirty percent of the year's yield of corn. The largest slaveholder at the Post was the widow Menard. François's relict, she owned nine of the Post's remaining sixteen slaves but she was listed as a *marchande* and produced no crop at all. The total white population was given at 107.

During the next few years the Arkansas continued its growth in population and long-term prospects. Already in 1793, when Captain Pedro Rousseau, commander of the war galiot *La Flecha*, visited the Post of Arkansas, he reported that the Post had about thirty houses "with galleries around, covered with shingles, which form two streets." Below the fort "were a dozen quite pretty houses of four by four arpents, where there are very beautiful fields of wheat on the highland." [159] While Rousseau thus seemed reasonably high on the place, a 1796 visitor, Victor Collot, had a somewhat different perspective. "Two ill-constructed huts, situated on the left," he sneered, "surrounded with great palisades, without ditch or parapet, and containing four six-pounders, bear the name of fort." When Collot passed through the Post a Spanish engineer was there investigating the possibility of a new fort made necessary, yet again, by the action of the river. The village proper

159. A. NASATIR, SPANISH WAR VESSELS ON THE MISSISSIPPI 165–66 (1968).

Collot described as "a little behind this fort," and, he said, "it may contain from forty to fifty whites." He noted that since the *habitants* had "no means of defense against the Indians, who are continually pillaging their cattle and robbing them of their industry, they are in general poor and miserable."[160]

Collot did single out Michael Wolf for praise: "A single farm, belonging to Mr. Wolf, a German, evinced what might be expected from a country thus fertile. He was employed in gathering his corn harvest, which yielded him two hundred fold. The quality of the wheat was certainly equal to that of the best departments of France; which leaves no doubt, that under a government favorable to agriculture, this cultivation would be attended with the greatest success. But with an administration so vicious as the present, Mr. Wolf was compelled to display a constancy and firmness of character which are rarely to be found."[161]

Mr. Wolf was indeed an industrious gentleman. In 1791 he produced, without the help of slaves, eighteen barrels of wheat and eighty barrels of corn. Though his household contained, besides himself, only his wife and three *enfans*, this output made him the second largest producer of wheat at the Post.

At almost exactly the same time as Collot arrived at Arkansas, a signal event in the history of the Post took place, one that provided a sure sign that the little settlement was struggling towards a kind of maturity. This was the creation of the parish of *Los Arcos*, the first canonical parish ever erected in the Arkansas country.[162] When Pierre Janin arrived on August 5, 1796, and established himself as first pastor, he was also the first resident priest that Arkan-

160. 2 V. COLLOT, A JOURNEY IN NORTH AMERICA 40 (1826).
161. *Id.* at 41.
162. For details, see p. 119, *infra*.

sas Post had had since Father Carette had left in despair thirty-eight years previous. Less than a year later, on June 27, 1797, Governor Carondolet made an effort to encourage economic development by making, in one instrument, grants of land at the Arkansas to ten different Americans. The largest, of one million arpents, was made to Elisha Winter; and two others, of 250,000 arpents each, were made to William and Gabriel Winter.[163] The Governor said in his grant that his object was "to encourage population and agriculture, by every means that the political circumstances of the time will admit." He admonished the commandant that no other American families besides the grantees should be admitted into the area; "but," he added, "the commandant may admit good colonists, such as Spaniards, French, Germans, and Dutch." It was made an express condition of the concession that the grantees take possession within a year, else the "concession shall be void." The census of 1798[164] shows that William Winter was resident, but the only other grantee under this concession enumerated was Joseph Stilwell who had been given 600 arpents.

The census for 1798, the last which survives from the eighteenth century, reported a white population of 341 at the Arkansas, more than triple that of 1791, and they were living in almost 120 different households.[165] Resident with them at the Post were three free persons of mixed blood and fifty-six slaves. Though the residents' occupations were not given in this census, the product of the *habitants* was. The corn harvest had actually decreased from 1,815 barrels in 1791 to 1,200 in 1798. Tobacco had been added as a crop in the report, but only six farmers grew it. In-

163. Translations of this grant are available in a number of places. I have used the one in 3 AMERICAN STATE PAPERS, PUBLIC LANDS 290 (1834).
164. See *Padron del Puesto de Arkansas, 1798*, AGI, PC, leg. 2365.
165. See *id.*, *passim*.

deed, only twenty-five of the households (about twenty percent of the total number) reported any crop at all. Madame Desruisseaux was still resident and was still a major farmer. She had produced 200 *minots* of wheat and 150 barrels of corn; Joseph Bougy had produced 200 *minots* of wheat and 100 barrels of corn; Pierre Lefevre had produced 150 *minots* of wheat; Jose Tessier was next in importance with 100 barrels of corn. These were the champion growers of the Arkansas. Only two farmers, Martin Serrano and Estevan le Vasseur, grew wheat, corn, and tobacco, and for this they deserve at least an honorable mention. Beauvais had died. Michael Wolf, our industrious German so admired by Collot, had done likewise.

Though some progress had been made, it seems more than apparent that the Arkansas Post of Louisiana was not, even by the end of the eighteenth century, primarily an agricultural village. With only twenty per cent of the population which submitted to the census reporting a harvest, it seems clear that the desire to create at the Arkansas a stable farming community had proved difficult to realize. The tiny gross agricultural output gives credence to the reports of early nineteenth-century travelers who time and time again assert that even at that late date Arkansas Post gave shelter mainly to a population of hunters and Indian traders.

The population was still heavily French. Familiar Arkansas names were reported: Desruisseaux, Gossiot, Bougy, Placid, Menard, Fagot, Caillot, Pino, Pertuis (nine of them in four different households), Jardelas, Le Vasseur, Soumande, Dardenne (ten of this name are found), La Vergne, Vaugine, Imbau (sixteen of them in four different households), Bonne, Duchassin, Guignolet, Barthelemi, Saussier, Lefevre, Janine, and Francoeur are among those listed. Martin Serrano with his wife and son, and Juan Batista Rodriguez, a bachelor, provided the tiny identifiably Spanish contingent of the population. But there were newcomers who were not French. Joseph Mason, a Kentuckian, had arrived. Christopher Cauffman had come from Virginia. Asher Brown, Joseph Fletcher, Joseph Greenawalt, John Curry, Silas Bailey, and Samuel Pitney had also arrived, presumably from somewhere in that new country called the United States.

The nationalities of almost seventy-five percent of the households at the Post at this time are either known or reasonably certain.[166] Seventy per cent of those known are French, and of the remaining unknown probably a greater percentage are. The French households, moreover, tended to be larger than the others. The American Joseph Stilwell with his wife and seven children was an exception.

Instruments bearing on the proof of Spanish land claims and presented to the Board of Land Commissioners in the early nineteenth century also yield some interesting data about the nationality of the residents of late eighteenth-century Arkansas.[167] The first board, established in 1804, passed on a total of 127 claims to Arkansas land. A surprising number of these claims were for land on the St. Francis River and on the Mississippi River north of the Arkansas, or around Esperanza, which was, as noted before, founded in 1797, and situated at modern-day West Memphis. There were about forty such claims, and twenty-five of them were advanced by or alleged to be derived from Americans. Six of the other claims name Benjamin Fooy (a Dutchman) or a member of his family as original grantee, and six are claims by Spaniards who were once members of the

166. Mrs. Dorothy Jones Core very kindly assisted me in identifying the nationality of the people listed in this census.

167. What follows is drawn from the MINUTES OF THE BOARD OF LAND COMMISSIONERS which are located in the Archives of the Secretary of State of Missouri, Jefferson City, Mo. Some of the claims that were allowed, of course, were fraudulent, and that makes it somewhat hazardous to use those records for the purpose of determining who was settled in Arkansas in the eighteenth century. See A DOCUMENTARY HISTORY OF ARKANSAS 26 (C. WILLIAMS ET AL eds., 1984) for allegations of fraud in connection with claims to land on the Cache and White rivers.

Esperanza garrison. Joseph Vallière, Augustin Grande, and Jacques Gossiot are the only original grantees in this area identifiable as Frenchmen. All of these grants but one, however, were made in 1800 or after and most of them after 1802. The single eighteenth-century grant was a concession to Joseph Stilwell "on the River St. Francis" for 600 arpents which had been made by Captain Charles de Villemont, Commandant of the Arkansas Post, on April 25, 1798. This grant was among a total of only eight confirmed in this area of Arkansas. Seven were confirmed to Americans, one to John Henry Fooy. None was confirmed either to or through a Frenchman; nor were any of the grants to the Spaniards confirmed at this time.

Plainly the settlers of Arkansas north of the Post were latecomers and largely American. Around the Post, up the Arkansas River, and on the southern part of the White River, things were different. About seventy-five claims were filed for land in that area, and of the original grantees or occupants whose nationalities are reasonably certain, forty were French, one Spanish, two German, and eleven American. Moreover, of the confirmed grants among these (twenty-one in all) thirteen of the original grantees or occupants were Frenchmen, one was a Spaniard, two were Germans, and four were Americans. The earliest grant in any of the Americans' chains of title dates from 1800, and the total number of acres confirmed to Americans was less than 1,000.

The original grantees or occupants who were French, however, produced evidence of title going back to the 1780s. Interestingly, the earliest document in any chain of title is from Captain Josef Vallière, commandant at Arkansas, dated September 25, 1787; it concerned Joseph Bougy's petition for 320 arpents of land. This confirms the picture which emerged above that serious settlement at the Arkansas did not much predate 1790. In fact, the next earliest document is a 1790 grant from commandant Josef Vallière to Louis Gotiot; later the same year, the new commandant Ignace Delinó made a grant to Pierre Lefevre. 1791 proved a big year for the Arkansas: Governor Miró made four grants that year, totaling about 1,250 arpents, to François Menard, John Levergnes, Leonard Keplar, and Michael Wolf. The last three grants were made on the same day (May 6), and it is clear from the surrounding evidence that they were made in an attempt to clear up titles based on prior possession.

The figures above show that forty of fifty-four original grantees or occupants of claimants' land in lower Arkansas were French, about seventy-five percent. With respect to land which was confirmed to claimants, thirteen of twenty, or sixty-five percent, had been originally granted to or occupied by a Frenchman. In both instances, the facts reveal that American penetration would seem to be almost exactly twenty percent.

IX

The procedure for obtaining and perfecting a land grant from the Spanish government of Louisiana can be reconstructed with remarkable ease from printed sources. That is partly because the number of unadjudicated claims based on Spanish land grants remained large well into the nineteenth century.[168] Since ultimate resolution of these claims depended on their validity under Spanish law, many people were drawn to ransacking the old books for ordinances and regulations dealing with grants from the Spanish royal

168. In 2 J. WHITE, *supra* note 139, at 10, 11, an 1829 letter from White to Henry Clay is reproduced in which White estimates that unsettled claims "in Louisiana, Alabama, Missouri, Arkansas, and Florida yet cover ten or twelve millions of acres."

domain; and many of these laws found their way into print at various times after the American takeover.[169]

As soon as O'Reilly had established himself in authority in New Orleans, he made an extensive trip into the interior of what is now the state of Louisiana to make inspections, hear complaints, and generally inform himself on the state of governmental affairs in some of the remote posts in Lower Louisiana. Of course he did not journey as far north as the Arkansas. Upon his return, he issued a set of regulations bearing on the concession of land. Under them, each newly arrived family was entitled to a plot of six or eight arpents in front by forty in depth. The grantees as *quid pro quo* were expected to build levees and ditches during the first three years of their possession and were obligated to keep the roads in repair. Within the same three-year period, moreover, they were "bound . . . to clear the whole front of their land to the depth of two arpents." If grantees did not fulfill these conditions, the regulations provided, "their land shall revert to the king's domain and be granted anew." During the initial three years of possession, which had the aura of a probationary period, written permission from the governor to make an alienation was required; and he was not to give it unless, "on strict inquiry, it shall be found that the conditions above explained have been duly executed."[170] There was also a requirement that the entire front of each concession be enclosed during the three-year period, but it was not made an express condition of the grant.[171] All grants were to be made by the governor and the government surveyor was to fix the bounds in the presence of the local commandant and two settlers. These last four were to sign a *procès-verbal* reciting the events, and three copies of it were to be made: One for the archives of

169. The most complete compendium is the work by Joseph M. White *supra* note 139.

170. J. WHITE, *supra* note 139, at 220.

171. *Id.* at 230.

the Cabildo, one for the governor, and one for the proprietor "to be annexed to the titles of his grant."

Though these regulations were clearly generated by local conditions encountered by O'Reilly on his visits, and while Opelousas, Attakapas, and Natchitoches were specifically mentioned in them more than once, it seems that the general intended these rules to be observed everywhere in Louisiana. They close with the general's injunction to the "governor, judges, Cabildo, and all the inhabitants of this province, to perform punctually to all that is required by this regulation."[172]

Not until 1797 was further regulation of land concessions made. In that year Governor Gayoso laid down some rules on who was qualified to receive grants. A stranger who was not a farmer or artisan, and who was unmarried and propertyless, was ineligible for a concession until he had been a resident for four years. Unmarried artisans, on the other hand, were privileged, and could qualify after having exercised their art or profession for three years. Married settlers could immediately receive 200 arpents plus fifty arpents for each child. It was specifically stated that a new settler would "lose [his lands] without recovery, if, in the term of one year, he shall not begin to establish himself upon them, or if in the third year he shall not have put under labor ten arpents in every hundred." Moreover, grants were to be made contiguously, as to do otherwise "would offer a greater exposure to the attacks of the Indians, and render more difficult the administration of justice, and the regulation of the police . . . ."[173]

When in 1798 the power to regulate land concessions passed to the intendancy, Juan Ventura Morales issued an extensive set of regulations on the subject.[174] No grant was

172. *Id.* at 231.
173. *Id.* at 231–33.
174. The discussion of Morales's regulations which follows is based on *id.* at 234–40.

to exceed 800 arpents. Grantees "on the river" were under the duty to build levees and canals, make and maintain roads, and construct necessary bridges. All settlers were to clear and put in cultivation within three years the whole front of their concessions to a depth of at least two arpents; if they did not, the rules provided, "the land granted [will be] remitted to the domain . . . ." O'Reilly's restraint on alienations during the "probationary" period was repeated, as was Gayoso's instruction on the necessity for contiguous grants.

An interesting feature of Morales's rules was that, for the first time, the point at which title passed to the grantee was precisely fixed. O'Reilly's regulations had not directly spoken to that point. Morales's regulations noted that some people had thought that title passed when their petition for a grant was filed, others when the order of survey was given, and still others when the survey was made. None of these people was right according to Morales. "Real titles" were required before the grant was perfected. These were to be issued when the surveyor's *procès-verbal* and a certified copy of it were sent to the intendant. At that point, the intendant, with the consent of the King's Attorney, would deliver "the necessary title paper." Those occupying lands without such titles were "to be driven therefrom as from property belonging to the crown," except that those who had been in possession ten years or longer would be allowed to stay after paying "a just and moderate retribution." Those not in such a position were given six months to perfect their titles if they could.

There is no evidence whatever that any of this vast array of regulation had the slightest impact in Arkansas. Only twenty-nine claims totalling just over 8,000 acres were confirmed in the entire state of Arkansas by the first board which reported in 1812. (By contrast, 1,311 claims in Mis-

175. *See generally*, on the subject of Spanish land claims in Missouri,

souri were confirmed.)[175] Among the Arkansas claims, fourteen were confirmed on the basis of settlement rights, seven on the ground of ten years' possession, and only eight on the strength of a "concession." Even these last were not complete titles under Spanish law. Four were "concessions" from commandants—one from Vallière, and three from De Villemont. Even under the most liberal construction of O'Reilly's laws, as we have seen, a local commandant had no power to grant lands from the royal domain. The other four "concessions" were from governors, three from Miró, and one from Gayoso. But none of these was supported by a "real title" and thus would have failed under Morales's regulations. There was not a single regular Spanish land title ever made out in the entire state of Arkansas. Captain Amos Stoddard estimated that 95 percent of the land claims in Upper Louisiana were incomplete,[176] but this estimate turned out to be low since only thirteen complete titles were ever made out in the whole Missouri Territory.[177] The lack of anxiety among Arkansas residents about complying with the law was, according to Lafon, a New Orleans engineer, easily explained. "Land situated so remote from population and commerce" he said, speaking of Arkansas Post, "was held in very little estimation, scarcely worth paying the fees of office for the file papers."[178]

The conveyancing practices of commandants and settlers at the Arkansas are illustrated by an extremely interesting pair of documents available in the Archives of the Secretary of State of Missouri in Jefferson City. The first is

---

Violette, *Spanish Land Claims in Missouri*, WASHINGTON UNIVERSITY STUDIES 167 (1921). Also useful are 3 L. HOUCK, *supra* note 95, at 34 *et seqq.* and J. SCHARF, HISTORY OF ST. LOUIS (1883).

176. A. STODDARD, SKETCHES OF LOUISIANA 245 (1811).

177. 1 SCHARF, *supra* note 175, at 32.

178. 3 AMERICAN STATE PAPERS, PUBLIC LANDS 294 (1834).

Joseph Bougy's petition (in French) requesting permission to settle at Arkansas Post: "To Monsieur De Valliere, Captain of infantry, Civil and Military Commandant of the Post of Arkansas: Joseph Bougy, *habitant* of the Post of Kaskaskia, humbly prays, saying that he would like to come to settle in this place of the Arkansas with his family; and [he prays] that it would please you to grant him eight arpents of the ordinary depth on the bank of this river. The applicant will pray for the saving of your days *etc.* Arkansas, 24 September, 1787. Mark X of Joseph Bougy"

The only other document in this chain of title was the following (in Spanish): "I certify the said land [as] belonging to the royal domain. Arkansas, 25 September, 1787. Josef Valliere."

This last document was the only semblance of a "grant" that Bougy had. It was actually only a statement by the commandant that the land was vacant. Beginning in the 1790s, the commandant who endorsed a petition for a land grant almost always prefaced his certificate of vacancy with a statement such as, "I consider the petitioner worthy of the favor which he asks." But during the Spanish period the commandants at the Arkansas never actually purported in writing to make grants from the royal domain.

A new formula introduced at the Post just before the American takeover, however, adopts a tone which stops just short of purporting to make a grant. Caso y Luengo, the last Spanish commandant at the Arkansas, seems responsible for the new language. A good example of it comes from February 26, 1803, when Pierre Lefevre petitioned for an extension of his grant so that he could cut enough trees to build a saw mill. He asked that Caso y Luengo "deign to accord [*acordar*] him an extension of the depth of his land, which he believes, far from prejudicing anyone, would be much to the advantage of the settlement." The commandant replied that since the "proposal would redound much to the benefit of this settlement, I

find no objection to me granting him what he asks. . . ."
This artful reply comes as close to using words of grant as
one can without actually doing so. Caso y Luengo used
these and similar words in many of his endorsements.
It is abundantly clear, however, that the settlers at the
Arkansas regarded their land as having been granted to
them as soon as the commandant endorsed their petitions.
For instance, on May 7, 1799, Charles Drouot, *habitant* of
the Post, petitioned Captain Carlos de Villemont for 240
arpents of land. De Villemont endorsed the request by re-
plying: "I consider the petitioner worthy of the favor which
he requests and it appears to me that the land he wants is
vacant and belongs to the royal domain." The next instrument in this chain of title is one signed by Drouot which
states: "I certify that I have ceded the above-mentioned
concession to Monsieur Pierre Lefevre, in faith of which I
have subscribed [this instrument] at the Arkansas. . . ."
Clearly, though erroneously, Drouot believed that the
commandant's endorsement was a "concession" that had
given him an alienable interest in realty. The practice of the
Board of Land Commissioners was also to describe commandants' endorsements as "concessions," whatever their
language. Petitioners for land in Arkansas often revealed a
belief that commandants had the power to give some kind
of title, for they frequently asked the commandant *accorder
une concession* or *conseder la . . . tierra.* After the American takeover Arkansas commandants were actually bold
enough to claim that they had possessed a power that in
fact the land regulations had clearly denied them. For instance, when in October of 1804 Henry Cassidy became
anxious about the title to land he claimed on the St. Francis, he obtained an affidavit from Caso y Luengo stating
that, when he was commandant, he "had conceded him a
portion of land in the place called the little prairie."
    The commandants and *habitants* of the Arkansas thus
very clearly ignored the extensive set of land regulations

promulgated by various eighteenth-century governors and others. It was simply too costly and too complicated to comply, especially when the benefits of compliance seemed in any case not very great. However, an interesting contrast to this insouciance is provided by the few eighteenth-century wills executed at the Arkansas that have survived. The stakes were higher in the case of wills since very often a great deal of personalty, especially debts and slaves, would purport to pass under them. For instance, in 1791 François Menard executed a will and codicil at the Post shortly before he died leaving to his wife his fourteen slaves (three of whom were runaways), his desk (*bureau*) full of notes and bonds, and his liquor and other merchandise, subject to a trust in favor of his illegitimate daughter Constance.[179] Menard also declared his ownership of a house in New Orleans situated in the *Rue de la Madame Boisclare*.

Captain Juan Ignace Delinó de Chalmette, called to Menard's bedside at four o'clock one morning, did quite a serviceable job of drafting the will and codicil. He caused it to be executed, moreover, in accordance with the formal requirements prevailing in Louisiana. O'Reilly's *Instructions* of 1770 to the post commandants had indicated that wills ought to be signed by the testator, surrogate notary, and five witnesses—two to aid the commandant's attestation and three others.[180] But O'Reilly's Laws of 1769 specifically said that "if there be no notary [attesting], there must be present five witnesses, residents of the place in which the will shall be made; if, however, it be impossible to procure the last-mentioned number, three may suffice." The *Nueva Recopilación de Castilla* was cited in support of this proposition.[181] Delinó had only three witnesses to the will

179. The will, executed July 27, 1791, is included in the papers in a case brought in 1793 by Menard's widow. *See* Spanish Judicial Records, Louisiana History Center, Louisiana State Museum, Feb. 14, 1793.

180. *Instructions*, § 11.

181. *See Instructions, supra* note 6, at 49.

and codicil but this, as just demonstrated, was probably authorized by O'Reilly's Laws. It is likely that this was in any event the custom at the Arkansas since the only other complete specimen of a will executed there in the eighteenth century is executed precisely the same way—indeed, with the same witnesses.[182]

The Spanish archives of Arkansas Post had grown quite large when, on March 23, 1804, they were delivered to Lieutenant James B. Many of the United States Army. There were over 200 items, dating at least to 1780, listed in the inventory which he signed by way of receipt for their delivery by Captain Francisco Caso y Luengo.[183] The archives themselves have, unfortunately, been lost, but the inventory reveals a good deal of interesting data.

The commandant's notarial duties consumed a great deal of his time. There were recorded in the archives eight wills, seven marriage contracts, five other contracts (*acuerdos* and *convenios*), a large number of bonds and receipts, numerous deeds (of land, houses, slaves, and livestock), and three deeds of emancipation. The commandant's judicial duties were also considerable. There were almost thirty probate proceedings and this kind of case probably accounted for a great deal of the commandant's judicial work.

182. The will of Louis Lefevre, executed October 13, 1793, has survived in a number of copies. I have made use primarily of the one in Probate Record Book AA, pages 14–15, at the Probate Clerk's Office, DeWitt, Arkansas. Deputy Circuit Clerk Tommy Sue Keffer brought this instrument to my attention. The witnesses to both the Menard and Lefevre wills were Juan Baptista Duchassin, François Vaugine, and Manuel Reyes. The only other will executed at Arkansas Post in the eighteenth century that I have discovered was that of Captain Balthazar de Villiers. It is in AGI, PC, *leg.* 107. But this is a Spanish translation of a French original and the attestation seems not to have been copied; only a signature is indicated at the end. The will was executed on April 14, 1782, and a codicil to it followed in May.

183. The inventory is in AGI, PC, *leg.* 140 and covers four pages.

It could be rather remunerative as well, especially if the estate was large and thus required some time to inventory and settle. For instance, on May 27, 1778, De Villiers had to travel two leagues downriver from the Post to inventory the goods of Pierre Laclède, the founder of St. Louis, who had died in his trading boat near the mouth of the Arkansas.[184] It took three days and fifteen pages to list all his goods. Interestingly, De Villiers also acted as coroner in this instance, for he noted that, having inspected the body, Laclède's "death had occurred naturally."

Adversarial litigation at the Arkansas may have been rare, but the condition of the evidence is such that statements on this subject are exceedingly hazardous. The inventory of the Post archives records the presence of five petitions (*instancias*), presumably written complaints whose function was the initiation of litigation. The existence of six *procesos* is also mentioned, and these are probably case files that had been advanced at least to the deposition stage. This seems a rather small number of cases, but perhaps both the *instancias* and *procesos* have to do with litigation that would eventually be decided in New Orleans. It is well to recall that matters within the commandant's exclusive jurisdiction could be initiated and determined "verbally" according to O'Reilly's instructions of 1770, so the number of suits adjudicated by the commandant may have been rather larger than the archives at first seem to indicate. In 1792 commandants were ordered to begin keeping a written book of judgments,[185] and the mention in the inventory of a "book which contains various *determinaciónes*" may be evidence that the Arkansas commandants conformed to that requirement. But without such a book it is impossible to tell what the litigation rate in eighteenth-century Arkansas was.

184. AGI, PC, *leg.* 191.
185. J. HOLMES, GAYOSO: THE LIFE OF A SPANISH GOVERNOR IN THE MISSISSIPPI VALLEY, 1789–1799, 67 (1968).

Still, some interesting conclusions can be drawn from even so meager a record as this. For instance, four of the five *instancias* and three of the six *procesos* involved merchants on one side or the other; François Menard alone was a party to five of these eleven cases. Marriage contracts seem to have been employed by relatively few people: Seven within a space of twenty-five years is not a very large number. The social status of the parties to them, moreover, tended clearly toward the *bourgeoisie*: Luis Dianna, Joseph Lambert, Caterina Bartolomé, Juan Larquier, Luisa Jardela, and Joseph Bartolomé, parties to marriage contracts, were all probably of this class. Likewise, those who executed wills were either propertied or of old French families. François Menard, André Lopes, Juan Bauptista Duchasin, and René Soumand were all merchants. Luis Lefevre, though hardly well off, was a member of an important Post family. Not much is known of the social and economic status of Pedro Burel but it is a reasonable guess that he was among the more well-to-do residents of Arkansas.

As was the case in the French period, therefore, it appears that the social and economic class of persons who adhered to European legal traditions and resorted to regular dispute settlement mechanisms was quite narrow and their number very small. They were the merchants and *habitants* of the Post in the technical sense. The hunters, the *coureurs de bois*, the bulk of the Arkansas population of roughly 600 at the end of the Spanish period, simply regulated their lives by whatever light nature could provide them. Many claimed to owe obeisance to no state and steadfastly refused to take part in the ordered, agrarian community that De Villiers and others had so desperately wished to create. They preferred instead to pass their lives in silent beauty and in danger.

III
The Influence of the Church in Eighteenth-Century Arkansas

Legal historians have long known that the church frequently provided an alternative to the state as an agency of social control and dispute settlement. In Louisiana, as elsewhere, the church did in fact aspire to be a partner with the secular government in creating and maintaining the moral order. "Today religion joins with the law," one observer of Louisiana noted: "The one suppresses bad thoughts, the other restrains guilty hands."[1] But the resources of the Louisiana church were simply no match for its ambitions, and nowhere was this truer than in the remote Post of Arkansas.

I

One of the means to which the French resorted in order to attract the loyalty, and therefore the trade, of the Indians of Louisiana was the creation of Jesuit missions to convert and minister to them. Across the Mississippi, contemporary Anglo-Americans were well aware of the part played by the Jesuits in the French effort to gain the affection of the Indians. One New Englander (perhaps a lawyer),

1. 1 Second Voyage à la Louisiane 271 (1803).

greatly alarmed by Law's plans to colonize Louisiana, warned in 1720 that French colonization would result in the disaffection from the English of the Indians inhabiting "the inland countries."[2] Law's colonists would "cut off all Intercourse and Traffic between us and the Indians,"[3] he maintained; and in the event of a war with France the Indians on the west side of the river could prove potent allies for the French.[4] He knew of the missionaries' efforts: "In every tribe there are some missionary priests, and tho' few or none of the savages have ever been made thorough converts to the truths of the *Christian* religion, yet in all other matters they look upon these good Fathers as Teutular *Gods*, and give themselves up entirely to be directed by their Councils."[5] The author concluded his estimation of the danger posed by the missionaries by noting sarcastically: "In short, Sir, he ought to be a *cunning* man that treats with the *Indians*, and therefore the *French* leave that business to the Jesuits."[6]

Even before the grand plans of Law's *Compagnie d'Occident* were laid there was a missionary among the Arkansas Indians. The first missionary to take up residence in Ar-

2. Some Considerations on the Consequences of the French Settling Colonies on the Mississippi, with Respect to the Trade and Safety of the English Plantations in America and the West-Indies 26 (1720) (Repr. 1928). Professor Beverley W. Bond, Jr., in his introduction to the reprint of 1928, says that "the author was from New England, a conclusion that is confirmed by the extensive acquaintance that is shown with the difficulties of a solicitor in the New England admiralty courts." *Id.* at 8.

3. *Id.* at 26.

4. *Id.* at 28.

5. *Id.* at 38.

6. *Id.* at 41. For some discussion of the political and commercial motives which lay behind the French government's desire to establish the Jesuits in Arkansas, *see* J. Delanglez, The French Jesuits in Lower Louisiana 54, 75–76, 434 (1935). *See also* C. O'Neil, Church and State in French Colonial Louisiana 29 (1966), where Iberville is

kansas was Father Nicholas Foucault who established himself among the Quapaws in 1700.[7] He was also the first martyr of the Louisiana territory: He left Arkansas late in July of 1702 in the company of two soldiers and two Koroa Indians; the Indians murdered him along the way under the pretext "of punishing the aged priest for leaving . . ."[8] Serious missionary efforts were evidently not made again until John Law's colonizing schemes of around 1720. At that time the Jesuits undertook to provide a priest for Arkansas; but the Capuchins grumbled that "the Jesuits promise more than they can keep,"[9] and events proved them right. The priest destined for Law's Arkansas colony died on the journey from New Orleans,[10] and only after Law's director Dufresne abandoned the concession in 1726 were the Jesuits able to furnish a replacement. In 1727, Father Paul du Poisson came to Arkansas; in the interim the place had enjoyed only an occasional visit from the peripatetic priests of the region.[11] Two years later Brother Philip Cruez was sent to help Du Poisson, but he died in

---

quoted as saying of the Indians of Louisiana: "We would then promptly put our missionaries among them, who will keep them on our side, and will draw a great number of people to religion." O'Neil concludes, *id.* at 30, that if "for a moment the missionary societies hesitated before Iberville's frankly political role for the missionary, they soon resolved the doubt in his favor."

7. F. Guy, "The Catholic Church in Arkansas, 1541–1803" 34 (n.d.). This unpublished manuscript is among the Guy Papers in the Arkansas History Commission, Little Rock. It is a much expanded version of a thesis submitted by Guy in 1932 for the M.A. degree at the Catholic University of America.

8. *Id.* at 35. Foucault had complained that the Quapaws had mistreated him in unspecified ways and he had therefore resolved to leave them. *See* J. DELANGLEZ, *supra* note 6, at 454 (1935).

9. C. VOGEL, THE CAPUCHINS IN FRENCH LOUISIANA (1722–1766) 86 (1928). Cf. J. DELANGLEZ, *supra* note 6, at 437.

10. 4 M. GIRAUD, HISTOIRE DE LA LOUISIANE FRANÇAISE 217 (1974).

11. F. Guy, *supra* note 7, at 37. Guy there documents visits from

November of 1729 of sunstroke.[12] That very month Du Poisson himself was killed in the massacre at Natchez; the Natchez Indians burst into the chapel there while he was praying and cut off his head with a hatchet.[13] Again the Arkansas was without a priest and had to be content with the episodic visits of wandering missionaries.

The only priest of the French period who stayed long enough to make much of an impact was the Jesuit Father Louis Carette who took up his post in 1750.[14] In August of 1758 he left in despair, taking the church records with him. Over the years, the good father had become increasingly disgruntled with the state of affairs at the Post of Arkansas. For one thing, there was no chapel at the location to which Captain De Reggio moved the Post in 1756, and no effort was being made to provide one. But the event which immediately precipitated Carette's departure involved the irreligious inclination of his French communicants. The commandant's dining room was the only place now to say a mass, "not a very suitable place, not only because it was a dining room, but on account of the bad conduct and freedom of language of those who frequented it."[15] The room

---

Father Lamaine in 1714, Father Charlevoix in 1722, and Father Le Boullenger in 1723.

12. *Id.* at 44.

13. *Id.*

14. *Id.* at 47. Father De Guyenne may have been resident for a brief time around 1732, and Father Avond was at Arkansas from about 1737 to 1740. See DELANGLEZ, *supra* note 6, at 437–39; Faye, *The Arkansas Post of Louisiana: French Domination*, 26 LHQ 633, 675–76 (1943). The 1744 visit of the missionary Father Laurat is documented in Bovey, *Some Notes on Arkansas Post and St. Phillipe in the Mississippi Valley*, TRANSACTIONS OF THE ROYAL SOCIETY OF CANADA 29 (1939). The record of the four baptisms he performed at the Post on July 10, 1744 may be found in *id.* at 39, 40 and in ABSTRACT OF CATHOLIC REGISTER OF ARKANSAS (1764–1858) 74 (D. CORE ed. & N. HATFIELD trans., 1976).

15. J. DELANGLEZ, *supra* note 6, at 444 quoting P. Watrin's BANISHMENT OF THE JESUITS.

was open to everything, even the fowls of the Post; and
after one mass a hen, flying over the altar, knocked over
the chalice, and sacrilegious remarks followed. One person
exclaimed: "There! The God's Shop is upset." "To these
sentiments," the Jesuit Father Watrin wrote of the inhabitants of Arkansas Post, "corresponded a life as little Christian."[16] Father Carette auctioned off his belongings, paid
his debts to the store, and left for New Orleans.[17] Watrin
remarked with regret that Carette had "labored to correct
the morals of the French, but reaped hardly any fruit from
his toil."[18]

The French never sent a replacement for Carette, and
with the suppression of the Jesuit order in Louisiana in
1763 came the end of any possibility of resident priests for
Arkansas for a considerable time. Under the Spanish, the
missionary system as a means of Indian control was deni-
grated in importance; the number of priests in Spanish
Louisiana was small and was not augmented until settlement became extensive enough to support parishes. Shortly
after O'Reilly took command he wrote a memorandum
outlining the religious needs of the colony and indicating
where priests ought to be sent, but he omitted mention
of Arkansas altogether.[19] It was simply too remote and
too tiny.

In 1770, to hear the Arkansas commandant tell it, there
was still no real chapel, much less a priest, at the Post. That
year Captain François Demaselliè re requested permission
of the governor to convert the "building where public
praying is done" into a shelter. It was, he said, only a one-
room building, "unadorned by any religious goods . . .

16. Quoted in *Id.*
17. *Id.*
18. *Id.*
19. *Nombre des Religieux que nous croyons necessaires dans la colonie*
. . . . Feb. 14, 1770, AGI, PC, *leg.* 2357.

where the chaplain used to sleep."[20] Some of the inhabitants had a different version: To them the building was considered "a chapel." As to the lack of adornments, they wrote to De Clouet, Demasellière's predecessor, to inquire what ornaments had been left there when Demasellière took over. There had been candlesticks and an altar cloth they knew; but now the "chapel" was bare. What, they wanted to know moreover, had become of the presents for the chapel that Madame De Clouet had left behind?[21]

After the creation of Ste. Genevieve Parish in 1770 the pastor there occasionally ministered to the people at Arkansas; and in 1790 responsibility for the Arkansas country was transferred to the recently created parish of New Madrid.[22] But visits by priests during this period were of necessity few and far between. The *habitants* of the Post were fortunate if a priest came once a year, and frequently a number of years elapsed between visits. As late as 1794 Father Sebastien Flavien de Besançon, a French Capuchin who was a refugee from the French Revolution, reported that the Post had no church, no chapel, not even a confessional.[23]

20. Demasellière to General, May 20, 1770. AGI, PC, *leg.* 107. Presumably the chaplain referred to is Father Carette.

21. Inhabitants of Arkansas Post to De Clouet, no date, 1770 (?), AGI, PC, *leg.* 107. Visiting priests also evidently considered the building in question a chapel. *See* REGISTER, *supra* note 14, at 26, where the missionary Sebbastien Louis Meurin attests to baptisms in 1764 "in the chapel of the fort of Arkansas."

22. F. Guy, *supra* note 7, at 53–54. The town of New Madrid was not founded until 1789.

23. R. BAUDIER, THE CATHOLIC CHURCH IN LOUISIANA 224 (1939). It is there stated that Father Sebastian Flavien had "established himself at the Post of Arkansas" in 1794. But he cannot have stayed long as he was very soon ordered down to New Orleans to be examined and obtain faculties. *See id.* He was certainly in Arkansas in May, June, and July of 1794. *See* REGISTER, *supra* note 14, at 26, 28. But he soon became the pastor of St. Charles on the German Coast. *See* note 33, *infra*.

Not until 1796 was the "Parish of Arcanzas" created.[24] Pierre Janin, its first and only priest and a native of France, arrived at the Post on August 5th of that year and soon thereafter built a chapel named for St. Stephen. But in 1799 he left to become the pastor at St. Louis and the parish became vacant.[25] It was never again filled, not even during the American period. Not until about 1835, the year before statehood, would there be a Roman Catholic parish again anywhere in Arkansas. Of course, with the American takeover in 1803, Louisiana would no longer have a state-subsidized church; and only four of the thirty-five clergymen in the old Spanish province chose to remain.[26]

II

The absence of much connected religious activity in Arkansas, and the impermanence of resident priests at the Post, meant that one effective alternative to social control by the state was altogether lacking. The truth is that for most of the eighteenth century the church was quite weak and ineffective throughout the colony, even in the sup-

24. The documents which recite the circumstances of the founding of this parish (sometimes called *Los Arcos*) are available on film in the Arkansas History Commission, Little Rock. *See* CALENDAR OF THE MICROFILM EDITION OF THE RECORDS OF THE DIOCESE OF LOUISIANA AND THE FLORIDAS AT THE UNIVERSITY OF NOTRE DAME (1967) for 1796.

25. F. Guy, *supra* note 7, at 54.

26. F. Guy, "The Catholic Church in Arkansas, 1541–1803" 25 (M.A. Thesis, Catholic University of America, 1932). In 1802 Father Juan Brady, a Carmelite monk and priest of the Parish of Our Lady of Carmen at the settlements of the Red and Ouachita rivers, visited the Post for a short time. The record of the baptisms he performed there is printed in A BAPTISMAL RECORD OF THE PARISHES ALONG THE ARKANSAS RIVER, AUGUST 5, 1796 TO JULY 16, 1802 (1982).

posedly civilized precincts of New Orleans. When the diocese of Louisiana and the Floridas was created in 1794,
Louis Peñalver y Cardenas was named its first bishop,[27]
and on December 22, 1795, he made extensive inquiries
into the moral and spiritual health of his diocese. He found
it none too good. Father Joaquin Portillo of New Orleans
reported to him that more than half the people in his city
lived in open sin.[28] Don Jasper de Aranda thought Portillo's
estimate conservative: He told the bishop that most of the
people lived in public concubinage and that all the blacks
did.[29] Portillo also said that he often preached to the inhabitants that they were worse than pagans. There were parents, he claimed, who, as soon as their sons arrived at the
age of puberty, gave them a black woman or mulatto girl.
Slaves did not get married, he reported, and their offspring
were very numerous.[30]

Bishop Peñalver's instructions to the parish priests of
Louisiana are very interesting for the light they shed on the
functions he expected pastors to fulfill.[31] They were to ex-
hort all parishioners who were ill for three days to make a
will and they were to urge all married people to live together. All those living in concubinage were to be compelled to separate. The priests were instructed, moreover,
to avoid discords and controversies and to mediate "whenever such a position does not offend God"; and they were
to advise their parishioners to do the same in all "injuries
and disputes."

The relationship between pastor and commandant in the
remote posts was a most interesting one. The bishop told
his pastors that the commandant was the most important

27. See CALENDAR, supra note 24, for Dec. 22, 1795.
28. See Id.
29. Id.
30. Id.
31. The following paragraph is based on Id. for Dec. 21, 1795.

person in their parishes. That was partly because the cooperation of the commandant was frequently necessary to effect a moral order tolerable to the church. For instance, if those living in concubinage failed to separate, they should, according to the bishop, be reported to the civil authorities to be punished in accordance with the secular law.[32] Likewise, if slaveholders worked their slaves on days of obligation, the commandants must be told to enforce the sabbath laws.[33]

Examples of the cooperation of church and state in the late eighteenth century are relatively numerous. When Paul de St. Piare, pastor at Ste. Genevieve, complained to the bishop of drunken Indians who committed great crimes in his parish, the bishop replied that the commandant should enforce the laws against selling liquor to Indians. "Preaching is insufficient," he said, "if civil authorities do not help."[34] When in 1797 advice was sought from the vicar-general of St. Louis on what to do about a blasphemer, the vicar-general advised threatening the offender with the civil authorities. As an alternative, he suggested sending the offender to New Orleans to the ecclesiastical court for punishment. Even this alternative, however, could involve secular authorities since only they had the power to arrest those who would not appear voluntarily in church tribunals.[35] The state's monopoly on force was also important when it came to having to deal with married persons who refused to live together and who attempted to effect an escape from the parish. In such a case, Bishop Peñalver instructed his priests to solicit the help of the

32. Id.
33. Bishop Peñalver so instructed Father Sebastian Flavien, pastor of St. Charles (German Coast) in a letter of Jan. 8, 1796. Id. for Jan. 8, 1796.
34. Id. for October 1, 1796.
35. Maxwell to Didier, id. for December 21, 1795.

royal justice—the commandant in places like Arkansas
Post.[36]

III

Because the church did not exert a sustained force over a
significant period of time in the Arkansas country, it is not
surprising that very little has been left behind to indicate
what influence it was in fact able to bring to bear. All that
has survived are marriage, baptism, and burial records,
most of them from 1796 and after.[37] But there is some interesting detail to be gleaned there, and the records show
both a conscientious determination to bring the settlement
into line with canon law and a practical willingness to
compromise with the conditions of the frontier.

Since they usually had no resident priest, future spouses
in Arkansas apparently often stipulated in their marriage
contracts that they would regularize their union *in facie ecclesiae* at the earliest opportunity, and then simply began
living together as husband and wife. It is clear that the
habitants regarded the signing of this contract as a kind of
civil marriage. This view could only have been reinforced
by the fact that the commandant "passed" the contracts in
his capacity as surrogate notary and official witness. In
1793 Father Pierre Gibault, the pastor of New Madrid parish, visited Arkansas and married five couples who had
previously contracted marriage "before witnesses" (one of
whom, presumably, was the commandant), due to the lack

36. Peñalver's instructions to parish priests in *id.* for December 21,
1795.

37. *See* REGISTER, *supra* note 14. When Father Carette left Arkansas
for New Orleans in August of 1758, he took the church registers of the
Post with him. *See* J. DELANGLEZ, *supra* note 6, at 446.

of a priest in the area.[38] Several of these couples also recognized certain children as their own, thus allowing them to take advantage of the post-marriage legitimation rule of the civil and canon law.[39] In 1797, after the founding of the Post parish, Father Janin married two couples who had previously been "married in the presence of the commandant of this post." Interestingly, the record also notes that in 1797 Bishop Peñalver ruled that the necessity for publishing the banns was waived for marriages previously contracted in this fashion.[40] Of course, these unions were otherwise of no effect; it could not be clearer that such couples were not married in the eyes of either the church or the state.[41]

Filhiol, the commandant at Ouachita Post (modern-day Monroe, La.), had got himself into serious difficulty witnessing these kinds of contracts, probably because an important family had complained about the "marriage" in this fashion of their daughter to an Indian whom they decidedly disliked.[42] In 1801 Filhiol was haled before the bishop's court to explain why he had allowed these forward marriage contracts and participated in their execution. Filhiol replied simply that it had been the custom and that he had stopped doing it when a parish priest was appointed for his post in 1799. In the end, the ecclesiastical court held that all Filhiol had done was witness a civil contract between parties, and it acquitted him. He had not actually officiated at a ceremony; he had only acted as a sur-

---

38. REGISTER, *supra* note 14, at 20, 21.

39. *Id.* at 11.

40. *Id.* at 41. See also *id.* at 25 where it is noted in a marriage record of October 15, 1792, that the couple had previously contracted before "Mr. DeValliere, commandant."

41. *See generally,* Baade, *The Form of Marriage in Spanish North America,* 61 CORNELL L. REV. 1 (1975).

42. What follows is based on CALENDAR, *supra* note 24, for August 19, 1801.

rogate notary. Evidently the commandants in these kinds of instances were smart enough not to pronounce any words purporting to create a marital bond.

Other entries in the Arkansas church records seem to indicate that many of the inhabitants had been cohabiting without even the benefit of a contract to regularize the arrangement when a priest should next appear. At least that is a plausible inference from the records of marriages in which children are recognized and no mention of a prior contract is made.[43] This presumption seems especially strong in cases where the illegitimate children are numerous and of a fairly advanced age.[44] This state of affairs is, in the nature of things, not at all surprising. Clearly, the inhabitants of Louisiana, and of Arkansas in particular, were not especially devout. It is a tribute to the persuasiveness of the priests of Arkansas that they were able to impose as much order on the place as they were.

In one respect, however, it appears that the teachings of the church had no impact at all. No records of the marriages of blacks have survived. This could be because no records were kept, or, more simply, because they have been lost. But records of the baptism and burial of blacks do survive in fairly large numbers and this makes both of these possibilities less likely. But it would not be a cause for wonder if the marriages of slaves did not take place *in facie ecclesiae*. The church, of course, regarded regular marriages as every bit as necessary to the health of black souls as of white ones, but there is evidence that the attitude of slaveowners made such marriages difficult and often impossible. In 1795, for example, Father Felix de Quintanar, the Capuchin pastor of Galveztown, complained to Bishop Peñalver that the slaveowners themselves officiated at the marriages of their slaves and just laughed when he offered

43. *See, e.g.,* REGISTER, *supra* note 14, at 20.
44. *See, e.g., id.* at 19.

to marry them for free. The owners claimed that what they did was "the usage not only in this town but in all the colony."[45] The bishop wrote back instructing the priest to get the commandant to help him persuade slaveholders not to officiate at slave marriages.[46]

Change in this custom must have come slowly if at all. No doubt slaveowners wanted no competition when it came to authority over their slaves and resented any attempt to dilute it. In 1801, the pastor of Attakapas noted that census-taking in his district was difficult because slaveholders did not want to reveal their holdings.[47] Clearly any intrusion by external authority into the master-slave relationship was going to meet great resistance. This was evidently true in Arkansas as well, although the number of slaves there in the eighteenth century could not have much exceeded sixty.[48]

45. CALENDAR, *supra* note 24, for Dec. 27, 1795.
46. *Id.* for Jan. 7, 1796.
47. *Id.* for Aug. 7, 1801.
48. In 1798 fifty-six slaves were reported to be resident at Arkansas Post. See *Padron de Puesto de Arkancas*, AGI, PC, leg. 2365.

Fin de Siècle

On October 1, 1800, the Spanish, by the secret treaty of St. Ildefonso, receded Louisiana to the French. Possession, however, did not immediately pass; in fact, that would not happen until late in 1803 when the French reoccupied Louisiana for three weeks mainly for the purpose of transferring the province to the Americans pursuant to the Treaty of Paris signed the preceding April.

Rumors first of the retrocession to France and second of the American takeover circulated freely in Louisiana and probably created a good deal of speculation and anxiety among the *habitants* at the Arkansas. No doubt the flurry of concessions which we noticed at Esperanza and at the Post beginning around 1800 occurred in preparation for the impending changes in sovereignty. But it is too much to expect that even such cataclysmic constitutional changes as these would have much immediate effect on the nature of the Arkansas population. For more than a hundred years it had already remained more or less unchanged by the succession of feudal lords, capitalists, and monarchs who had pretended to have governmental authority over it. Our expectations are confirmed by the accounts of Arkansas left by those who visited its settlements in the opening years of the nineteenth century.

François Marie Perrin du Lac, a French traveler who passed through Arkansas in 1802, reported at Esperanza

6. Captain Carlos de Villemont, Commandant of Arkansas Post from 1794 to 1802. The picture was painted when De Villemont was about thirteen years old. (*Courtesy of Mr. and Mrs. Howard Stebbins, Little Rock.*)

"some miserable houses . . . almost entirely in ruin [and] guarded by a dozen soldiers commanded by a sublieutenant."[1] The *Village des Arkansas* he described as follows: "The habitants, almost all originally French emigrants

1. F. PERRIN DU LAC, VOYAGE DANS LES DEUX LOUISIANES . . . EN 1801, 1802 ET 1803 . . . 360 (1805).

from Canada, are hunters by profession, and grow only corn for the nourishment of their horses and of a small number of oxen used in plowing. More than half the year one finds in this village only women, children, and old people. The men go to hunt deer, the skins of which are less valued than those from the northern country; buffalo which they salt for their use; and some beaver which they still find at a little distance. On their return home, they pass their time in playing games, dancing, drinking, or doing nothing, similar in this as well as in other things, to the savage peoples with whom they pass the greater part of their lives, and whose habits and customs they acquire."[2]

Du Lac also remarked that the Post had "a garrison of fifteen or sixteen men commanded by a captain, who is far from being able to control the savages who pass few years without killing some traders or hunters."[3] He reckoned the population at "not more than 450 *habitants*."[4] In the same year an American resident of New Orleans described Arkansas Post "as almost altogether military," meaning, probably, that there were very few agricultural settlers there. He went on to say that it was a place "frequented by hunters and traders, and from where descend, in the spring, boats loaded with pelts, and bear oil the best of which is used in that colony, for the needs of the kitchen, like lard, and it is almost as good, and the common is used for the lamps and other purposes."[5]

Late in 1803, on the eve of the American takeover, an abstract of papers in the offices of the Departments of State and Treasury noted that the *habitants* at the Arkansas were "mostly French" and said simply of the Post: "Here there

2. *Id.* at 367.
3. *Id.* at 368.
4. *Id.*
5. View of the Spanish Colony of the Mississippi, 1802, by a Resident Observer on the Premises 60 (1802).

are but a few families, who are more attached to the Indian trade (by which they chiefly live) than to cultivation."[6] The Americans were about to inherit a largely ungoverned and ungovernable population at the Arkansas.

6. *An Account of Louisiana. 1803.* 11, 6 (OLD SOUTH LEAFLETS, no. 105).

IV

The First American Legal System in Arkansas 1804–1812

In New Orleans on December 20, 1803, the vast and largely undefined territory of Louisiana was formally delivered by France to the United States,[1] and W. C. C. Claiborne, who had been appointed by Jefferson to exercise all the powers previously held by the Spanish Governor-General and Intendant[2], immediately took up his duties. In his first proclamation, issued the day possession was transferred, Claiborne ordained that "all laws and municipal regulations which were in existence at the cession of the late government [shall] remain in force, and all civil officers charged with their execution . . . are confirmed in their functions during the pleasure of the Governor . . ."[3] This meant, of course, that the Spanish commandant at the Arkansas was authorized to continue exercising his civil authority.

I

Claiborne's authority was extensive, in fact enormous, and a few weeks after taking office he confessed to James

1. 2 STATS. AT LARGE 245.
2. THE LIFE AND PAPERS OF FREDERICK BATES 19 (J. MARSHALL ed., 1926) [hereinafter cited as BATES].
3. I OFFICIAL LETTER BOOKS OF W. C. C. CLAIBORNE, 1801–1816, 308–09 (1917).

Madison his "political uneasiness" over the "great latitude
of the powers" with which he was temporarily entrusted.
His Spanish predecessor, Claiborne claimed, "when exercising the Sacred Character of Judge, . . . often vended his
decisions to the highest bidder."[4] Speaking of the condition
of the judicial business of the province, Claiborne said:
"The state in which I found the jurisprudence of the country embarrasses me extremely." A large backlog of cases
had developed; some had been pending upwards of twenty
years. The new governor was appalled by the size of the
task: There was an enormous accumulation of depositions,
all in Spanish, which he could not read; and knowledge of
the "Spanish laws and habits of practise" would be an obvious qualification for anyone who would be called upon
to decide these cases. But, Claiborne lamented, "Characters with such qualifications and Men to whom may safely
be confided so important a trust are not easily to be found."
He himself felt a "great reluctance in exercising any judicial authority." He therefore established a Court of Pleas
consisting of seven magistrates and having a civil jurisdiction extending to cases not exceeding three thousand dollars, but its jurisdiction he did not "at present extend beyond the limits of the city."[5]

Very soon, however, Claiborne set himself the task of
appointing magistrates for the outlying districts. In appointing Julian Poidras Civil Commandant of Pointe Coupée he said simply: "The same powers in *civil matters* which
heretofore were exercised by the commandant of the district under the Spanish government, will devolve upon
you. . . ."[6] He told Poidras to keep a record of all official
acts and to report occasionally on the state of his district.
"Doubtful questions and cases of great importance, which

4. *Id.* at 322 (January 2, 1804).
5. *Id.* at 324–25 (January 2, 1804).
6. *Id.* at 333 (Claiborne to Poidras, January 14, 1804).

can admit of delay," Claiborne said, "can be reported to me. . . ."[7] A similar instruction was given to other district commandants.

In February the governor sent Dr. John Watkins to some of the districts north of the city "as high up as Baton Rouge" with blank commissions which he was "to fill up with the names of the persons you may select as commandants of the different districts." Commandants presently serving who wished to be reappointed were to be given preference.[8] For the entirety of Upper Louisiana Claiborne appointed Amos Stoddard as "First Civil Commandant"; he was to "exercise the same powers in *civil matters*" which had been exercised by his counterpart under Spanish rule— that is, the lieutenant governor. Stoddard was specifically given the authority to "lessen the number of deputy commandants" in his district and "to appoint such characters to exercise these offices temporarily as you may deem most deserving."[9] Some months later Claiborne wrote to him and said that he had learned that Stoddard had pursued the policy of reappointing the old Spanish commandants. "I have found it good policy to recommission several of the former Commandants," Claiborne said; "but we should both take care, that these men should execute their powers with justice and in mercy." The governor admonished Stoddard that "the conduct of the several Commandants acting under your authority should be strictly watched, and carefully investigated." This was especially true with

---

7. *Id.* at 333–34. Claiborne wrote to Lieutenant Henry Hopkins on January 20, 1804, and appointed him Civil Commandant of the Districts of Attakapas and Opalousas; he used almost the same words in describing Hopkins's duties as he did those of Poidras. *See id.* at 336–38. *See also id.* at 386–87.

8. Claiborne to Watkins, February 9, 1804, *id.* 367–68. Watkins's report and recommendations are very interesting and may be found in 2 *id.* at 3–13.

9. Claiborne to Stoddard, January 24, 1804, 1 *id.* at 350.

respect to the "distant posts" where the commandants "were frequently guilty of oppression and injustice."[10] According to Stoddard, under the Spanish regime the dividing line between Upper and Lower Louisiana was Esperanza. But Claiborne's letter books contain no appointments in Arkansas; the only mention of government there occurs on April 14, 1804, when Claiborne casually remarked to Henry Dearborn that by "letters this moment received the Post of Arkansas, has been delivered to Lieutenant (James) Many and everything in that quarter is going well."[11] Arkansas was one of the last posts delivered. Only Natchitoches, which was evidently surrendered late in April of 1804, and Ouachita, delivered in the middle of the same month,[12] seem to have been given over to American control later.

Claiborne, as we have already noted, had no use for his judicial duties and from the very beginning he made no bones about it. "Amidst all my duties here," he confided to Madison, "the most embarrassing are those which I have to discharge in my Judicial Character." He went on to say that he "avoided taking any cognizance of civil suits as long as I could."[13] He declared it his "favorite wish, to exercise no judicial authority,"[14] and regretted that he was "compelled to exercise judicial powers."[15] He knew nothing about civil law, and freely confessed it. "I will readily

10. 2 *id.* at 222–23.
11. Claiborne to Dearborn, April 14, 1804, *id.* at 96. Claiborne exercised control over important business touching on Arkansas, a further indication that he considered it under his jurisdiction. For instance, on February 8, 1804, he gave Jacob Bright "permission to establish a store on the Arkansas, for the purpose of carrying on trade with the inhabitants of that District, and such Indians as may still visit that Post." *Id.* at 367.
12. *Id.* at 145, 147.
13. *Id.* at 197.
14. *Id.*
15. 1 *id.* at 372.

acknowledge my want of information on Spanish law,"
he said, "yet I profess to be acquainted with the Laws of
Justice." [16]

When dealing with legal matters arising in the outlying
districts Claiborne exhibited a similar vagueness about substantive law. In his circular to the commandants of the districts, apparently sent on March 30, 1804, he said that in
the passage of sovereignty from one country to another "it
often happens that laws are evaded and municipal regulations entirely neglected." It now behooved the "civil magistrates to recall the citizens to obedience of the law, and to
establish that order in society so essential to the preservation of morals and the promotion of Good Government."
He proceeded then to instruct the commandants to tend to
the erection and maintenance of a good militia, to regulate
the behavior of the slave population, to see to it that roads,
bridges, and levees were maintained, and to license and
police the sale of liquor. In the case of slaves and liquor,
he specifically mentioned the laws and regulations made
under the Spanish regime which he deemed still to be in
force. But the law of property and obligations, of tort
and contract, he entirely omitted from mention. "Property
[and] liberty" were to "be protected"—but he did not say
how. Commandants were simply to "keep constantly in
view the principles of impartial justice." [17]

In a similar vein, when dealing with individual cases
which came to his attention from the local commandants,
Claiborne sidestepped difficulties by telling the commandant to take steps which "Justice and the ancient usages of
the country will justify"; [18] to do "everything relative there-
to that justice may require"; [19] to inflict "such punishment
upon the said [defendant] as in your judgment (and agree-

16. *Id.* at 357.
17. *Id.* at 71–74.
18. *Id.* at 92.
19. *Id.* at 107.

ably to the usages of the Country) [the defendant] may have merited"; and to end a dispute "consistent with justice and the usages of the Country."[20] In one fairly complicated case Claiborne directed the commandant to "take for your guide, the immutable Principles of Justice, and there can be no doubt but your proceedings will be satisfactory."[21]

In a complex case involving the proper way to foreclose a mortgage, the governor did make "an unremitted series of enquiries on the Subject at Length" and wrote a long letter explaining to an anxious commandant at Ouachita what he should do. In the course of this letter Claiborne explained why he could not devote so much energy to every case that was referred to him: "It is one of the serious inconveniences of the present state of things in this country that we are under the necessity of being governed as nearly as possible, by a system, in most points incongenial with the principles of our own Government by Laws to which we are almost utter strangers, and forms of practice as intricate as they are new to us; add to this that the executives of the Collony [sic] have often exercised a dispensing power over those laws, and the people consequently have been habituated to the uncertain operation of rules occasionally modified by the wisdom or caprice of those in power."[22]

In almost every other instance Claiborne papered over difficulties by instructing the local magistrates "to render that justice which the nature of the case requires"[23] or "to act as you may think proper and as Justice to the innocent requires."[24]

20. *Id.* at 133.
21. *Id.* at 286.
22. *Id.* at 223–24.
23. *Id.* at 127–28.
24. *Id.* at 132.

II

As we have noted, it fell to Captain Amos Stoddard to act as the agent of the United States to take possession of Upper Louisiana on March 10, 1804, in St. Louis;[25] and he was directed to exercise therein all the functions previously exercised by the Spanish commandants.[26] Stoddard immediately authorized the Spanish commandants in his several districts to continue exercising the civil authority which they had enjoyed when the territory was under Spanish rule.[27]

However, though the matter is obscure, it appears that little attention was at first paid to government at the Arkansas. During the Spanish dominion over Louisiana, as noted before, Arkansas Post was not considered to be in Upper Louisiana. When De Lassus, the last Spanish lieutenant governor at St. Louis, gave Stoddard an account of the personnel who served under him, the southernmost settlement mentioned was New Madrid.[28] The same was true when he advised his commandants that he had delivered possession of "this place and all of Upper Louisiana to Mr. Amos Stoddard." Finally, when Delassus was ordered to come to New Orleans and bring with him all artillery, ammunition, and goods belonging to the king, his last stop for this purpose was Esperanza.[29] Indeed, Stoddard

25. 2 L. HOUCK, HISTORY OF MISSOURI 357–58 (1908).
26. 1 BATES, *supra* note 2, at 20–21.
27. *Id.* at 21.
28. This document is among the Chouteau Papers in the Missouri Historical Society in St. Louis.
29. 2 L. HOUCK, *supra* note 25, at 365, 369. The original of Delassus's journal is extant in the Missouri Historical Society in St. Louis. Governor Harrison had replaced the Spanish officers with officers of the United States Army as civil commandants in all the districts except New Madrid. *See* W. ENGLISH, THE PIONEER LAWYER AND JURIST IN MISSOURI, 21 UNIVERSITY OF MISSOURI STUDIES NO. 2, 47 (1947). In New Madrid, Pierre Laforge, a civilian and French notary, was appointed.

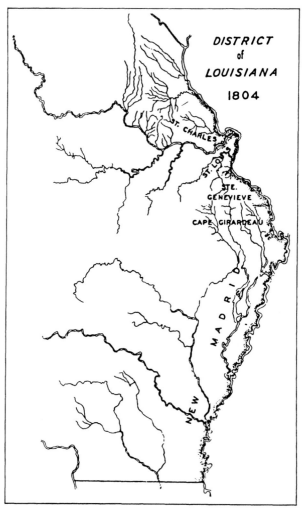

7. District of Louisiana, 1804. (*Courtesy Records Management and Archives Service, Office of the Secretary of State, State of Missouri.*)

See 2 L. HOUCK, *supra* note 25, at 382. According to English, New Madrid District at this time extended down to the present boundary of Louisiana. W. ENGLISH, *supra* at 47, n. 8.

himself said that Esperanza marked the old Spanish boundary between the two Louisianas.[30] Though Stoddard therefore did not consider most of Arkansas within his jurisdiction, it is nevertheless also true that Governor Claiborne gave Arkansas almost no thought.

Curiously, however, when in October, 1804, the old Spanish Province of Louisiana was divided into two parts by act of Congress—the Territory of Orleans with New Orleans as its capital, and the District of Louisiana with Vincennes as its capital—Arkansas was included in the latter. The dividing line was the thirty-third parallel, the present boundary between the states of Arkansas and Louisiana.[31] The debates in Congress gave no hint as to why the boundary was drawn where it had never been drawn before; indeed, no discussion of the issue has left its mark on the record. As James Primm has noted, the "former Spanish Illinois and Arkansas were lumped together in a new District of Louisiana. . . ."[32] It was nevertheless a profoundly important event; as shall be seen, it determined the legal system under which Arkansans were destined to live.

During the Spanish regime Upper Louisiana had been divided into five administrative districts: St. Charles, St. Louis, Ste. Genevieve, Cape Girardeau, and New Madrid.[33] On the division of Louisiana, governmental authority over the new District of Louisiana was vested in the Governor and the three Judges of Indiana Territory;[34] and in the early fall of 1804 they held a session of the legislature and passed a law retaining the old Spanish subdivisions and providing for courts of Common Pleas and

30. A. STODDARD, SKETCHES, HISTORICAL AND DESCRIPTIVE, OF LOUISIANA 205 (1812).
31. 2 STATS. AT LARGE 283.
32. J. PRIMM, LION OF THE VALLEY: ST. LOUIS, MISSOURI 76 (1981).
33. 2 L. HOUCK, *supra* note 25, at 378.
34. 2 STATS. AT LARGE 283.

Quarter Sessions for each of these districts.[35] According to Houck, these courts were actually established.[36] Arkansas was nominally included in the District of New Madrid, but early in 1805 it was reported that civil authority had still not yet reached the Post: The *habitants* there were submitting their disputes to the American commandant, Lieutenant James B. Many, in stubborn imitation of their previous practice.[37] It is probable that Arkansas retained a military government longer than any other place in Louisiana.

III

Arkansas was hardly the only place in Louisiana where the old legal ways would prove difficult to replace. In Lower Louisiana, by the act creating the Territory of Orleans, Congress had provided that, in the main, the laws previously in force would continue in force until modified. But Congress had also introduced some important common-law features: Jury trial in capital cases, constitutional rights to *habeas corpus* and reasonable bail, and the prohibition against cruel and unusual punishments were extended to the inhabitants.[38]

Despite the relatively measured pace of legal change in Orleans Territory "discontent among the inhabitants developed early," and "dissatisfaction over legal innovations was a salient grievance."[39] For one thing, the use of English in the courts caused considerable confusion, and apparently the governor's preference for *viva voce* testimony

35. 2 L. HOUCK, *supra* note 25, at 378.
36. *Id.* at 382–84.
37. 13 THE TERRITORIAL PAPERS OF THE UNITED STATES 170 (1948).
38. 2 STATS AT LARGE 283.
39. G. DARGO, JEFFERSON'S LOUISIANA: POLITICS AND THE CLASH OF LEGAL TRADITIONS 116 (1975).

over written depositions compounded this difficulty.[40] Real difficulties erupted in 1805 when Congress passed a second organic act for Louisiana that incorporated the provision of the Northwest Ordinance requiring "judicial proceedings according to the course of the common law."[41] Incredibly, such was the strength of the substantive civil law in Louisiana that in November of 1805 the Territorial Court, in the person of Judge Prevost, held that "the term common law in Orleans Territory could only mean the common law of that territory or the common law of that land, which was the civil law."[42] Interestingly, however, only a few months before, the territorial legislature had found many features of common-law procedure attractive and had provided for juries in civil cases, *viva voce* testimony in open court, and compulsory attendance of witnesses.[43] Special issues were to be put to the jury to guard against their lack of legal knowledge.[44] The same year, the legislature adopted wholesale "the common law of England" as to crimes and provided that "the forms of indictment, . . . the method of trial, the rules of evidence, and all other proceedings whatsoever . . . shall be . . . according to the common law." The only exception was for the crimes of slaves: They were still to be "punished according to the laws of Spain for regulating her colonies."[45]

Thus the people of Orleans Territory had come a considerable way toward the complete reception of the common law by swallowing whole the substantive law of crimes and much of common-law civil procedure. But these innova-

40. See *Remonstrance of the People of Louisiana*, U.S. CONG., DEBATES AND PROCEEDINGS, 8th Cong., 2d Sess., 1597–1608 (1807).
41. See G. DARGO, *supra* note 39, at 128; Brown, *Legal Systems in Conflict: Orleans Territory 1804–1812*, 1 AMERICAN J. LEG. HIST. 35 (1957).
42. Brown, *supra* note 41, at 40.
43. *Id.* at 42.
44. *Id.* at 43.
45. *Id.* at 44–45.

tions caused considerable grumbling, especially in the out-lying districts, where preference for the old commandant system was being voiced. At the same time that Prevost handed down his decision interpreting the Northwest Or-dinance a remarkable pamphlet appeared, *instructions* from some of the rural planters to their delegates in the ter-ritorial legislature, complaining about the encroachments of the common law. According to this pamphlet, were it not for "the small share of . . . ancient jurisprudence that our fabricators of laws have deigned not to meddle with," the social order would have been entirely overturned. By accepting uncritically so much of an alien legal system, the tract maintained, the legislature had committed an act "more fatal to us . . . than the invasion of the Goths and Vandals was to the Roman Empire."[46] Clearly, opposition to further inroads on the civil law was hardening.

In 1806 the Orleans legislature, evidently stung by the mounting opposition to the common law, set its face against the introduction of further change. It passed a bill which, had it been signed, would have as to substantive civil matters established the civil law in Louisiana. The bill identified the sources where the civil law was to be found: The Insti-tutes, the Digest, the Code of Justinian, the Commentaries of Domat, the *Recopilación de Castilla*, the *Siete Partidas*, and the *Recopilación de las Indias*, even the ordinance of Bilbao, all receive mention. Claiborne vetoed the bill and the legislature adjourned in a huff.[47]

It is clear from a "manifesto" drafted by the legislators in defense of their decision to adjourn that there would sim-ply be no retreat from the position that private law in Lower Louisiana ought to remain as it had been. The law of successions, wills, domestic relations, contracts, prop-erty, and conveyancing had to stay untouched. The "Mani-festo" maintained: "Everyone knows today and from a

46. G. DARGO, *supra* note 39, at 133–34.
47. *Id.* at 136–37; Brown, *supra* note 41, at 46–48.

long experience how successions are transferred, what is the power of parents over their children and the amount of property of which they can dispose to their prejudice, what are the rights which result from marriages effected with or without contract, the manner in which one can dispose by will, the manner of selling, of exchanging or alienating one's properties with sureness, and the remedies which the law accords in the case of default of payment. Each of the inhabitants dispersed over the vast expanse of this Territory, however little educated he may be, has a tincture of this general familiar jurisprudence, necessary to the conduct of the smallest affairs, which assures the tranquility of families; he has sucked this knowledge at his mother's breast, he has received it by the tradition of his forefathers and he has perfected it by the experience of a long and laborious life. Overthrow this system all at once. Substitute new laws for the old laws; what a tremendous upset you cause!"[48]

On March 31, 1808, the Orleans legislature passed an act which provided for the promulgation of a "Digest of the Civil Laws now in force in the territory of New Orleans," and Claiborne this time decided not to exercise his veto. The digest subsequently produced covered the law of domestic relations, estates in land, wills, successions, contracts, quasi-contracts, sales, and some rudimentary commercial law.[49] In short, it adopted a civil-law scheme for the private law of what would become the state of Louisiana.

48. Quoted in G. DARGO, *supra* note 39, at 139.

49. The table of contents of the bill is printed in Brown, *supra* note 41, at 54–5.

IV

By the act that created the District of Louisiana and placed the Upper Territory under the government of the Indiana Territory, Congress had provided that "the laws in force in the said district . . . at the commencement of this act . . . shall remain in force . . ."[50] The legislature for the new district, which as we saw consisted of the governor and judges of the Indiana Territory, promulgated a number of basic laws in their first session in Vincennes and they became effective on October 1, 1804.[51]

Practically the entire common law of crimes was imported wholesale in the first act of this legislature: Treason, murder, arson, burglary, robbery, larceny, perjury, embezzlement, assault and battery, forgery, and conspiracy, all outfitted with their common-law definitions, were outlawed and penalties for their commission were imposed. A conviction for treason carried with it the death penalty and forfeiture of property. Murder and arson brought the death penalty. Burglary earned a culprit a fine plus imprisonment if he could not find a surety; a burglar who succeeded in stealing something and who offered violence or was armed with a dangerous weapon was to suffer death. Robbery was treated the same way as burglary. A conviction for perjury brought with it a fine and three hours in the pillory. Larceny carried a fine and a duty of restitution, and the thief who had insufficient property to discharge the sentence could be bound to labor for a term not exceeding seven years "to any suitable person who shall discharge such sentence." Embezzlers were fined and pilloried, and those found guilty of assault and battery were fined and could be made to enter into a peace bond.[52]

50. 2 STATS. AT LARGE 283.
51. LAWS FOR THE GOVERNMENT OF THE DISTRICT OF LOUISIANA . . . .
(1804).
52. Id. at 3–14.

In the same legislative session a very elaborate court system was erected. A General Court was established, the "Supreme Court of record" for the entire District, with original jurisdiction in civil cases "of the value of one hundred dollars and upwards," original jurisdiction over all crimes (and exclusive original jurisdiction over capital ones), and appellate jurisdiction over all inferior courts. Jury trial was made mandatory in this court in all criminal cases and in any civil case if either party requested it. The right to counsel was guaranteed there in both civil and criminal cases, compulsory process against witnesses was provided for, and *viva voce* testimony in open court was to be the rule at trials.[53]

Inferior tribunals were also established. A General Quarter Session of the Peace was to sit in each district, consisting of at least three Justices of the Peace, each of whom had power "to take all manners of recognizances, and obligations as any such justice of the peace in any of the United States may, can or usually do"; evidently the court had the power to try all but capital crimes.[54] On the civil side, a Court of Common Pleas was established in each district staffed by "a competent number of persons," to "hold pleas of assize, *scire facias*, replevins and hear and determine all and all manner of pleas, suits, actions and causes, civil personal real and mixed according to law." They could also issue replevins, writs of view, writs of partition, "and all other writs . . . as occasion may require." They were in addition empowered to issue subpoenas against witnesses.[55] The General Court could hear appeals from these lower tribunals by *certiorari*, error, or *habeas corpus* depending on the circumstances.

Nor were small claims forgotten. A long statute of twenty pages, entitled "A Law Establishing Courts for the

53. *Id.* at 92–95.
54. *Id.* at 88–92.
55. *Id.* at 95–98.

Trial of Small Causes," gave every Justice of the Peace jurisdiction over "every action for debt or other demand" within his district; justices were directed "to hear and determine the same according to law." Only simple debts were within the jurisdiction, however; "debts on a bond, actions of covenant, actions of replevin, or upon any real contract, actions of trespass on the case for trover and conversion or slander, actions of trespass *vi et armis*, or actions wherein the title of lands shall in any wise come in question" were explicitly excluded from cognizance. First process in a Justice Court was by summons, unless the plaintiff alleged that he or she would "be in danger of losing his or her demand unless the defendant be arrested," in which case a *capias* was to issue. Elaborate bail regulations followed, as did similarly detailed instructions on execution. A complicated appeal procedure to the Court of Common Pleas was set out for the benefit of an aggrieved party.[56]

A probate judge was also established in each district "to take proof of last wills and testaments and to grant letters testamentary and letters of administration"; but he was not allowed to render "definitive sentence and final decrees" on his sole authority. These had to be rendered by a combination of the probate judge and two justices of the Court of Common Pleas. Together, the statute directed, these individuals "shall constitute the court of probate, a majority of whom" was empowered to proceed to judgment.[57]

Nor was this an end to the complex governmental structure erected. The governor was directed to appoint a sheriff[58] and recorder[59] in each district and the Court of Quarter Sessions was directed to appoint constables;[60] these officers were to be remunerated by fees, and an elaborate fee sched-

56. *Id.* 18–36.
57. *Id.* at 124–27.
58. *Id.* at 14–15.
59. *Id.* at 101–07.
60. *Id.* at 127–31.

ule regulated what they could charge.[61]

A most interesting feature of the product of this first legislature is that, except for a code regulating slavery[62] and the establishment of some elementary liability rules covering the activities of boatmen,[63] there was no attempt to tinker with the private law observed under the Spanish regime. Moreover, neither jury trial nor the right to counsel was extended to the tribunals below the level of the General Court at this time. As in the case of Lower Louisiana, the Americans were proceeding with caution.

Nevertheless, and again as in the case of Lower Louisiana, the *habitants* of the upper territory were quite unhappy with the change in regime. Some of the more influential citizens had no doubt gotten wind of what the new legislature was going to do or had already done, and ten days before the work of the first legislature became effective a convention of citizens from the various parts of Upper Louisiana was held in St. Louis to discuss grievances. The original plan, according to Judge Rufus Easton, was for this convention to produce a resolution asking Congress for a *government militaire* identical in all important respects to the old Spanish one. Easton reports that the plan had the following outline:

"1. To have a Governor residing in the territory possessing both civil and military jurisdiction;

"2. Commandants for each district to possess like powers with an appeal to the Governor in certain cases;

"3. No trial to be by jury except in such cases as in the opinion of the Governor or Commandant Justice should absolutely require it for special causes to be shown, and the practice of lawyers to be entirely prohibited."[64]

61. *Id.* at 36–59.
62. *Id.* at 107–21.
63. *Id.* at 15–18.
64. 2 L. Houck, *supra* note 25, at 394.

In the original draft of this resolution the governor and judges of the Indiana Territory were compared to "foreign Bashaws, . . . Pro-proctors and Pro-consuls . . . sent out to rule over the people."[65]

There is other evidence that many people in the District of Louisiana preferred the military rule of commandants to the new ways of republicanism so dear to the Jeffersonian heart. Both Frederick Bates[66] and Amos Stoddard[67] allude to this attachment to old ways, and Stoddard himself says that the commandants in the exercise of their judicial functions "were in most instances upright and impartial in their decisions."[68] The merchants of St. Louis found jury trial especially distasteful since juries prolonged trials and increased costs. They had observed after the American takeover in Illinois that jury trials "enriched the lawyers whether justice triumphed or not."[69] Indeed, the new modes of trial and the professional lawyer class were widely believed to have exerted a stifling effect on commerce in St. Louis for a number of years after the American takeover.[70]

Nevertheless, the petition which the St. Louis convention of 1804 ultimately produced was much more temperate and moderate than the one originally proposed. So far as procedural matters were concerned, it asked only that judges be selected from the District, that they be able to speak French and English, and that judicial records be kept in both languages. As for substantive matters, the members of the convention were apparently resigned to the eventual importation of the common law. They asked only that "every private engagement comfortable to the laws

65. *Id.*
66. Bates, *supra* note 2, at 242–43.
67. A. Stoddard, *supra* note 30, at 281.
68. *Id.*
69. J. Primm, *supra* note 32, at 80.
70. *Id.* at 86.

of Spain, entered into during the time Louisiana was ruled by the Laws of Spain . . . be maintained; [and] that judgments rendered by the Spanish courts that were not final under Spanish law be provided an avenue for appeal."[71] Nor was any grievance concerning jury trial or the legal profession advanced.

Why, in comparison to their Lower Louisiana brethren, the inhabitants of the District of Louisiana proved in the end so fainthearted and pusillanimous in their opposition to the common law is a question that needs to be answered. The absence of a professional lawyer class in Spanish Illinois, ironically thought by the *habitants* a great advantage, may have made the substitution of the common law more easily achieved. With a real stake in the outcome, and with the forensic skills necessary for creating an attachment to ideas, professional lawyers might have been able to salvage some of the old system.

But there is more. In the lower territory, the French outnumbered the Americans seven to one at the time of the takeover.[72] By contrast, in the last decade of the eighteenth century Upper Louisiana had witnessed a considerable influx of Americans; perhaps a third of the population of St. Louis and its environs at the beginning of the American period were of Anglo-American extraction.[73] Of course the French still dominated in numbers and prestige; but to the extent that national origins carry with them some attachment to a legal culture, the civilian capacity to resist in Upper Louisiana was diluted by the presence of persons whose legal culture was derived from England. Indeed, half of the delegates to the convention of 1804 were Americans "who had taken up their residence under the Spanish government prior to the acquisition of the territory by the

71. 2 L. HOUCK, *supra* note 25, at 391.
72. G. DARGO, *supra* note 39, at 9–10.
73. J. PRIMM, *supra* note 32, at 74.

United States."[74] Houck even claims that the delegates "principally represented the American settlers."[75]

More fundamentally, some have seen at work a deep cultural difference between the two Louisianas. One commentator has ventured the following assessment of the comparative sophistication of the settlers in the upper and lower territories: "On the whole, the inhabitants of upper Louisiana were analogous to their neighbors across the Mississippi in Prairie du Rocher, Cahokia, and Kaskaskia. Uneducated, unaware of and uninterested in events beyond their immediate daily concerns, they were not particularly concerned with the abstract question of what were to be the laws in force. The French in lower Louisiana were the reverse. They were attached to the civil law and its institutions and a certain nostalgia for a Latin rather than an Anglo-American civilization intensified this attachment."[76]

V

On March 20, 1805, the District of Louisiana became the Territory of Louisiana,[77] but the former administrative units of the old District were maintained. Thus Arkansas remained nominally part of the District of New Madrid, the seat of which was a 250 mile trip by river from Arkansas Post. Obviously, the Arkansas settlements were so inconsequential that they did not even figure in the plans of their new American masters. A succession of American military commandants at Arkansas Post from 1804 to 1806 styled themselves "Civil Commandants" when recording

74. 2 L. HOUCK, *supra* note 25, at 392.
75. *Id.*
76. Brown, *Law and Government in the "Louisiana Purchase": 1803–1804*, 2 WAYNE L. REV. 168 at 178 (1956).
77. 2 STATS. AT LARGE 331.

conveyances,[78] and it is thus likely that during that period they exercised the judicial authority possessed by their counterparts under the Spanish regime. It was hardly practicable for the *habitants* of the Arkansas to look to a court in New Madrid to order their affairs and settle their disputes. Finally, on June 27, 1806, New Madrid District was divided and a District of Arkansas created.[79] The need for such a governmental unit was plain: The town of New Madrid was at least a ten days' journey from the Post and was a large inconvenience to citizens who wished access to the courts. Moreover, service of process and the execution of judgments over such a large territory would have been extremely difficult.

Judges were appointed to serve on a Court of Common Pleas for the District of Arkansas at the time the district was created, but there is no evidence that this court ever sat. Certainly no record of its sessions survives. If it did in fact exercise any authority, it was short-lived, for on July 7, 1807, Frederick Bates, the Secretary and Acting Governor of the Territory of Louisiana, issued his proclamation reuniting the Districts of Arkansas and New Madrid.[80] Bates expressed the conviction that the object of securing law enforcement for Arkansas would "be better promoted by a reunion of that distant and inconsiderable settlement with the district from which it was originally taken."[81]

78. Core, *The American Takeover in Arkansas*, 16 GPHSB 3 (1973).

79. 13 Territorial Papers of the United States 540 (C. Carter ed., 1948) [Hereinafter cited as Territorial Papers]. A law regulating the sessions of the courts in Arkansas was passed on June 27, 1806. *See* 1 Laws of a Public and General Nature, of the District of Louisiana, of the Territory of Louisiana, of the Territory of Missouri, and the State of Missouri up to the Year 1824 ch. 19 (1842).

80. The proclamation appears in full in 1 Bates, *supra* note 2, at 152–53.

81. This sentiment was contained in Bates's letter to the Louisiana Territorial Legislature on July 1, 1807. The letter appears in full in *id*. at 150–51.

The Arkansas Post of the Territory of Louisiana was not at all different from its eighteenth-century Spanish predecessor. Change in the character and extent of its population came very slowly. John B. Treat, sent to Arkansas Post by the Americans to open a government trading post there for the Indians, wrote in 1805 that the pursuits of the population at the Post were "either farming, trading, or hunting . . . but I must admit, that agriculture here is yet in its infancy. . . ." He reported a population of "between sixty and seventy families, nine, or ten of which are from the three states Virginia, Maryland, and Pennsylvania; the others (one or two Spaniards excepted) are all French either natives; or those who emigrated from the Illinois, New Orleans, and two or three from Europe." Thus, according to Treat, Americans composed about fifteen percent of the population. All the Post population, Treat said, lived in the village or within a three or four mile radius of it. The black population he put at sixty.[82] A year later Thomas Ashe reported that the "village of the Ozark" contained sixty houses "inhabited by persons of several nations, and who reside there for the purpose of conducting a very lucrative trade with the Indians, who resort to the village from the high country. . . ."[83] In 1808, Fortescue Cuming passed by Esperanza and noted that "immediately below Mr. Foy's (whose negro quarter gives his pleasantly situated settlement the appearance of a village or hamlet) was formerly a Spanish fort no vestige of which now remains."[84] Cuming thought the Post barely deserving of notice. He wrote that it "consists chiefly of hunters and Indian traders, of course is a poor place, as settlers of this description never look for anything beyond the mere necessities of life, except whis-

82. 13 Territorial Papers, *supra* note 79, at 278–79.
83. T. Ashe, Travels in America in 1806, 305 (1808).
84. F. Cuming, Sketches of a Tour of the Western Country, in 4 Early Western Travels 293 (E. Thwaites ed., 1904).

key."[85] A soldier stationed at the Post from 1807 to 1809
wrote that "the land [around here] is remarkably fertile,
tho the cultivation of it has been much neglected, the inhabitants being mostly a heterogenious mass of French and
the Arkansas Indians . . . [and] there are but few families
who are not more or less connected with the natives. Their
general pursuit is hunting; those who are less indigent
carry on a little trade in peltries and furs. They are remarkably fond of amusements, particularly of dancing, cards,
and billiards." The writer believed that emigration from
the Southern and Western states would soon transform the
place. "[I]f it were inhabited by a more civilized people,"
he predicted, "it would be a paradise. . . ."[86]

It is easy to see how such a place as this would not seem
to justify a separate administrative unit for its government and no doubt the nature of the Arkansas settlements
weighed heavily in the decision to abolish the District of
Arkansas. But Frederick Bates had been in Louisiana only
three months when he issued his proclamation reuniting
the districts of Arkansas and New Madrid. He had of necessity acted without any firsthand knowledge of the facts.
(In December of 1807 he wrote his brother that he had
been only as far south as Ste. Genevieve.)[87] But his duties
as a member of the Board of Land Commissioners would
soon take him to Arkansas, and there the *habitants* would
have a chance to convince him that he had erred in abolish-
ing Arkansas as a separate governmental unit.

The Board of Land Commissioners had been set up in
1804 to try the validity of French and Spanish land claims
in Upper Louisiana. Bates resolved as early as July 14,
1807, to visit Arkansas in April of the following year. "The
claimants," he wrote to Albert Gallatin, "have once with

85. *Id.* at 299.
86. A. Stewart to Thomas Moulton, Feb. 27, 1809. Missouri Historical Society, St. Louis.
87. 1 Bates, *supra* note 2, at 238.

difficulty attended at Saint Louis, and it is now believed that many even of those who live abundantly on their plantations have not cash to defray the expenses of attendance."[88] He planned to travel to Esperanza to gather evidence for claims in that community and in and around Arkansas Post as well. However, when he arrived at Esperanza he found only one resident of Arkansas Post, Joseph Stilwell, there to meet him.[89] He decided, therefore, to continue his journey and arrived at the Post on July 2, 1808.

Frederick Bates was just past his thirty-first birthday when he arrived at the Arkansas settlement. There was very little in his background that could have prepared him to appreciate such a place very highly.[90] While his family could not accurately be described as well-heeled, they were Virginia gentry; and Bates, although not furnished with a formal college education, wrote vigorous English, "possessed a considerable knowledge of the Latin classics, and . . . was versed in history and the science of government."[91] In 1794 he had begun to study law as a clerk in Virginia, and when he moved to Detroit in 1797 as a member of the Army quartermasters' corps, he continued to read law in his spare time.[92] He enjoyed some success as a merchant in Detroit after his discharge from the Army, but his real interests evidently lay in politics, as he began seeking territorial offices even before Michigan Territory was formally erected. In 1804 he was appointed land commissioner and in 1805 he was made an Associate Judge of the Michigan Territorial Court. He took his seat on that court on July 1, 1805, when the new territory came into being.[93]

88. *Id.* at 160.

89. 2 *id.* at 12.

90. Bates was born on June 23, 1777, in Goochland County, Virginia. 1 *id.* at 6.

91. *Id.*

92. *Id.* at 8.

93. *Id.* at 9.

His charge to the grand jury at Detroit in August of 1805 was elegant, learned, and politically sophisticated.[94] As his biographer has noted, "it seems probable that the finely phrased address must have been rather high flown, and in part perhaps incomprehensible to the frontiersmen who listened to the dignified Virginian on the bench."[95] Bates also amused himself by writing poems—some amatory, some satirical, some in imitation of eighteenth-century English poetry.[96]

Bates was thus not very well equipped, either by way of temperament or educational background, to conceal his contempt of the ignorance which he encountered on his trip to Arkansas. His distance both intellectually and socially from most of the people he met there no doubt made it difficult for him to form an objective appraisal of their capacities; and there is evidence that he could sometimes affect an unpleasantly rhetorical posture without a great deal of provocation.[97] Still, his appraisal of Arkansas is extremely interesting and is entirely consistent with the assessment made by Fortescue Cuming who, as noted before, visited Arkansas Post in the same year as Bates.

On July 22 Bates wrote Albert Gallatin a letter from the Post reporting on his experiences. "The claims in this part of the country," he wrote, "have been brought forward with much irregularity. The people are for the most part so entirely unacquainted with every kind of business, except that of the chase, it is not at all to be wondered at that af-

94. The charge is set out in its entirety in *id.* at 14–15.

95. *Id.* at 14–15.

96. *Id.* at vii. Professor Marshall there remarks that Bates's poems "no doubt served their purpose in developing his art of writing, but as poetry they do not deserve a place in literature."

97. In his letter of June 17, 1807, to Abraham Fuller Hull, Bates says: "You ask me for an account, a political one I presume, of Louisiana. If I had a description of chaos, by one of the heathen philosophers, I would send you an extract from it." *Id.* at 143. This is a mild example of Bates's heavily rhetorical style.

fairs requiring method, order and an observance of legal forms should be totally unintelligible to them."

He continued: "Contrary to my expectations, a great number of claims remained to be entered when I arrived on the 2d instant. The next day the People appeared to be ignorant that the time for receiving them had expired, and having procured Agents, presented themselves very generally with their papers. . . . Considering the remote and sequestered situation of these claimants I was even induced to receive and reduce to writing the testimony in relation to these antedated and illegal entries. The papers and testimony will be carefully preserved, subject to those orders which you may think proper to give with respect to them." [98]

While in Arkansas Bates not only gathered evidence for the Board of Land Commissioners, he also delivered commissions to Benjamin Fooy of Esperanza and Captain George Armistead, Commandant of Fort Madison at Arkansas Post, naming them Justices of the Peace for the District of New Madrid. These commissions had been signed in blank by Governor Meriwether Lewis in May; it was left to Bates to fill the positions with persons whom he considered fit to hold them. [99] The citizens of Arkansas, moreover, had importuned Bates while he was there to resurrect their old district: A letter to him from Perly Wallis, a lawyer in Arkansas, dated September 1, 1808, stated that "the people are anxious for our separation and organization." [100] In fact, by the time Wallis's letter was written the district had already been separated by Governor Lewis's proclamation of August 20, [101] no doubt at Bates's sugges-

---

98. 2 *id.* at 7–8.

99. *Id.* at 30. It was noted in the records that the commissions for Fooy and Armistead "were dated 18th May—left blank by the Governor, and filled by the Secy. [*i.e.*, Bates] when he visited the Arkansas in July." *Id.*

100. *Id.* at 23.

101. The proclamation is set forth in full in *id.* at 15–16.

tion. On that day, and the three ensuing ones, Lewis set his head to "the civil organization and the reestablishment of the district of Arkansas," appointing judges to serve on the Courts of Common Pleas and Quarter Sessions and of the Court of Oyer and Terminer, a clerk for the various courts, a Recorder and Judge of Probate, a Sheriff, a Treasurer, and a Justice of the Peace and Notary Public.[102] John Honey, the Clerk of the Courts, Treasurer, Recorder, and Judge of Probate, took the commissions with him to Arkansas and arrived there on November 15. He administered the oaths to those who accepted the commissions as judges, and on November 30 Captain Armistead wrote to Bates that the "judges have excepted [sic] there [sic] commissions and nex [sic] Monday we shall have a cort [sic]."[103] And the next Monday they did indeed have a court,[104] evidently the first technically possessing anything like a general jurisdiction to sit in Arkansas since its annexation to the United States five years before.

Lewis appointed to this court, no doubt at Bates's suggestion, four Arkansas citizens of standing and renown: Charles Refeld, Benjamin Fooy, Francis Vaugine, and Joseph Stilwell. Charles Refeld refused his appointment "though not without expressing his gratitude in the highest form and with many gestures to the Governor for the honor which he done him in placing so much confidence [in] his integrity and abilities."[105] Benjamin Fooy accepted the proferred position but did not show for the first term of court. Thus only Vaugine and Stilwell were present at the court's first session.

102. *Id.* at 30.

103. *Id.* at 45.

104. The records of this court survive in the QUARTER SESSIONS REC- ORD BOOK and the COMMON PLEAS RECORD BOOK in the Arkansas History commission, Little Rock.

105. 2 BATES, *supra* note 2, at 59.

VI

Judge Honey voiced his doubts about these lay judges only a few weeks after they first sat.. "Mr. Vaugine and Stilwell," he wrote to Bates, "excepted [sic] the commissions as Judges. But knowing them not to be (tho very good men) very well acquainted with the proceeding in courts I was particular in making enquirees [sic] for a suitable person to recommend to the Governor in place of Mr. Refeld."[106]

The lack of learning on the part of the lay judges of the Territory of Louisiana was a matter of concern to many observers, including, of course, those professional lawyers who had been drawn to the new American possession by the hope of establishing a practice.[107] But lawyers had no interest themselves in accepting these low-paid positions.[108] In St. Louis and its environs, even in Ste. Genevieve, a fairly large number of lawyers were very soon after the American takeover induced to begin practice. At the first term of the Superior Court for the Territory of Louisiana the judges decided that all attorneys who had been admitted while the territory had been attached to Indiana would be admitted to the Bar, and seven men were sworn on the first day of the term.[109] However, it would be some time before Arkansas could boast a bar that large. A lay judiciary was simply a necessity for some time.

Charles Refeld, the man who refused his commission, was born in Danzig, Poland, in 1754 and had established himself as a merchant in Arkansas Post as early as 1794.[110] Benjamin Fooy, a native of Holland, had rendered long

106. *Id.*
107. W. ENGLISH, *supra* note 29, at 63.
108. *Id.* at 49.
109. *Id.* at 25.
110. Core, *Refeld Notes*, 15 GPHSB 24 (1972).

service to the Spanish on both sides of the Mississippi and had moved to the Chickasaw Bluffs (Memphis) in 1794. In March of 1797 Fort San Fernando de las Barrancas, located on the bluffs, was razed in preparation for delivering the area to the Americans and a new post, called Esperanza, had been established across the river in Arkansas. Two of the old fort's blockhouses were reassembled there, and a number of logs from the old stockade "made the trip across the river to become the new stockade at Esperanza."[111] Fooy relocated in Esperanza where he acted as interpreter and advisor on Indian affairs to Sergeant Augustin Grande, the commandant.[112] At the time of his appointment to the bench he was evidently a farmer and merchant. Francis Vaugine, a member of one of the most distinguished French families of colonial Louisiana, was born in Louisiana in 1768 and was a well-respected merchant at the Post where he had been resident since 1792.[113] Joseph Stilwell, the final member of Arkansas's first court, was born in New Jersey in 1752. Late in the eighteenth century he moved to New Orleans and in 1797 he was granted a tract of land in Arkansas. He arrived at the Post in 1798.[114]

Arkansas's first American court, therefore, consisted of a Dutchman, a native Louisianian of French background, and an Anglo-American, all without legal training. Before it is concluded, however, that the motliness of this court was its most distinguishing characteristic, it needs to be

111. Roper, *Benjamin Fooy and the Spanish Forts of San Fernando and Campo de la Esperanza*, 37 THE WEST TENNESSEE HISTORICAL SOCIETY PAPERS 41, at 46, 51 (1982).

112. *Id.* at 51, 52. In J. HOLMES, GAYOSO, THE LIFE OF A SPANISH GOVERNOR IN THE MISSISSIPPI VALLEY 229 (1968) it is stated that Fooy was for a time commandant at Esperanza.

113. Core, *The Vaugine Arkansas Connection*, 21 GPHSB 6 (1978).

114. R. DHONAU, STILWELL HERTAGE IN ARKANSAS, 1798–1976, 1–5 (1976).

noted that two of its members spoke and understood French, at least two could do the same for English, all were literate, all had lived in Arkansas for at least ten years, and all had had some experience with business and governmental affairs. To assemble a group with that much sophistication in the Arkansas in 1808 was no mean feat when one considers the descriptions which nineteenth-century travellers have left us of Esperanza, the Post, and their populations.

It proved extremely difficult, however, to assemble this group with any regularity. It was supposed to meet three times a year, in April, August, and December.[115] During the four years that the court existed, therefore, it should have held thirteen terms, but it in fact managed to hold only eight. For four of those terms only two judges, Francis Vaugine and Joseph Stilwell, a bare quorum, kept the court. From August, 1810, to December, 1811 there was no court at all: Only Francis Vaugine showed up, dutifully noted in the record that he was the only judge to appear, and adjourned until the next term.

No doubt some of the judges simply regarded holding court as too much trouble. Probably Benjamin Fooy did not especially relish the triennial trek from Esperanza to Arkansas Post: Even though the sessions rarely lasted longer than a week, he sat only three terms. There was also the difficulty of attracting and keeping a qualified clerk and recorder. John Honey, first Recorder, Clerk of the Courts, Probate Judge, and Treasurer, was only nineteen years old when he came to Arkansas and he stayed only about six months.[116] His replacement, John Harvey, stayed less time

115. What follows is based on the record books of the Court of Common Pleas and Court of Quarter Sessions which I first examined when they were in the custody of the Clerk of the Supreme Court of Arkansas. They are now in the Arkansas History Commission, Little Rock.

116. Core, *John William Honey*, 22 GPHSB 8 (1979).

than that and on November 16, 1809, Bates wrote an exasperated and extremely short letter to the judges of the District of Arkansas announcing Harvey's resignation. He enclosed blank commissions for the vacancies created by this resignation and invited the judges to use their "best efforts in filling them worthily." He ended with a terse warning that on their "success in this attempt will probably depend the existence of your settlements as a *Separate District*."[117] The judges did fill the vacancies, and in 1810 the Arkansas Court of Quarter Sessions was even given jurisdiction over capital offenses.[118] But some time after August, 1812, and before the end of that year, the District of Arkansas was again abolished,[119] and this marked the effective end of Courts of Quarter Session and Common Pleas for Arkansas. It is true that late in 1813 Arkansas County was erected,[120] and the next year a new court of laymen was appointed.[121] This court met twice in 1814: But the first time it convened only to appoint a clerk;[122] and the second time it adjourned because of "the parties litigant not being timely noticed."[123] As we shall see, Congress would soon intervene to insure that Arkansas was provided a stable and professional legal system.

One reason that Arkansas's first experiment with a republican form of government failed had to do with resistance to it by the French *habitants*. By 1810, the Arkansas population had grown to 1,064; 183 people lived in the Es-

117. 2 BATES, *supra* note 2, at 115–16.
118. LAWS, *supra* note 79, ch. 78, § 1.
119. A proclamation of the governor reannexing the District of Arkansas to the District of New Madrid is mentioned in the act creating the county of Arkansas passed December 31, 1813. *See id*, ch. 99, § 3.
120. LAWS, *supra* note 79, ch. 99.
121. 2 BATES, *supra* note 2, at 192.
122. COMMON PLEAS RECORD BOOK 139.
123. *Id.* at 141.

peranza and St. Francis area, the rest in and around the Post and up the Arkansas and White rivers.[124] Though a few French families, many of whom would achieve prominence, did settle in Arkansas after the American takeover, almost all of the increase in population was due to American immigration. Nevertheless, the French may still have accounted for upwards of half of the Arkansas population in 1810. Henry Brackenridge wrote in 1811 that the Arkansas settlements were "the least considerable of the territory"; and he said of the Post that it contained 450 inhabitants and "was a French settlement . . . with about the same proportion of Americans as in the other towns."[125] In the same year, Amos Stoddard described Arkansas Post as containing "thirty or forty houses only" and its inhabitants as "altogether of French extraction."[126]

One measure of the disdain with which the French regarded American legal institutions is the infrequency of their appearances in the courts.[127] About two hundred civil actions were initiated in Arkansas in the period between 1808 and 1812 and of these only eleven were brought by Frenchmen. But the effective rate of appeal to the American courts by the French was even less than these figures would at first indicate. Only two Frenchmen accounted for these eleven civil actions: François Michel brought four of them and John Larquier seven. Michel was not a resident of Arkansas until 1804.[128] Lest it be thought that Larquier was an especially litigious fellow, it needs to be said that his adversary in every instance was Pierre Lefevre whom he

124. This census is reported in several sources. *See, e.g.,* H. BRACK-ENRIDGE, VIEWS OF LOUISIANA 118 (1814).

125. *Id.* at 212, 231.

126. A. STODDARD, *supra* note 30, at 206.

127. What follows is taken from COMMON PLEAS RECORD BOOK, 1–136.

128. *See* R. DHONAU, FRENCH MICHELS CAME TO MISSOURI AND ARKANSAS 6 (1978).

was suing for debts. No doubt many of these claims grew out of the same transaction (Larquier owned a saloon and billiard hall in the middle of the town) and some may even be duplicate entries of the same case.

It seems clear, then, that the old French *habitants* of Arkansas, amounting to perhaps half of the population, brought less than five per cent of the civil actions during this period. Of course this is partly attributable to the fact that many of the French were hunters who had always shied away from regular courts anyway, preferring self-help to legal niceties. We discovered earlier that except for a small number of gentry and *bourgeois*, people with a real attachment to French legal culture were not frequently encountered at the Arkansas. But it is striking that so few of even the respectable French families ever resorted to a court in this period. Even if they were otherwise inclined to do so, a very real practical difficulty that lay in their way was their inability to speak English. Almost all of the jurors were Americans; and though, at least at times, André Fagot acted as interpreter,[129] conducting a trial must have been at the very least a strain under such circumstances.

Another indication of the alienation of the Arkansas French from their new legal regime is revealed when the composition of trial juries is examined. Seventeen civil juries were empanelled in Arkansas between 1808 and 1812. The average number of French jurymen was less than one and the median was zero. In criminal cases the French were only a little more visible.[130] There were thirteen criminal juries empanelled: The average number of French jurymen was 1.5 and the median was one. Whether the French were systematically excluded from service, or were simply reluctant to serve and it seemed not worth the trouble to

129. Fagot's appointment as interpreter occurred on April 13, 1809 and is recorded in QUARTER SESSIONS RECORD BOOK at 10.

130. What follows is taken from QUARTER SESSIONS RECORD BOOK 1–79.

compel them to do so, we cannot tell. It seems likely that both of these propositions were operating to a degree.

When the grand jury in April, 1809, presented Perly Wallis, a contentious and impolitic lawyer at the Arkansas, for an unnamed offense, he moved that the trial jury "be composed of persons entirely who speak the English Language."[131] Though he withdrew his motion when the prosecutor objected to it, no doubt many of the Americans harbored desires similar to Wallis's. Matters would be much simpler for them if only the French could be encouraged to indulge what was anyway their natural inclination to avoid contact with the new legal system. There seems to have been no similar effort to exclude the old *habitants* who were English-speaking. Many of them sat regularly on juries: German-Americans, who had probably lived previously under common-law systems in effect in the English colonies, were not uncommonly called on to serve.

The picture that emerges is one of skepticism and aloofness on the part of Arkansas's old French *habitants* and a determination on the part of the American newcomers to encourage that attitude. There is only one apparent exception to an otherwise perfect impression of alienation.[132] The grand juries that were empanelled at the beginning of each term of the Court of Quarter Sessions always contained a number of Frenchmen. The average number of French grand jurymen was 6.6 and the median was seven. Sometimes, moreover, the foreman was French. Perhaps this reflects a desire on the part of the deputy attorney general to obtain the best possible information on crimes committed in the community. Perhaps, also, the French wished to protect themselves against American prejudice or, it may be, to indulge some prejudices of their own. This would have tended to overcome their otherwise clear and

131. *Id.* at 26.
132. What follows is taken from *id.*

demonstrated determination to stay as far away as possible from legal proceedings of any sort. Unlike Spanish criminal procedure, under which any citizen could initiate a criminal action, American criminal procedure required an indictment or presentment for all crimes, even misdemeanors. But French participation in the process of the grand jury tended to diminish towards the end of the period 1808–1812 and, as we shall see, it would very soon thereafter virtually disappear.

The aloofness of the French almost surely reflects their very low opinion of those American ideals of self-government which manifested themselves in the new legal system. Henry Brackenridge, a common lawyer from Pennsylvania, who later became a civilian with an extensive practice in New Orleans, commented in 1811 somewhat condescendingly on the reluctance of the Louisiana French to accept common-law institutions, especially the jury:[133] "There are some things in the administration of justice, which they do not yet perfectly comprehend; the trial by jury, and the multifarious forms of our jurisprudence. They had not been accustomed to distinguish between the slow and cautious advances of even-handed justice, and the despatch of arbitrary power. In their simple state of society, when the subjects of litigation were not of great value, the administration of justice might be speedy and simple; but they ought to be aware, that when a society becomes extensive, and its occupations, relations and interests, more numerous, people less acquainted with each other, the laws must be more complex. The trial by jury, is foreign to the customs and manners of their ancestors; it is therefore not to be expected that they should at once comprehend its utility and importance." No doubt the French of Arkansas viewed American legal process with the kinds of skepticism which Brackenridge ascribes

133. H. BRACKENRIDGE, *supra* note 124, at 144–45.

to the Louisiana French generally. It remains to wonder how the French settled their differences if they eschewed the ordinary court system. In the absence of direct evidence, this is the hardest kind of question to answer. It is possible that they did their best to counterfeit their old *government militaire* and submitted their disputes informally to the head of their militia. Though this seems odd, and is at best mere speculation, we know that when the English took over Quebec in 1764 civil disputes among the French were settled "by arbitration by the *curé* or the captain of militia."[134] The French of Quebec simply were not willing to apply to the common-law courts of the English for relief. At the Arkansas there was no priest, so a civilian military commandant would have been the only recourse for the old French *habitants*. For a later period, as we shall see, there is some direct evidence that this occurred.

VII

One of the most wrenching changes wrought by the new American legal system was the introduction of a professional lawyer class into Arkansas. Even nonforensic lawyers were unknown in Arkansas under both French and Spanish rule. Contentious, forensic professionals, adversary players in a public trial process, itself a jarring innovation, must have been especially obnoxious to the old French *habitants*. Still, the legal profession was relatively late in coming to Arkansas. This is not surprising since the Louisiana Territorial Assembly had been so tardy in providing Arkansas with a court system. The Post, moreover, with a

---

134. Hay, *The Meanings of the Criminal Law in Quebec, 1764–1774*, in CRIME AND CRIMINAL JUSTICE IN EUROPE AND CANADA 72 (1981).

population of only 450, most of whom were Indian traders and hunters, could not have held out much attraction for an aspiring practitioner. The prospects for remunerative work would simply have been too small.

Anxiety over the validity of Spanish land grants in Arkansas seems to have been responsible for the first documented appearance of lawyers there. When Frederick Bates arrived at the Post in July of 1808 to receive evidence on behalf of the Board of Land Commissioners, two men presented papers and appeared on behalf of Arkansas claimants. One was Joshua G. Clark of Natchez, the other Perly Wallis of Ouachita Post.[135] The failure of any resident land agent or lawyer to appear at so important an event is virtually conclusive evidence that there was no resident legal professional at the Arkansas at this time. We hear no more of Mr. Clark as a lawyer, but Mr. Wallis would long figure in the legal records of Arkansas.

Perly Wallis was in all probability the first person to appear as a lawyer before a court sitting in Arkansas. On December 5, 1808, when the Court of Common pleas for the District of Arkansas first convened, Wallis moved his admission. The court granted his motion on the ground that he had "produced to the court sufficient document of his good and moral character and of his having been a practicing attorney in a former court of this district."[136] Probably Wallis had appeared previously in the Justice Court of Captain George Armistead, the American officer in charge of the garrison at the Post.[137] There is no evidence that any other court ever sat at the Post previous to the convening of the 1808 Court of Common Pleas.

135. 2 BATES, *supra* note 2, at 12, 13.
136. COMMON PLEAS RECORD BOOK 2.
137. Armistead's court is mentioned as having previously sat in Arkansas when a Mrs. Moore presented the Court of Common Pleas with a bill for the quarters in which Armistead's court had been held. *Id.*

There is some difficulty in determining what provision was first made by the District of Louisiana for admitting attorneys to practice in its courts. The book that purports to contain all the laws enacted by the first Louisiana legislature in 1804, which was published in that year,[138] contains no provisions for regulating the practice of law. But a compilation of Louisiana and Missouri laws passed before 1824, published in 1842, contains an elaborate act, attributed to 1804, dealing with the admission of attorneys. Under it, any two judges of the Superior Court were empowered to grant licenses to practice law. An applicant was required to be twenty years old and to produce a certificate from any court of the United States where he resided "that he is a person of honest demeanor, or a license of his admission to practice in any court of any one of the United States." The judges were to admit an applicant "if after examination they shall be of opinion that he is duly qualified."[139]

Even if this law had ever been in effect, it would have been repealed by a later statute of 1807 regulating the practice of law.[140] By that act, any one judge of the Superior Court could admit a person to practice. But applicants had to have "studied law within this territory two years at least, under the direction of some practicing attorney or person of legal knowledge, or [to] have been admitted before in some court of record in some of the United States or territories as a practising attorney. . . ." The applicant, moreover, had to produce a certificate of good moral character and pass an examination by the judge.[141] Persons previously admitted by the General Court did not have to meet these requirements.

Perly Wallis was not admitted to practice by the General

---

138. Laws, *supra* note 51.
139. Laws, *supra* note 79, ch. 7.
140. *Id.*, ch. 38, § 58.
141. *Id.*

Court of Louisiana until October 26, 1809,[142] and his 1808 admission by the Arkansas Court was therefore almost certainly illegal. The only colorable ground that Wallis had urged for his admission in 1808 was his previous practice in the District of Arkansas; if the act of 1804 alluded to above was not in fact ever in effect, and if justice courts had the power to admit persons to practice before 1807, then Wallis might just possibly have been regularly admitted in 1808. But all this seems highly fanciful.

If Wallis was admitted under somewhat questionable circumstances, some later admissions at the Arkansas were even more irregular. Wallis seems to have been not only the first lawyer allowed to practice in the courts of the District of Arkansas; for more than a year he was the only one practicing there. For obvious reasons, this situation was at the least awkward and would eventually draw enterprising practitioners from elsewhere. But ingenious means had to be resorted to at first in order to deprive Wallis of his monopoly.

In the November term of 1809, Patrick Darby, evidently from the Territory of Orleans, presented a power of attorney from George Hook, an important merchant of Ouachita Post; and the record nonchalantly noted that "the court permit him to plead on the tenor of his power of attorney."[143] The following term, on April 21, 1810, Hezekiah Kirkpatrick and J. L. Henderson produced their licenses to practice in the Territory of Orleans and moved their admission "*pro tempore*, until a sufficient number of licensed attorneys shall appear in the said court to enable each of [the] parties to engage some regular attorney." The court

---

142. 2 MISSOURI SUPREME COURT RECORD BOOK 379. This book is in the Missouri Historical Society in St. Louis. Wallis presented his license to the Court of Quarter Sessions for the District of Arkansas on November 5, 1809. QUARTER SESSIONS RECORD BOOK 32.

143. COMMON PLEAS RECORD BOOK 17.

however denied the motion stating emphatically that "no attorney shall be allowed to plead unless he comes forward qualified as the law directs."[144] The next day Patrick Darby reappeared and asked whether "any person, vested with a Power of Attorney, may be permitted to plead at the Bar"; and the court thereupon ruled that "any person vested with an aforesaid power may be permitted to do so."[145]

Thereafter, Darby, Kirkpatrick, and Henderson are seen regularly engaged in the practice of law. It is clear, moreover, that they thought of themselves as allied in some way. Sometimes they associated with each other in representing clients.[146] Kirkpatrick and Henderson once combined to move the court to establish some elementary pleading rules.[147] When in August of 1810 Darby was "excluded in future from pleading at the bar under any pretense whatever under Power of Attorney or otherwise for his repeated contempts of the court,"[148] he was very soon readmitted on the motion of Kirkpatrick.[149] Wallis's absence from this cartel is obvious.

Late in 1811 the first truly regular practitioner appeared in an Arkansas court. He was Anthony Haden and on the first day of the December term he duly presented his license from the General Court of the territory and was permitted to plead.[150] Haden had been a lawyer since 1805 at least, for in that year he was at work at the first American court to sit in Cape Girardeau.[151] John Miller is also seen

144. *Id.* at 18.
145. *Id.* at 20.
146. *Id.* at 21 (Darby and Kirkpatrick); *id.* at 22 (Kirkpatrick and Henderson).
147. *Id.* at 22–23.
148. *Id.* at 49.
149. *Id.* at 50. Before the court readmitted Darby he is said at *id.* to have made "such acknowledgments as are satisfactory to the court."
150. *Id.* at 74.
151. 3 L. HOUCK, *supra* note 25, at 23 (1908).

at Arkansas doing the work of a lawyer in the December
term of 1811, but no hint is given as to his background.
Alexander S. Walker appeared in the records as an attorney
for the first time on December 9,[152] but he was not formally licensed until almost two years later.[153] Perhaps these
last two had taken advantage of the power of attorney
ruse. But Darby and Henderson dropped from sight forever; Kirkpatrick made two appearances this term, one of
them as Haden's "assistant,"[154] and then was heard of no
more. The court had evidently indulged its initial xeno-
phobic urge, and had sent the interlopers packing for Orleans Territory.

Though the Arkansas judicial records for 1808 to 1814
several times refer to the files of the court,[155] no files have
in fact survived. But the Record Books are still extant, and
they contain enough matter to allow at least a partial re-
construction of the courts' business and the manner in
which it was accomplished.

The chief business of the courts was, of course, judicial,[156] and from the beginning the records reveal at least a
patina of common-law professionalism. John W. Honey,
the Clerk of the Courts, and his successors had somehow
provided themselves with enough of the common lawyer's
lingo to make their books comfortable reading for a legal
historian. For instance, an entry in an 1809 debt case in
which the defendant had judgment concluded with cen-

152. COMMON PLEAS RECORD BOOK 63.
153. *Id.* at 70.
154. *Id.* at 72.
155. *See, e.g., id.* at 2.
156. The courts also possessed general administrative powers. Indeed, they were the county government. Thus they approved or dis-
approved bills presented to the county (COMMON PLEAS 2; QUARTER
SESSIONS 48), appointed constables (QUARTER SESSION 6), and erected
townships (QUARTER SESSIONS 61).

turies-old boiler-plate: "and the plaintiff for his false clamour in mercy *etc. etc.*"[157] Present also are allusions to the forms of action so familiar to the historian: Debt is by far the most common (a good fifty percent of the court's business), but covenant, replevin, false imprisonment, slander, defamation, trespass *vi et armis*, and unidentified actions on the case are also noted. On the criminal side, we encounter assault and battery (eighty percent of the court's business), larceny, receiving stolen goods, even one indictment for murder. Special statutory crimes are represented as well, probably the most exotic being "heating an Indian with whiskey thereby making said Indian drunk."[158] Honey had brought with him a manuscript copy of some at least of the acts of the Louisiana territorial legislature, and the records show that the court conscientiously consulted it on matters of limitations[159] and continuances.[160] On one occasion, in the December term of 1811, the court even notes that argument had been held on a legal point "and several cases cited."[161] Nor were the names of the actions used in the records necessarily merely borrowed furbelows: In 1813 an action of covenant was demurred to on the ground that the instrument on which it was based was not under seal, and the demurrer was sustained.[162]

Obviously there was an effort being made to conform the workings of the courts to many of the main points of common-law practice and procedure. But the records also contain some interesting episodes of sheer amateurism. The most remarkable and revealing of these is the court's first attempt to establish pleading rules. At the April term of 1810, on the motion of Messrs. Kirkpatrick and Hen-

---

157. COMMON PLEAS RECORD BOOK 5.
158. *Id.* at 2.
159. *Id.* at 37.
160. *Id.* at 114.
161. *Id.* at 80.
162. *Id.* at 60.

derson, the following incomplete order was entered: ". . .
it is ordered to be a rule of this court as to the manner and
form of pleading, that the plaintiff first appear and open
the case; that the defendant then reply to the argument of
the plaintiff and that the plaintiff then conclude; but if the
defendant adduce any new matter in his defense which is
not in direct answer to the argument of the plaintiff. . . ."[163]
Though the sentence breaks off before finishing, its drift is
plain enough, and in December of 1811 another attempt,
this time a complete one, was made at establishing rules of
pleading: "It is ordered to be a rule of this court in all civil
actions that the plaintiff open the case, the defendant then
reply, and the plaintiff shall then conclude which shall
finish the argument except in case the plaintiff or defendant
[sic] in his conclusion adduce any new matter or law the
defendant shall by leave of the Court have right to answer
to such new matter."[164]

What these rules seem to indicate is that pleading at
Arkansas Post in the early nineteenth century was, sometimes at least, done orally. Perhaps this was in conscious
imitation of the verbal procedure employed in eighteenth-
century Spanish Arkansas; just as likely, it reflects a lack of
learning on the part of the Arkansas bar. That is not to say
that the lack of sophistication which these rules reveal
makes them in any sense undesirable. No doubt they
served well, and modern pleading rules, except that a writing is required, do not differ markedly from them. The
point being urged is that their naïveté bears no relation to
the prolixity of the common-law pleading rules and practices in vogue elsewhere at this time in America.

163. *Id.* at 22–23.
164. *Id.* at 66.

V

The Professionalization of the Arkansas Legal System and the Obliteration of Civil-Law Traditions 1812–1836

On June 4, 1812, when the Territory of Louisiana became the Territory of Missouri, a popularly elected House of Representatives was for the first time provided for. It was composed of one representative for every 500 free white male inhabitants. Another chamber, called the Legislative Council, was created at the same time; its members were to be appointed by the President from a list provided by the House. A Superior Court, consisting of three judges, was erected and given jurisdiction in all criminal matters and exclusive jurisdiction in capital cases. In civil cases it had original and appellate jurisdiction if the amount in controversy was more than one hundred dollars. The General Assembly of Missouri was given the authority to establish inferior courts to which the governor had the power of appointment.[1]

I

The first election for members of the Missouri Territorial Assembly was held on the second Tuesday in November, 1812. Arkansas was at that time part of New Madrid

1. 2 STATS. AT LARGE 743.

County (the old name of "District" had been dropped) and the county was allotted two representatives. Neither of the members elected for New Madrid was from Arkansas. Indeed, it is not likely that a polling place for this election was even provided in Arkansas since the government there had entirely collapsed.[2]

On December 30, 1813, the Arkansas country was again, and this time permanently, separated from New Madrid when the County of Arkansas was created. A census taken that year for the purpose of apportioning the legislature revealed, incredibly, that the County of Arkansas had only 287 free white male inhabitants; the total white male population of the Territory was 11,393.[3] This meant, of course, that Arkansas County was not necessarily entitled to return a member to the House of Representatives. Nevertheless, it appears that when the General Assembly convened on December 5, 1814, a member from Arkansas was authorized to be present. At the second session of this legislature, convened in January of 1815, Henry Cassidy, a lawyer, represented Arkansas County.[4]

The first election held in the Arkansas country of which a record survives occurred in 1816. Nine polling places were established, one in each of the townships into which the new County of Arkansas had only recently been divided.[5] Three election judges were appointed for each precinct and Edmund Hogan was elected representative from Arkansas.[6]

The townships had been created and the election judges appointed by George C. Bullitt, a common lawyer from

2. 3 L. HOUCK, A HISTORY OF MISSOURI 2 (1908).

3. *Id.* at 5.

4. *Id.* at 6.

5. RECORD BOOK OF THE GENERAL COURT 276. This book is in the Arkansas History Commission, Little Rock.

6. 3 L. HOUCK, *supra* note 2, at 7.

Ste. Genevieve, who had recently arrived at the Post of Arkansas to become the first professional lawyer ever to sit on an Arkansas bench.[7] With the creation of the County of Arkansas late in 1813 a new Court of Common Pleas had been appointed, but it kept only one regular term, in April of 1814, and that one was immediately adjourned because "of the parties not being timely noticed."[8] It was obvious that the remote Arkansas country, still with a white population that could not have exceeded 1,500, required special attention if any sort of regular governance was going to be initiated there. Therefore in 1814 Congress enacted a bill creating "an additional judge for the Missouri Territory." This judge was given the jurisdiction "now possessed and exercised in said district by the court of common pleas, as well as that possessed and exercised by the superior court within the said district." Its jurisdiction, moreover, was exclusive. An appeal to the Superior Court in St. Louis was also provided. The court was to sit twice annually, and the act pointedly stated that the new judge "shall reside at or near the village of Arkansas."[9] It was this judgeship that George Bullitt took up in the fall of 1814.

The polling place which Judge Bullitt appointed for the election of 1816 for the township of Arkansas was "at the Court House of the County of Arkansas."[10] Travellers also make mention of Bullitt's court house.[11] Evidently this was

7. Bullitt was admitted to practice in Louisiana by the General Court of the Territory of Indiana at its first meeting on October 1, 1804, at St. Louis. W. ENGLISH, THE PIONEER LAWYER AND JURIST IN MISSOURI 25 (1947). He was a member of the first House of Representatives of the Territory of Missouri. 3 L. HOUCK, *supra* note 2, at 3.

8. COMMON PLEAS RECORD BOOK 141. The judges were Joseph Stilwell, Samuel Mosely, and Francis Vaugine.

9. 3 STATS. AT LARGE 95.

10. RECORD BOOK OF THE GENERAL COURT 278.

11. *See, e.g.,* T. FLINT, RECOLLECTIONS OF THE LAST TEN YEARS 255, 263 (1826).

a rented house in or near the village since the only building ever erected for public use in Arkansas Post was the jail.[12] It may even be that more than one building was in use at different times during Bullitt's five-year tenure, but there nevertheless seems to have been at this time a building set aside more or less exclusively for the use of the court. Otherwise the designation "court house" could have carried very little meaning. This was an event of more than a little significance in the gradual professionalization process which the Arkansas legal system was experiencing.

In 1815, the County of Lawrence, which included much of what is now northern Arkansas, was created out of New Madrid and Arkansas Counties.[13] Late that year, or early the next one, a surveyor laid out and platted a county seat, the town of Davidsonville on the Black River.[14] The town site was purchased by the county in December of 1815 from a man who had acquired it two months before from five Frenchmen.[15] Before the town was abandoned in the late 1820s[16] it grew to a fairly considerable size, though it never contained more than a few hundred residents.[17] The circuit court of the Territory of Missouri for the southern circuit began sitting in Lawrence County, presumably in Davidsonville, in 1816.[18] A courthouse, said to have been a

12. E. BEARSS and L. BROWN, STRUCTURAL HISTORY, POST OF ARKANSAS, 1804–1853, 47 (1971); W. HALLIBURTON, A TOPOGRAPHICAL DESCRIPTION AND HISTORY OF ARKANSAS COUNTY, ARKANSAS FROM 1541 TO 1875, 120, 137 (1901?). In 1816 George Armistead's house "near the Village of Arkansas" was in use as the Courthouse. E. BEARSS and L. BROWN, supra, at 47.

13. 3 L. HOUCK, supra note 2, at 7.

14. See C. DOLLAR, AN ARCHAEOLOGICAL ASSESSMENT OF HISTORIC DAVIDSONVILLE, ARKANSAS 7 (1977).

15. L. DALTON, HISTORY OF RANDOLPH COUNTY, ARKANSAS 174–75 (1947).

16. See L. STEWART–ABERNATHY, THE SEAT OF JUSTICE: 1815–1830, AN ARCHAEOLOGICAL RECONNAISANCE OF DAVIDSONVILLE 8 (1980).

17. L. DALTON, supra note 15, at 175.

18. The records of this court are available on microfilm at the Ar-

8. Territory of Missouri, 1816. (*Courtesy Records Management and Archives Service, Office of the Secretary of State, State of Missouri.*)

two-story brick structure, was eventually built there; but it almost certainly was not constructed until 1822.[19]

kansas History Commission, Little Rock.

19. C. DOLLAR, *supra* note 14, at 33–37.

As noted before, a common-law procedural structure
had been erected in the District of Louisiana immediately
upon the American takeover, but the legislature had at first
said very little about the substantive rules of decision to
which resort was to be had in settling civil disputes. Theoretically, this left intact the Spanish civil law of the old
province of Louisiana. However, because there were few
people in Upper Louisiana who knew the first thing about
substantive civil law, cases in Missouri Territory were often decided on common-law principles because the former practices could not be determined.[20] In 1807, John
Coburn, then a judge of the Louisiana Superior Court,
wrote to James Madison and explained to him the difficulties that his court was facing: "We found the few un-
digested Laws, which were in operation, extremely inadequate to the proper administration of Justice, and the
Government of the Territory. The mass of Law heretofore
in force was composed of crude and very discordant materials. The usages and customs, derived from the Spanish
Government. The laws organizing the Territorial Government, with perhaps the ordinance of 1787, and with those
the whole system of English Common Law, together with
the Laws enacted by the Governor and Judges of the Indiana Territory. From this extensive source, proceeded the
administration of Justice, and in practice it was found totally inadequate to the peculiar institutions of the Territory.
The usages and customs of the Spanish Government, said
to be in force in Louisiana, are extremely difficult to ascertain and in many instances not susceptible of proof. There
being no regular record kept of the decisions, rendered by
the several Commandants; and although the Courts have
in several instances resorted to parole proof, to ascertain a
particular usage; the dangers attendant on this practice are
obvious. . . . There are doubts existing, whether those

20. W. ENGLISH, *supra* note 7, at 55.

usages and customs are really engrafted into the system of Laws by the Acts of Congress organizing the Territory. To remedy the evils arising from this source and to meet the wishes of the French inhabitants, we were induced to incorporate in our Laws, several leading commercial customs; existing in the Country for a series of years. Those customs are peculiar to the Country, and are perhaps necessary for the convenience of the trading society. For example, we permit a debtor in certain contracts to have the alternative, to pay his creditors in peltry, lead or cash. We permit the Merchant who advances the merchandise for a trading voyage with the Indians; to retain a species of lien on the peltries and furs produced by the voyage, in preference to subsequent or other debts contracted by the voyager. It is our wish to assimilate by insensible means, the habits and customs of the American and French inhabitants; by interweaving some of the regulations of the latter into our Laws, we procure a ready obedience, without violence or complaint. We consider the policy as good and founded upon substantial justice."[21]

Almost all of the cases that arose involving contract or tort principles were so simple that ordinary moral propositions, a kind of natural law, could be resorted to for their solution. The common-law jury was, of course, perfectly suited to a substantive legal system based on commonly shared assumptions about how a moral world was ordered.

The civil law did, however, differ considerably from the common law in a few important substantive particulars. The law of descent and distribution was one of these and the law of marital property another. In 1807 a statute was passed adopting common-law canons of descent and giving widows something very close to common-law dower.[22]

21. 2 J. ROBERTSON, LOUISIANA UNDER THE RULE OF SPAIN, FRANCE AND THE UNITED STATES 355 (1911).

22. LAWS OF A PUBLIC AND GENERAL NATURE OF THE DISTRICT OF LOUISIANA . . . . ch. 39 (1842).

This statute also gave parents the right to disinherit their children, a power denied them under the civil-law doctrine of *legitime*. By its adoption of dower the statute effectively shattered forever in the upper territory the community property system and the long-time Louisiana custom of marriage contracts between future spouses. It might well have been theoretically possible to counterfeit a community property regime by ante-nuptial common-law contract, but that would have required a technical skill which few, if any, lawyers in the upper territory possessed. The same year a law allowing divorces and delineating the grounds therefor was enacted.[23]

In 1810, the General Court of Louisiana was given a general chancery jurisdiction.[24] Interestingly, it appears that issues of fact were to be tried to a jury should one be requested by either party, a procedure which had been not uncommonly employed in the eighteenth-century English colonies.[25] Obviously the adoption of a common-law legal system was by this time virtually complete.

Early in 1816, while Judge George Bullitt was presiding at the Post of Arkansas, the General Assembly of the Territory of Missouri went almost the entire distance and adopted as the rule of decision for civil suits "the common law of England, which is of a general nature, and all statutes made by the British Parliament in aid of or to supply the defects of the said common law, made prior to the fourth year of James the first. . . ." An important general exception was made for those "laws of this territory" which were "contrary to the common law." The statute specifically excepted from its operation, moreover, "the doctrine of survivorship in cases of joint tenants" and the

23. *Id.*, ch. 30.
24. *Id.*, ch. 239.
25. *See generally*, Arnold, *A Historical Inquiry into the Right to Trial by Jury in Complex Civil Litigation*, 128 U. Pa. L. Rev. 829 (1980).

"doctrine of entails."[26]

None of these developments could have done much to quiet the resentments of the French population of Arkansas, though they must have realized for some time that the death of their legal culture was inevitable. During the five years that George Bullitt held his court at the Arkansas their alienation from the republican ways of their new masters became complete.[27] The average number of Frenchmen on grand juries dwindled to three during his tenure; after 1816 it was less than one. Bullitt presided over fifty-nine juries, on which the average number of Frenchmen was just under one; the median was zero.

II

There is, moreover, hard evidence that Frenchmen who found themselves on *venires* were systematically and deliberately excluded from empanelled juries. For murder trials in 1815 three *venires* of forty-eight persons each were returned by the sheriff; they contained seven, eight, and ten Frenchmen respectively. In none of these cases was a single Frenchman seated on the jury. Though the court still had an interpreter,[28] it may be that difficulties caused by a language barrier furnished the primary motive for these exclusionary practices. But whatever the motive for exclusion, it appears clear that most Frenchmen were unwelcome when it came time to choose a jury. Nor did they very often appear as plaintiffs while Bullitt was on the bench.

26. LAWS, *supra* note 22, ch. 154.
27. What follows is taken from the RECORD BOOK OF THE GENERAL COURT, the QUARTER SESSIONS RECORD BOOK, and the COMMON LAW RECORD in the Arkansas History Commission, Little Rock.
28. André Fagot was appointed interpreter on April 3, 1809. QUAR-

The Americanization of Arkansas which was rapidly taking place is visible in another way in the legal records. In 1815, the General Assembly gave George Bullitt's court jurisdiction over "all county business," but even before then not a little of his energies was devoted to creating townships,[29] licensing ferries,[30] and appointing commissioners to view and mark out roads.[31] All of this was made

TER SESSIONS RECORD BOOK 10. In May of 1817, August Surville was named interpreter. COMMON LAW RECORD 2.

29. Arkansas County was first divided into townships in 1814 when nine townships were created. They were Hopefield, St. Francis, Cash, Arkansas, Big Rock, Caddeau (*sic; recte* Cadron), Hot Springs, Cadow, and Little Missouri. QUARTER SESSIONS RECORD BOOK 173. On May 7, 1816, Chicot Township was created. RECORD BOOK OF THE GENERAL COURT 275. In May of 1817 Cadron Township was divided so as to create Mulberry Township. COMMON LAW RECORD 11. On October 9, 1817, Bullitt declared the Town of Arkansas incorporated and its boundaries were defined. *Id.* at 39.

30. The first issuance of a ferry license that I have noticed occurred on September 9, 1814. On that date John McElmurry was granted a license to operate a ferry "across the Arkansas River at or opposite the said John McElmurry's place of residence . . . at the settlement of the Cadron." RECORD BOOK OF THE GENERAL COURT 159. The court also set the rates which ferrymen could charge, and they varied with the width of the stream on which the ferries operated. Usually license proceedings were commenced by petition of the hopeful licensee or of someone on his behalf. Sometimes, however, a grand jury presentment initiated such proceedings. For instance, on April 6, 1815, the grand jury presented to the court "the necessity of having public ferries established on the Arkansas River and they recommend the Little Rocks on the said River as a proper place for the establishing of one under the Direction of Edmund Hogan living on and about the said place." *Id.* at 180. Four days later, Hogan moved that he be granted a license "to keep a public ferry on the Arkansas River at a place on the said River called the Little Rocks" and Bullitt granted the motion.

31. Typically the grand jury would recommend to the court that a road be viewed and marked out, and Bullitt would then appoint commissioners for that purpose. *See, e.g.*, RECORD BOOK OF THE GENERAL COURT 158 (September 8, 1814; roads from Arkansas Post to Hot

necessary by the wave of American immigration that began about 1815 and which would push the Arkansas population past 14,000 by 1820.[32] It would also engulf the old *habitants* of the Post of Arkansas.

William Darby, in his 1818 edition of *The Emmigrant's Guide*, gave a description of Arkansas Post which readers will by now find all too familiar: "The post or town of Arkansaw is about forty-five miles above the entrance of that stream into the Mississippi. This is one of the most ancient establishments in Louisiana, being formed before the beginning of the last century. Its advance has not been in proportion to its duration. It has remained poor and inconsiderable, like all other places where the inhabitants depend upon hunting and trade with savages for their subsistence and commerce. The inhabitants are mostly French, many of them of mixed blood."[33]

As we shall see, this assessment of the Post was somewhat out of date when it was published. Nevertheless, many visitors to Arkansas on the eve of the creation of Arkansas Territory remark on the existence of large numbers of hunters in the area and comment on their attitudes toward civilization and law. Writing of social conditions which he encountered in Missouri Territory in 1818 and 1819, the naturalist Henry R. Schoolcraft said: "The hunter population in the territory, presents a state of society of which few

---

Springs, from Arkansas Post "toward" St. Louis, and from Cadron to Hot Springs). Commissioners were supposed to report the route chosen to the court, but they very frequently failed to do so. When they did report, Bullitt would occasionally reject their recommendation. *See, e.g.*, COMMON LAW RECORD 52 (October, 1818).

32. 1 D. HERNDON, THE CENTENNIAL HISTORY OF ARKANSAS 995 (1922). The decade between 1810 and 1820 witnessed the "greatest proportionate increase in population during any decade . . . ." The growth was 1250 per cent. *Id.*

33. W. DARBY, THE EMMIGRANT'S GUIDE (1818).

have any just conception, and of which, indeed, I confess myself to have been wholly ignorant, previous to my tour through those regions where they are located. Composed of the unruly and the vicious from all quarters, insulated by a pathless wilderness, without the pale of civil law, or the restraints upon manners and actions imposed by refined society, this population are an extraordinary instance of the retrogression of society. So far as is not necessary for animal existence, they have abandoned the pursuit of agriculture, the foundation of civil society, and embraced the pursuit of hunting, so characteristic of the savage state in all countries.

"This society is composed of persons from various sections of the Union, who have either embraced hunting from the love of ease or singularity, or have fled from society to escape the severity of the laws, and to indulge in unrestrained passion. Learning and religion are alike disregarded and in the existing state of society among the Missouri hunters, we are presented with a contradiction of the theories of philosophers of all ages, for we here behold the descendants of enlightened Europeans in a savage state, or at least in a rapid state of advance towards it. These hunters are chiefly located on White River, Arkansaw, and Red River. Their numbers may be computed at 1000 or 1500. The late division of territory will throw them nearly all into Arkansaw."[34]

Writing of the White River country in 1819, Schoolcraft noted: "The only inhabitants on the upper parts of White River, so far as inhabitants have penetrated, are hunters, who live in camps and log cabins, and support themselves by hunting the bear, deer, buffaloe, elk, beaver, racoon, and other animals who are found in great plenty in that region. They also raise some corn for bread, and for feeding

34. H. SCHOOLCRAFT, A VIEW OF THE LEAD MINES OF MISSOURI 175 (1819).

their horses, on preparing for long journeys into the woods or other extraordinary occasions. They seldom, however, cultivate more than an acre or two, subsisting chiefly on animal food and wild honey, and pay no attention to the cultivation of garden vegetables, if I except some cabbages, noticed at a few habitations. When the season of hunting arrives, the ordinary labours of a man about the house and corn field devolve upon the women, whose condition in such a state of society may readily be imagined. They in fact pursue a similar course of life with the savages; having embraced their love of ease, and their contempt for agricultural pursuits, with their sagacity in the chase, their mode of dressing in skins, their manners, and their hospitality to strangers.

"The furs and peltries which are collected during repeated excursions in the woods, are taken down the river at certain seasons in canoes, and disposed of to traders, who visit the lower parts of this river for the purpose. Here they receive in exchange for their furs, woollen clothes, rifles, knives and hatchets, salt, powder, lead, iron for horse shoes, blankets, iron pots, shoes, and other articles of primary importance in their way of life. Those living near the cultivated parts of Lawrence County, in Arkansaw Territory, also bring down in exchange for such articles, buffaloe beef, pork, bears' meat, bees' wax, and honey; which are again sold by the traders along the banks of the Mississippi, or at New Orleans. Very little cash is paid, and that in hard money only, no bank bills of any kind being taken in that quarter. I happened to be present, on my return from the head waters of White River, at one of these exchanges, where a further opportunity was offered of observing the manners and character of these savage Europeans."[35]

Schoolcraft described the self-help and feuds to which the Arkansas hunters resorted for the settlement of dis-

35. *Id.* at 249–50.

putes: "Justice, which in civilized society is administered through all the formalities of the law, is here obtained in a more summary way. Two hunters having a dispute respecting a horse, which one had been instrumental in stealing from the other, the person aggrieved meeting the other, some days afterwards in the woods, shot him through the body. He immediately fled, keeping in the woods for several weeks, when the neighboring hunters, aroused by so glaring an outrage, assembled and set out in quest of him. Being an expert woodsman, he eluded them for some time, but at last they got a glimpse of him as he passed through a thicket, and one of the party fired upon him. The ball passed through his shoulder, but did not kill him. This event happened a few days before our arrival, but I know not how it has terminated. In all probability several lives will be lost before a pacification takes place, as both parties have their friends, and all are hot for revenge."[36]

It is clear from Schoolcraft's descriptions of his journey that a few of the hunters of Arkansas had been civilized to some extent. Indeed he once interestingly wrote of a "half hunter, half farmer" who had been his guide.[37] Still, Schoolcraft's description of the population of the northern reaches of the White River would lead us to think that even as late as 1818 and 1819 the population there was composed largely of persons who derived their livelihood mainly from hunting. Around Arkansas Post, to hear some tell it at least, the situation had changed dramatically by 1817. In that year a person who modestly described himself as a "distinguished and enlightened French emigrant" described Arkansas in glowing terms and gave the following estimate of the population of the Post: "Nearly all the inhabitants of the Arkansas post and its environs, are French;

36. H. SCHOOLCRAFT, JOURNAL OF A TOUR INTO THE INTERIOR OF MISSOURI AND ARKANSAS . . . . 46 (1821).

37. H. SCHOOLCRAFT, SCENES AND ADVENTURES IN THE OZARKS 129 (1853).

many of them very amiable and sociable. All unite in wishing for us as neighbors, unless it be the few who live by hunting and trading; but the greater part have given up this mode of life for the cultivation of the land."[38]

The same writer spoke excitedly about the new settlers on the White, St. Francis, and Arkansas rivers. More than a hundred American families, he said, had established themselves as squatters on the Arkansas within the previous few years. "This is without doubt," our correspondent wrote, "the most beautiful and agreeable part of the U. States, both in temperature of climate and fertility of soil." He concluded with a truly remarkable burst of enthusiasm: "The river is as beautiful as the Seine, and only wants a Rouen or a Paris in miniature."[39]

This last proposition was an understatement of gargantuan proportions. In 1819 a member of S. H. Long's expedition wrote that within the Arkansas Territory "there are but few villages, and the settlements are as yet very scattered. The principal villages are the Post of Arkansas, situated about sixty miles above the mouth of the river; Davidsonville, on Big Black river; a small village at the commencement of the high lands on the Arkansa, at a place called the Little Rock. . . ."[40]

While the French hunters around the Post may have largely been coaxed into a kind of agricultural environment, due no doubt partly to the example set by the American immigrants and partly to the exhaustion of the game, the settlement of Arkansas Post and the state of agriculture there did not very much impress the British naturalist Thomas C. Nuttall who first visited the place in 1819. He left an extremely interesting account of his visit to the village, the most detailed description that we have from the

---

38. *Missouri Gazette*, Sept. 6, 1817, quoted in E. BEARSS and L. BROWN, *supra* note 12, at 5.
39. *Id.* at 7.
40. 17 EARLY WESTERN TRAVELS 127 (E. THWAITES ed., 1905).

period. Nuttall found the town spaced over an elevated prairie and containing thirty or forty houses. There were three principal merchants "who kept well-assorted stores of merchandise supplied chiefly from New Orleans, with the exception of some heavy articles of domestic manufacture obtained from Pittsburgh." Of some individuals Nuttall had a high opinion. In Dr. Robert McKay he found "an intelligent and agreeable companion." Joseph Bogy, to whom Nuttall had a letter of introduction, treated him "with politeness and respect," and, Nuttall continued, "I soon found in him a gentleman, though disguised at this time in the garb of a Canadian boatman." Mr. Drope, a merchant to whom he was also introduced by letter, "received me with politeness, and I could not but now for awhile consider myself as once more introduced into the circle of civilization."[41]

When, however, it came to an overall appreciation of the Post Nuttall was scathing in his denunciation of it. The state of agriculture at the place he found abysmal: "In this infant settlement of the poor and improvident," he said, "but little attention beyond that of absolute necessity, was as yet paid to any branch of agriculture."[42] He described the village proper as "an insignificant village containing three stores, destitute even of a hatter, a shoe-maker, and a taylor, and containing about 20 houses. . . ."[43] He went on to say that "after an existence of near a century, [it] scarcely deserved geographical notice, and will probably never flat-

41. T. NUTTALL, A JOURNAL OF TRAVELS INTO THE ARKANSAS TERRITORY DURING THE YEAR 1819, 83 (S. LOTTINVILLE ed., 1980).

42. *Id.* at 84–85.

43. *Id.* at 86. At 83, Nuttall says that "the town, or rather settlement of the Post of Arkansas, was somewhat dispersed over a prairie, nearly as elevated as that of the Chickasaw Bluffs, and containing in all between 30 and 40 houses." He was evidently speaking here of the settlement as distinguished from the village proper. This would explain the discrepancy in the number of houses which he reports.

ter the industry of the French emigrants, whose habits, at least those of the Canadians are generally opposed to improvement and regular industry."[44] Nuttall had a very low opinion of the French in Arkansas and was not at all reticent in expressing it. Speaking of the state of medical practice, he said that "such is the nationality of these ignorant people, that French quackery has hitherto been preferred to the advice of a regular physician."[45] If the present was far from pleasant, the future, in Nuttall's view, was altogether dismal: "The poverty of the land in the immediate vicinity of this place will probably operate as a perpetual barrier to its extension. The encroachment of the river upon the precipitous and friable bank in front of the town, and the enlargement of the ravines by which it is intersected, renders that site altogether precarious, and prevents the practicability of any thing like a convenient landing for merchandise."[46]

Nuttall then delivered a stinging and lengthy *coup de grâce*: "The love of amusements, here, as in most of the French colonies, is carried to extravagance, particularly gambling, and dancing parties or balls. But the sum of general industry is, as yet, totally insufficient for the support of any thing like a town.

"The houses, commonly surrounded with open galleries, destitute of glass windows, and perforated with numerous doors, are well enough suited for a summer shelter, but totally destitute of comfort in the winter. Without mechanics, domestic conveniences and articles of dress were badly supplied at the most expensive rate. Provision produced in the country, such as beef and pork, did not exceed six cents per pound; but potatoes, onions, apples, flour, spirits,

44. *Id.* at 86. Nuttall remarked in a letter written from the Post that "nearly all of the inhabitants at this place are French . . . ." Beidleman, *The Arkansas Journey of Thomas Nuttall,* 15 AHQ 254 (1956).

45. T. NUTTALL, *supra* note 41, at 86.

46. *Id.* at 88.

wine, and almost every other necessary article of diet, were imported at an enormous price, into a country which ought to possess every article of the kind for exportation to New Orleans. Such is the evil which may always be antici- pated by forcing a town, like a garrison, into being, previ- ous to the existence of necessary supplies. With a little in- dustry, surely every person in possession of slaves might have, at least, a kitchen garden! But these Canadian de- scendants, so long nurtured amidst savages, have become strangers to civilized comforts and regular industry. They must, however, in time give way to the introduction of more enterprising inhabitants."[47]

Nuttall's prediction turned out to be very quickly real- ized. When he returned to the Post almost exactly a year later, he observed that changes had taken place due to the erection of the Territory of Arkansas and the establishment of its capital at the Post. "Interest, curiosity, and specula- tion," he said approvingly, "had drawn the attention of men of education and wealth toward this country, since its separation into a territory; we now see an additional num- ber of lawyers, doctors, and mechanics." The post was, Nuttall said, "a growing town." Finally, he noted excitedly that "the herald of public information, and the bulwark of civil liberty, the press, had also been introduced to the Post within the present year, where a weekly newspaper was is- sued." Nuttall was speaking of the *Arkansas Gazette*.[48]

Even so, despite the apparent improvements, when James J. Audubon visited Arkansas Post in December, 1820, about a year after Nuttall had bid farewell to it, he described it as a "poor, nearly deserted village [which] flourished in the time that the Spanish and French kept [an] agreeable small town." Audubon continued: "At present

47. *Id.*
48. *Id.* at 248–49. The history of the *Gazette* while at the Post is ad- mirably told in M. Ross, Arkansas Gazette: The Early Years, 1819– 1866, 3–42 (1969).

the decripid visages of the worn out Indian traders are all that give it life."[49] The territorial legislature had met there two months previous to his visit and had voted to move the capital to Little Rock. Whatever lift had been given to the prospects of the Post by the creation of the territory would soon be lost, if it had not been already.

For the French, none of these developments was welcome. The influx of lawyers noted by Nuttall was inevitably accompanied by the creation of new courts and a number of new public offices. The *Arkansas Gazette* was regarded by the French with great suspicion, as productive of strife and trouble. The turbulence generated by the exercise of republican liberties was not much to their liking, nor was the glorification of the popular will which lay at the base of it. Participating in government had never been of much interest to them.

Washington Irving made these and other observations about Arkansas Post based on a visit he made there on November 15, 1832. He wrote in his journal that the old French settlers had been "accustomed to be governed by commandants whose will was law. One who was capricious would exact all kinds of services . . . another would squeeze them." Now that "the government is . . . changed," Irving sarcastically remarked, "they have equal rights with their meddlesome, quarrelsome, litigious, electioneering fellow citizens of the U.S. . . ." Nevertheless, he added, "they retain their old, passive acquiescence in the despotism of public affairs," and "do not intermeddle or distress themselves in elections or worry themselves about public affairs." Most of the French, Irving reported, were "at a settlement below [the] frontier on [the] river where they retain [the] French language." They "have nothing of that spirit that sets up two newspapers in the little village of Little Rock and sets neighbors by the ears

49. D. Peattie, Audubon's America 147 (1940).

calling each other hard names and reviling each other because they differ on abstract points." Irving also noted pointedly that the French "do not like Americans, [who they say] trouble themselves with cares beyond their horizon and import sorrow thro the newspapers from every point of the compass."[50]

Irving quite obviously was much struck by the clash of cultures that he encountered at Arkansas Post, for his journal, usually epigrammatic, quite expansively described what he saw there. He very clearly regarded the decaying little village he discovered in Arkansas as a paradigm of the events which attended the change to American sovereignty in Louisiana. Irving also saw the transformation of the legal system as a crucial element in the cultural metamorphosis which had occurred. In a story called "The Creole Village," based on the notes he made at the Post, he remarked on the passivity of the French *habitants* at Arkansas and their retention of "their old habits of passive obedience to the decrees of government, as though they still lived under the absolute sway of colonial commandants, instead of being part and parcel of the sovereign people. . . ." He then said: "A few aged men, who have grown gray on their hereditary acres, and are of the grand old colonial stock, exert a patriarchal sway in all matters of public and private import; their opinions are considered oracular, and their word is law." The "*Grand Seigneur*" of Arkansas Post was a central figure in this story, and he was certainly Frederick Notrebe, the richest Frenchman of the village, and, interestingly, the highest-ranking Frenchman in the Arkansas militia. He would have been a perfect substitute for the *government militaire* for which the *habitants* still obviously yearned.

In the same story, Irving describes an imaginary Ameri-

50. THE WESTERN JOURNALS OF WASHINGTON IRVING 166–68 (J. MC-DERMOTT ed., 1944).

can town, based partly on Little Rock, which he uses as a foil to the sleepy old Post of Arkansas. "The place," he said, "already boasted a court-house, a jail, and two banks, all built of pine boards, on the model of Grecian temples." There lived there "the usual number of judges and generals and governors; not to speak of . . . lawyers by the score." Irving ended his story by posing a rhetorical question: "Alas! with such an enterprising neighbour, what is to become of the poor little creole village!"[51]

III

Only twice has an Arkansas court written an opinion dealing with the reception of the common law in Arkansas. In 1831, in the case of *Grande vs. Foy*,[52] the Superior Court of the Territory of Arkansas heard an appeal in which it was claimed that the action of ejectment was not available in Arkansas. In a discursive and sometimes incoherent opinion, written by Judge Edward Cross, which purported to trace the action of ejectment to the reigns of Edward II and Edward III, the court noted the reception statute of 1816 and concluded that it authorized the use of the common-law action. It rejected the argument that an 1807 statute, repealed by the time this case was brought, had been the only foundation for the action. That statute had provided that plaintiffs in ejectment were not to employ the fictitious allegations of lease, entry, and ouster. Where, however, the court asked, had the action itself ever been authorized directly? The court remarked that

---

51. *The Creole Village* was first published in 1837 in THE MAGNOLIA. It is most conveniently available nowadays in J. McDERMOTT, *supra* note 50, at 171 *et seqq.*

52. HEMPSTEAD'S REPORTS 105.

9. Edward Cross, Judge of the Superior Court of the Territory of Arkansas. In 1831 he wrote that the common law had been "adopted as far back as 1807, and indeed prior to that time, and it is not very material whether by common consent or by statute."

common-law actions of trespass *vi et armis*, ejectment, case, debt, and covenant had been mentioned in the acts of the Territory of Louisiana as early as 1807. Did the legislature, the court inquired, intend in these instances to refer to civil-law forms of actions that had been "authorized by the laws and regulations in force at the time Louisiana was acquired?" The court continued: "If so, it is doubtful whether the laws of France or Spain should have been resorted to, to find their definitions, and the manner of proceeding in them, inasmuch as the province of Louisiana had been acquired from the latter by virtue of the treaty of San Ildefonso in October, 1800. It would certainly be conjectural altogether to say the laws of either of these governments were intended, and to say both would be absurd."[53] The court then concluded that the common-law actions were intended and thus the common law of actions must have been adopted in the upper territory long before the reception statute of 1816. What, then, had become of the civil law of actions which the 1804 act creating the District of Louisiana declared was to remain in force? The court stated: "We would answer, that many [of these laws] have been abolished, or superseded by our statutes, and others have shared the fate of all ancient customs, when there no longer exists any necessity for their observance. The conclusion, therefore, is well founded, that the common law was, at least partially, adopted as far back as 1807, and indeed prior to that time, and it is not very material whether by common consent or by statutes."[54]

The court then held that the common law of ejectment was in force by virtue of the reception statute of 1816, even though it had specifically saved from its operation any previous statutes of the Territory which were contrary to the common law. The 1807 statute, the defendant argued, since it was contrary to the common law, had kept the common-law action from being received; and since that statute had been repealed after the passage of the reception statute the action of ejectment did not exist. The court, in a confused passage, held that the 1807 statute was not contrary to the common law since it was possible for lessees at common law to bring the action without the fiction.

Clearly, and understandably, the court wished to provide litigants with a method for trying title to land. Just as

53. *Id.* at 108.
54. *Id.* at 109.

understandably, it did not wish to revert to the civil-law modes of civil procedure, for it had not the slightest idea where it might discover what those were. The truth is, as we have seen, that eighteenth-century Arkansas procedure had been simplicity itself. There had been there no real civil law of actions. But the court knew the common law and was disinclined to ransack old books for foreign methods for settling disputes. It had no intention of lending any respectability to civilian legal traditions.

In 1838, two years after Arkansas became a state, the Supreme Court of Arkansas, in *Small vs. Strong*,[55] was called upon to decide the effect of another statute passed by the legislature of the Territory of Louisiana in 1807. The defendant had executed a bond to certain merchants and they had assigned it to the plaintiff. When sued on the bond, the defendant attempted to set off a debt owed him by the merchants by virtue of a bond executed by them in favor of a third party who had assigned it to the defendant. The defendant claimed that when this second bond came into his hands the debt to the merchants had been automatically set off and cancelled and that the plaintiff-assignee could be in no better position than the merchants were. To support his position, the defendant cited an 1807 statute that made bonds assignable but also provided that there was no intention "to change the nature of the defence in law, that any defendant may have against the . . . original assignor"[56]— that is, against the merchants in this case.

The court, in a singularly lucid opinion written by Chief Justice Ringo, reasoned that the 1807 statute had intended to leave the civil law of negotiability intact, and by virtue of the civil-law doctrine of *compensatio* the defendant might well have been entitled to the set off he claimed. Without more, the court continued, the defendant would be en-

55. 2 Ark. 198 (1838).
56. LAWS, *supra* note 22, ch. 38, § 53.

titled to judgment since under the civil law the mere existence of a mutual indebtedness had operated as a set off. It cited *Pothier on Obligations* in support of this view,[57] the only example of a citation to a civilian legal authority by an Arkansas court that has so far come to light. However, the court concluded, the reception statute of 1816 had adopted the common law of set offs, and the common law did not recognize the civil-law principal of *compensatio*. Therefore, the plaintiff was entitled to recover.

The court could just as well have held that the 1807 statute had positively adopted, rather than simply preserved, the civil law of set offs and that it was not the purpose of the 1816 reception statute, by its own terms, to undo positive enactments in derogation of the common law. Indeed, the 1816 statute and the court in *Grande vs. Foy* had so stated.[58] Clearly, the civil law was not much favored by the common lawyers of Arkansas, especially when it conflicted with the customs of merchants and restricted the currency of private paper at a time when hard money was scarce.

Both *Grande vs. Foy* and *Small vs. Strong* expose to view a determination by the Arkansas professional lawyer class to extirpate the civil law entirely from their legal system. Arkansas, unlike its nearest southern neighbor, would completely and deliberately separate itself from its eighteenth-century cultural and legal traditions.

---

57. *Id.* at 204.
58. LAWS, *supra* note 22, ch. 154. The court in Grande vs Foy stated that "the legislature, by the act of 1816, have certainly introduced no part of the common law in consistent with statutory provisions in force at the time of its passage . . . ." HEMPSTEAD'S REPORTS 109–10.

IV

Immigration was of course much encouraged by the creation of Arkansas Territory, and, as Nuttall noted, the number of lawyers was greatly increased as well. From the beginning, they enjoyed great power and prestige. The first territorial legislature consisted of the twenty-one-year-old Robert Crittenden, Secretary of the Territory and a lawyer, and the three judges of the Territorial Superior Court, all but one of whom, James Woodson Bates, left Arkansas immediately after the session was over, never to return.[59] At the first session of the Superior Court, five new lawyers were admitted to practice, and the following term six more were licensed.[60] This added substance to the warning contained in the first issue of the *Arkansas Gazette*, published November 20, 1819, that "there are a sufficient number of lawyers in the Territory—more than make fortunes from their practice."[61] The same article contained a familiar plea: "Farmers, men who cultivate the soil, are the men whom we need; to them are the greatest inducements held out, of acquiring property."[62] The number of lawyers who inserted professional cards as advertisements in the *Gazette* in its first years attests that the warning was not much heeded.[63]

The lawyer class in Arkansas would very shortly include within it some of the richest and most powerful men in the territory. They would become the governors, congress-

59. For the work of this first session, see 1 D. HERNDON, *supra* note 32, at 158–62. Its product formed part of the first book published in Arkansas. *See* LAWS OF THE TERRITORY OF ARKANSAS . . . TOGETHER WITH THE LAWS PASSED BY THE GENERAL ASSEMBLY OF THE TERRITORY OF ARKANSAS, AT THE SESSIONS IN 1819 AND 1820 (1821).

60. COMMON LAW RECORD 75, 98, 99, 122, 125.

61. *Arkansas Gazette*, November 19, 1820, p. 2, col. 2.

62. *Id.*

63. *Id.*

men, and senators of the state upon Arkansas's admission to the Union in 1836. A late nineteenth-century Arkansas lawyer could thereafter write, without the slightest trace of self-consciousness, that in "America it is the lawyers who are the natural leaders of the people; it is they who dominate every legislative assembly." He continued: "America is therefore a country ruled by its lawyers; and the history of the bench and bar of any state is the history of its political development. This is particularly so in its early and formative period. . . ."[64]

There was within the territorial legal profession a class structure which seems to have been evident very early. Generally speaking, the lawyers who practiced in Arkansas before the creation of the territory fared very badly thereafter. Their practices languished and they were largely eclipsed by the newcomers, many of whom became rich through land speculation.[65] Though none of the newcomers seems to have attended law school,[66] they were in general better educated than those whom they found practicing in Arkansas on their arrival. They were quick to let their superiority be known.

A probable manifestation of this class structure is contained in the earliest surviving opinion of an Arkansas trial court. It was written in 1824 by Judge Thomas P. Eskridge who was sitting on circuit at Arkansas Post. The case which generated the opinion was an accounting in Equity

64. Rose, *Bench and Bar of Arkansas,* in 1 F. HEMPSTEAD, HISTORICAL REVIEW OF ARKANSAS 425 (1911).

65. Chester A. Ashley is probably the best example. *See generally,* S. Ruple, "The Life and Times of Chester Ashley of Arkansas; 1791–1848" (Master's Thesis, University of Arkansas, 1982).

66. None of the judges of the Superior Court of the Territory of Arkansas had attended a law school either. *See* Smith, *Arkansas Advocacy: The Territorial Period,* 31 ARK. L. REV. 449 at 449 (1978). But two of the nineteen men who sat on that bench were college graduates, and most had attended a secondary school. *Id.* at 449–50.

and the issue was the *res judicata* effect in Equity of a judgment in an action of account at law. What better context
could a common lawyer ask for exhibiting his technical
learning? At the end of his opinion, Eskridge remarked on
the lack of learning exhibited by the non-establishment
bar. "The court may be permitted to remark, in conclusion," he said, "that it hopes that this decision may operate
as a salutary admonition to the gentlemen of the Bar. It is a
fact too well attested to admit of doubt that most cases
which are lost may be ascribed to the inattentions of the
Bar."[67]

In 1837 the lawyers of Arkansas organized their first bar
association. On the 24th of November of that year nineteen of them, all but three from Little Rock, gathered and
adopted an elaborate constitution.[68] The association had
some very interesting rules which reflected its guild character. Election to the society had to be by unanimous
vote.[69] All "disagreements or difficulties," which arose
"between members of this Association, in the discharge of
their professional duties" were referred to the Committee
on Professional Courtesy; their recommendation was to be
sent to a plenary meeting of the group, the decision of
which was "binding upon the parties."[70] Members were
forbidden to speak ill of each other, it being provided that

67. Eskridge's opinion is reproduced in Appendix V.

68. *Constitution of the Bar Association of the State of Arkansas Adopted at
an Aggregate Meeting of the Profession Held in the City of Little Rock on the
24th Day of November, 1837* (1838). The founding members were Chester
Ashley, William Mck. Ball, S.D. Blackburn, John J. Clendenin, J. W.
Cocke, William Conway, Edwin Cross, P. T. Crutchfield, William
Cummins, Absalom Fowler, Nathan Haggard, Samuel P. Hall, S. H.
Hempstead, Lemuel P. Lincoln, Albert Pike, William C. Scott, F. W.
Trapnall, and George C. Watkins. Some discussion of the new associa-
tion and its constitution can be found in J. CALLOWAY, THE TRAPNALL
LEGACY 17–18 (1981).

69. *Constitution, supra* note 68, Art. I, § 4.

70. *Id.*, Art. III, § 8.

"on all occasions, members shall scrupulously observe towards each other at the bar, the most marked courtesy and cordiality of bearing."[71] By unanimous vote of the association, a member offending against this rule could be compelled to make a retraction.[72]

Like most guilds, the new bar association had as one of its aims the creation of a cartel, and its rules reflected that purpose. For instance, no member could ever require of another an affidavit in the course of practice: A member's word must suffice.[73] Another section of the constitution declared that, in suits on the endorsements of promissory notes and bills of exchange, if the parties were represented by members, records of the protests of Notaries Public would be received as competent evidence.[74] There were other privileges granted members, and it was specifically stated that all privileges were to be observed "only between members of this Association."[75] As to lawyers who were not members the rule was that "no relaxation of the rigid rules of practice shall be made."[76] No member, moreover, could "give aid or countenance, advise or consent [to], or be in any manner connected in any case whatsoever with any non-member."[77] Finally, the most obvious mark of the cartel character of the society was the minimum fee schedule which occupied more than two pages of its twelve-page rule book.[78] The members pledged solemnly "to each other, as gentlemen, not to receive . . . fees or compensation" below the scheduled minimums.[79] A second violation

71. *Id.*, Art. VII, § 1.
72. *Id.*, Art. III, § 8.
73. *Id.*, Art. VII, § 4.
74. *Id.*, Art. VII, § 7.
75. *Id.*, Art. VII, § 8.
76. *Id.*
77. *Id.*, Art. VII, § 9.
78. *Id.*, Art. VI, § 1.
79. *Id.*

of the fee schedule could bring expulsion and a recommendation to the Supreme Court that the offender be disbarred.[80] An expelled member was to be ostracized: He would "in no instance be recognized as the professional peer or social companion of any member."[81]

80. *Id.*, Art. IV, § 1.
81. *Id.*, Art. IV, § 3.

Conclusion

Though it had exerted its influence in Arkansas for upwards of 150 years, the civil law proved extremely easy to eradicate in the end, owing mainly to the general weakness of *bourgeois* legal and moral values in eighteenth-century Arkansas. While a French settlement of sorts was established on the river in 1686, the European population of Arkansas was always tiny: Even as late as the time of the American takeover it could not have much exceeded six hundred. The size of the population alone, therefore, would have made its mores vulnerable to American immigration and to the legal assumptions which accompanied it.

But the weakness of civil-law traditions in Arkansas is attributable as much to the nature of the French population there as to its size. Throughout the eighteenth century and into the nineteenth the bulk of it was formed by *voyageurs* and *coureurs de bois* whose attachment to civilized European habits was extremely tenuous at best. Some of them conscientiously forswore allegiance to any organized state. A few *bourgeois* families, and some gentry, did establish themselves in Arkansas, and they conformed their affairs as much as possible to civilian legal norms, as their marriage contracts and wills testify. But their number was always extremely small and their influence over the rest of the population minuscule.

The inability of the French and Spanish governments to create a stable agricultural community of *bourgeois* at the Arkansas is easily explained. The strategic mission of Arkansas Post was to serve as an *entrepôt*, and this meant that a location near the Mississippi River was indicated. But flooding made agriculture there impossible. Even with its relocation to *Écores Rouges* in 1779, though some improvement followed, Arkansas Post nevertheless continued to be, in the main, a supply point and home base for hunters because it was dangerous and remote.

The establishment of a community with stronger ties to an organized and even-handed legal system was also rendered difficult by military necessity. Louis XV's pardoning of Jean Baptiste Bernard and the other deserters in 1756 was simply a political act, effected without any knowledge of the facts. The trial of the American traitors in 1782 had been irregular in the most fundamental way possible, yet their executions were carried out. In both instances there were political reasons which those in authority thought compelled the relaxation of legal principle. Both of these cases expose to view the kinds of exigencies which worked to weaken the regard for the regular processes of the law at the Arkansas.

It is probable that the seriousness with which a people attend to procedural rules more clearly indicates their attachment to law than does any other single datum. Based on this criterion, the regard for law at the Arkansas was feeble indeed for most of the eighteenth century. It seems unlikely that Bernard and the other deserters of 1756 were given any trial at all. Captain De Villiers thought that regular legal procedure was mere "pettifogging," an unnecessary bit of bureaucratic camouflage, especially at "miserable posts," of which Arkansas furnished for him the prime example. The American traitors of 1782 did receive a trial, but in the end due process was sacrificed to military need.

Some regularity began to appear in the last decade of European sovereignty, as Lachenese's trial for wounding in 1791 reveals, but the loss of the archives makes it impossible to gauge with any accuracy the extent of procedural sophistication which existed in late eighteenth-century Arkansas.

The church maintained only an episodic presence in Arkansas, exactly what we would expect in a community of inconsequential size whose population inclined heavily toward individualism. The church thus found itself unable to influence the people of Arkansas very directly, and the parish of *Los Arcos*, not created until 1796, had a pastor for only three years. The disestablishment of the church incident to the American takeover, and the subsequent immigration into Arkansas of mostly Protestant Americans, did nothing to bolster a Catholicism which was in any case only very weakly established.

The powers of government in Arkansas during its first 120 years of European settlement were all vested in a single person, the commandant of the garrison. He was judge, sheriff, coroner, chief of police, recorder, lawyer, head of immigration and naturalization, ambassador to foreign nations, and commander-in-chief of the army. At times, though Captain De Villiers professed a devotion to free-market principles in terms that would have touched Adam Smith, the commandant even possessed a monopoly over trade with the Indians; indeed, he occasionally claimed to be entitled to preferential payments from hunters whom he had supplied. What little power he did not possess the commandant arrogated.

It would be hard to imagine a system of government and law more profoundly different from the one that the Americans planned to establish after Jefferson's purchase of the sleepy French province. But because Arkansas was of so little consequence the Americans at first devoted almost no thought to changing the government there. Indeed, the American military commandants continued to exercise the judicial powers of their Spanish and French predecessors at least until 1806 and probably until 1808. No doubt the French population approved wholeheartedly of this arrangement. When in 1808, partly at the instance of Perly Wallis, an American lawyer, a regular common-law court sat in Arkansas for the first time, the French refused to have anything to do with it and the Americans were just as glad. There is even evidence that the French partially counterfeited their old governmental arrangements by submitting their disputes to the *grand seigneur* of the village for settlement. They preferred aristocratic military rule to a panel of civilian judges aided by a jury of ordinary people; they disliked the boisterous frontier lawyer of which Arkansas provided paradigmatic examples; and they were bewildered by a bureaucratic republicanism which set up three courts and several other county offices where only one person had theretofore nicely sufficed. Nor could they have been very happy about the taxes which this diffusion of power and authority had made necessary. Before the coming of the Americans, except for a small duty levied on imports, the *habitants* of Arkansas had never paid a tax, not even a tithe.

It is most interesting that the only major differences between the two legal systems which held sway in Arkansas were procedural. There were a few interesting differences in the substantive law of persons and property. But the law of crimes was not appreciably different after the American takeover, for under both legal systems it had remained more or less undeveloped. That is mostly because, as Professor Milsom has said, "Crime has never been the business of lawyers."[1] Moreover, so far as the living law was

---

1. S. MILSOM, HISTORICAL FOUNDATIONS OF THE COMMON LAW 374 (1969).

concerned, the private law of torts and contracts both before and after the change in regimes was a kind of natural
law. Disputes were settled by a resort to notions of logic
and ordinary equity. A most fundamental innovation came with the introduction of the common-law modes of trial and the adversarial
system. The latter created, or made necessary, an entirely
new class of persons trained to operate the legal apparatus.
They would derive power and advantage from their spe-
cialized knowledge and property from its sale. It was in
this respect that the substitution of legal systems had its
most profound impact. It was as much a social and political change as a legal one.

About 1820 many, perhaps most of the French farmers
moved upriver to Jefferson County. Some of them went so
far as to create a new town there with the bravely hopeful
name of New Gascony. Father Edmond Saulnier, sent
from St. Louis in 1832 to revive the Arkansas church,
found at the Post of Arkansas a village "comprising all in
all twenty-five houses, two of which are built of brick. . . ."
There Frederick Notrebe, Washington Irving's *grand seigneur*, informed him that "the inhabitants were poor" and
"that the majority of the French [had moved to] Pine
Bluff."[2] Of the approximately fifty people whom Saulnier
could muster for mass on Christmas Eve, he said they
were "very indifferent and ignorant; they had forgotten
nearly everything."[3] Saulnier's effort to get the *habitants* of
the Post to subscribe for the cost of a chapel met with failure, and his successor was ridiculed for a similar effort:
"This one won't stay long," the people of the Post jeered.[4]

2. Holweck, *The Arkansas Mission Under Rosati*, 1 St. Louis Catholic Historical Review 247 at 248 (1919).
3. *Id.* at 249.
4. *Id.* at 259.

Just before Arkansas achieved statehood, a chapel was established three miles below Pine Bluff, and plans were laid for one at New Gascony; as for the Post, it was still thought that it was impossible to get a chapel built there "because the people do not pull together."[5]

The gradual assimilation of the French into the American culture can be seen in the registers of the Roman Catholic priests of Arkansas, where intermarriages with Americans are quite common by the end of the territorial period.[6] Today, one may occasionally be lucky enough to encounter an Imbeau or a Bogy or a Menard in Arkansas. But almost all of the families with the old names have long ago shared the fate of Desiré and Françoise Michel whom the Americans disrespectfully transformed into Daisy and Fannie Mitchell.[7] But we have seen that beneath the weight of nineteenth-century American immigration a great deal more was lost than phonology and orthography. A legal culture, to be sure often in only the most moribund condition, but alive nonetheless, had been overcome as well. Jefferson's intention that the common law be introduced into Upper Louisiana was effected with a vengeance, and every opportunity to turn away from the civil law was gladly taken. A total substitution of cultures, of which legal values were an important part, had been very quickly achieved.

5. *Id.* at 265.
6. ABSTRACT OF CATHOLIC REGISTER OF ARKANSAS (1764–1858) (D. CORE ed. & N. HATFIELD trans., 1976).
7. *See* R. DHONAU, FRENCH MICHELS CAME TO MISSOURI AND ARKANSAS: MITCHELLS AND RELATED FAMILIES 13 (1978).

Appendix I

The Eighteenth-Century Legal Records of Arkansas Post

As noted in the text, the archives of Arkansas Post were delivered by Francisco Caso y Luengo to Lieutenant James B. Many on March 23, 1804.[1] The inventory of the archives which Many accepted that day on behalf of the American government was four pages long and it revealed that a very considerable volume of papers had been handed over.[2] A diligent search has, however, failed to uncover them. Though it is possible that they may be rediscovered, that eventuality unhappily seems remote. It is natural to wonder what their fate was.

One of the first acts of the legislature for the District of Louisiana ordered that the Spanish civil records be delivered to the appropriate American civil officials. Papers relevant to litigation pending in the districts were to be delivered to the "prothonotaries of said districts."[3] Wills were to be handed over to the judge of probate and deeds and other conveyances to the recorder of each district.[4] If this was done in the case of the Arkansas records, they would have been sent to New Madrid since that was where the civil officers who nominally had jurisdiction over Arkansas until 1806 resided. The Spanish records of New

---

1. *See* text *supra* at 110.
2. AGI, PC, *leg.* 140.
3. LAWS . . . OF THE DISTRICT OF LOUISIANA . . . UP TO THE YEAR 1824
. . . . ch. 13, § 22 (1842).
4. *Id.*, § 23.

Madrid have in fact survived and are now in the Missouri Historical Society in St. Louis. Unfortunately, they contain no Arkansas documents. Nor does the present day courthouse at New Madrid. In the nature of things, however, and despite the fact that Arkansas was part of New Madrid district until 1806, and twice again thereafter, it would seem most unlikely that the Arkansas papers would ever have been transferred there. Even if they were, they should have been transferred back again when Arkansas County was created.

André Fagot, the first notary public appointed for Arkansas in the American period, was educated in France[5] and thus would have known the civil-law tradition that the notary was to keep his own notarial records and act as a public depository of official acts. In the state of Louisiana, the tradition of notaries keeping their own official act books persisted for a long time; not until after the Civil War was a central office for the keeping of notarial records established.[6] As to official acts passed by notaries after the American takeover in the Upper Territory this was true also.[7] It seems altogether likely and natural, therefore, that Fagot would have succeeded to the notarial records of the Arkansas; and his one surviving act book indicates that he was in fact giving notarial copies of acts passed in the Spanish period, lending support to this view.[8]

If this was the case, it may well be that the Post archives came into the possession of Fagot's family after his death and were subsequently lost. This happened frequently

5. *See* Core, *André Fagot*, 17 GPHSB 3 (1974).

6. R. WALDO, NOTARIAL ARCHIVES OF ORLEANS PARISH i-ii (1946).

7. The statute passed in 1807 which provided for notaries in each district and defining their duties talks about the notary's "register and other public papers." LAWS, *supra* note 3, ch. 34, § 5.

8. *See, e.g.*, NOTARIAL BOOK OF ANDRÉ FAGOT 19, Arkansas County Court House, DeWitt, AR., where Fagot certifies copies of documents relevant to a 1799 transaction at the Post.

enough in the lower territory.[9] In fact, W. H. Halliburton reported that before the Civil War he visited Fagot's widow and saw "a large number of papers she had retained in an old trunk belonging to her husband." Halliburton noted that these papers "referred to various subjects, some written in English, some in French, and some in Spanish."[10] A permissible and unhappy inference would be that Halliburton had happened on the archives of Arkansas Post and had failed to rescue them.

Another possible explanation for the disappearance of the archives has to do with the removal of the Arkansas County records during the Civil War. They were hidden in a log cabin two miles from DeWitt and were returned to the courthouse after the war "with but little loss or damage."[11] Perhaps the archives were lost at that time, but on balance it seems more likely that they came into the hands of Fagot's widow on his death. Attempts to locate Fagot's descendants have so far been unavailing.

9. *See* R. WALDO, *supra* note 6, at ii.
10. W. HALLIBURTON, A TOPOGRAPHICAL DESCRIPTION AND HISTORY OF ARKANSAS COUNTY, ARKANSAS FROM 1541 TO 1875, 46 (1901?).
11. *Id.* at 154.

Appendix II

The Locations of Arkansas Post
1686–1985

Tonti's trading post, which was in operation from 1686 to about 1699, was at the Quapaw village of Osotouy. This village was then located at the base of Little Prairie in Arkansas County, almost certainly at what is now called the Menard Site.[1]

John Law's colony, established in August of 1721, was also located at Little Prairie, as a careful examination of the journals of visiting Frenchmen reveals. The Jesuit Father Charlevoix visited the place on December 2, 1721, and reported that it was situated a little more than eleven leagues (about 26.5 miles) from the mouth of the Arkansas River, opposite the village of Kappa (Quapaw).[2] In March of the following year Bénard de La Harpe visited the colony; he

---

1. See Ford, *The Quapaw Village of Osotouy on the Arkansas River*, 28 ANTHROPOLOGICAL PAPERS OF THE AMERICAN MUSEUM OF NATURAL HISTORY, Part II, 133, at 137–42 (1961). As Ford remarks, conclusive evidence of his conjectural identification of the location of Tonti's post would "be the discovery of remains . . . ." *Id.* at 181. But, as he points out, to "find the site of a cabin made of horizontal logs with archaeological techniques seems very difficult, for it is not necessary to disturb the soil to erect this type of building." *Id.* Still, Ford makes an extremely compelling circumstantial case for his identification of the Tonti site.

2. P. DE CHARLEVOIX, JOURNAL D'UN VOYAGE FAIT PAR ORDRE DU ROI DANS L'AMÉRIQUE SEPTENTRIONALE 163–64 (1744).

placed it at 10.5 leagues from the mouth of the Arkansas, and about a quarter of a league inland "at the commencement of the prairies where it is situated. . . ."[3] Five years later Father Du Poisson put the Post, still situated where Law's colony was, at a little more than eleven leagues up the Arkansas, across from the village of Kappa.[4] These contemporary sources are in remarkable and unanimous agreement, though they are sometimes difficult to understand and require close scrutiny to determine their meaning. It is clear that the prairie mentioned in these sources is Little Prairie since it is at the indicated distance from the mouth of the Arkansas. One could not reach the Grand Prairie without travelling four or five leagues farther up the river. Little Prairie is the closest place to the mouth of the Arkansas that was relatively free from flooding and was thus the obvious position for a settlement.

This location for Law's establishment is also confirmed by later sources. In 1765, Captain Phillip Pittman reported that the colony had been situated nine leagues from the mouth of the Arkansas.[5] His league was three miles long and thus his location for the colony, twenty-seven miles from the Mississippi by river, is in exact agreement with the writings of Charlevoix, La Harpe, and Du Poisson.

In October of 1738, during the Chickasaw Wars, the Jesuit Father De Vitry visited his colleague Father Avond at Arkansas Post, and since his journal has been consistently misread, it will be well to examine it in some detail. De Vitry reported that on October 29 he entered the mouth of

3. JOURNAL HISTORIQUE DE L'ÉTABLISSEMENT DES FRANÇAIS À LA LOUISIANE 312–16 (1831).

4. J. DELANGLEZ, THE FRENCH JESUITS IN LOWER LOUISIANA 431 (1935).

5. P. PITTMAN, THE PRESENT STATE OF THE EUROPEAN SETTLEMENTS ON THE MISSISSIPPI 41 (1770) (Reprinted with an introduction by R. Rea, 1973).

the Arkansas and travelled upriver to the mouth of the White.[6] The next day, he set off "up the Arkansas . . . for the French settlement situated four leagues from here."[7] This clearly indicates that the Post was four leagues from the mouth of the White River and not four leagues from the mouth of the Arkansas as has been claimed by some.[8] This puts the Post above the Arkansas forks and in the vicinity of Little Prairie. There is no reason to believe that it had yet been moved downriver to a position below the forks as some have suggested.[9]

There is no evidence, moreover, that the Post was in a different location when it was attacked in May of 1749 by the Chickasaws and Abekas. Although Stanley Faye maintained that it had been relocated downstream below the forks during the time that Montcharvaux was commandant,[10] (that is, between 1739 and 1748),[11] his citations do not bear him out. Moreover, Captain De Villiers, writing in 1778, put the first establishment in Arkansas above the forks and says that it had remained there until it was attacked. In other words, it was still at Little Prairie. This identification is confirmed by De Villiers's description of the first settlement as being "at the *entrée* of a little prairie."[12] By 1778, De Villiers noted, the position of the old

6. *Journal of Father Vitry of the Society of Jesus, Army Chaplain during the War Against the Chickasaws*, 28 MID-AMERICA 30 at 34 (1941).

7. *Id.*

8. *See, e.g.*, R. MATTISON, REPORT ON THE HISTORICAL INVESTIGATIONS OF ARKANSAS POST, ARKANSAS 84 (1957) (Typescript in Arkansas History Commission, Little Rock).

9. *See, e.g., id.*

10. Faye, *The Arkansas Post of Louisiana: French Domination*, 26 LHQ 633 at 681 (1943).

11. *See* Appendix III.

12. De Villiers to Gálvez, June 11, 1778, AGI, PC, *leg.* 191.

settlement had been "separated from the river by a cut-off." [13] It would be hard to imagine a better description of Little Prairie and Lake Dumond. [14] Therefore it seems right to think that the Arkansas Post was not moved before May of 1749.

Shortly thereafter, however, it was moved. Before September of 1749 the governor ordered its relocation five leagues higher "to a bluff where [the] Indians are settled." [15] The exact date of removal is not certain, but De Villiers claimed that it took place the same year as the attack. [16] Probably this is correct. The place to which the Post was moved, evidently in 1749, was called *Écores Rouges* and is located where the Arkansas Post National Memorial is today. Archeological remains of several forts built there have been discovered, [17] and probably some of them are of the fort constructed in 1751–52. [18]

This location proved inconvenient for Mississippi ship-

13. *Id.*

14. De Villiers, however, put the old settlement at two, or perhaps three, leagues from the forks. *Id.* That is about one league short of Little Prairie. However, it is clear that he had not visited the place when he wrote this letter. Moreover, he once claimed a location for *Écores Rouges* which was two leagues closer to the forks than it actually was. His distances are not, therefore, always very accurate.

15. ILLINOIS ON THE EVE OF THE SEVEN YEARS' WAR, 1747–1755, 116 (T. PEASE & E. JENISON eds.) in 29 COLLECTIONS OF THE ILLINOIS STATE HISTORICAL LIBRARY (1940).

16. De Villiers to Gálvez, *supra* note 12. However, De Villiers put the attack (wrongly) in the year 1754. According to Governor Kerlérec, the relocation of the post occurred in 1752. *See* T. PEASE & E. JENISON, *supra* note 15, at 879.

17. *See* P. HOLDER, ARCHAEOLOGICAL FIELD RESEARCH ON THE PROBLEM OF THE LOCATIONS OF ARKANSAS POST, ARKANSAS, 1686–1804 (1957).

18. A description of and bill for the materials employed in this construction, together with some description of the finished product itself, can be found in an appendix to R. MATTISON, *supra* note 8.

ping and the Post was therefore moved downriver in 1756 to a place in Desha County below the forks about ten miles from the mouth of the Arkansas,[19] where it was flooded almost every year.[20] This post has come to be called Fort Desha, and is the location from which Layssard wrote his letters in 1758. It is also the place described by Pittman in 1765,[21] though some have suggested, wrongly, that he did not know what he was talking about.[22] De Villiers called it Fort St. Louis.[23]

In March of 1779 the Post was moved back to *Écores Rouges* in the hopes of establishing a more stable agricultural community. De Villiers named the place Post Carlos

19. De Villiers to Gálvez, August 3, 1777, AGI, PC, *leg.* 190. The new fort there was complete by late in 1758. ANC, C¹³ᴬ 42:121.

20. For an engineer's report on the construction of the new fort and repairs made there in 1758 made necessary by flooding and "*un coup de vent*" (presumably a tornado), *see* ANC, C¹³ᴬ 40:349–50 (Transcript in Little Rock Public Library).

21. P. PITTMAN, *supra* note 5, at 40–41.

22. *See, e.g.*, Faye, *supra* note 10, at 681, n. 45. This post appears on Nuttall's 1819 map. *See* T. NUTTALL, A JOURNAL OF TRAVELS INTO THE ARKANSAS TERRITORY DURING THE YEAR 1819 74–75 (S. LOTTINVILLE ed., 1980). Nuttall also noted that the Post had been located near Lake Dumond at one time, but he got his chronology wrong. He asserted that the first establishment was the one below the forks: "The first attempt at settlement on the banks of the Arkansas, was begun a few miles below the bayou which communicates with White River. An extraordinary inundation occasioned the removal of the garrison to the borders of the lagoon near Madame Gordon's [*i.e.*, Lake Dumond], and again disturbed by an overflow, they at length chose the present site of Arkansas." *Id.* at 87. The first number of the *Arkansas Gazette* noted that "two places on the river below were attempted for the establishment of Spanish garrisons, but were drowned out by the high water." *Ark. Gaz.*, November 20, 1819, p. 2, col. 2. Both the Gazette and the Nuttall accounts are accurate in that they ascribe only two previous locations to the Post, and Nuttall is correct about where they were located. But these accounts also contain some inaccuracies.

23. *See* text, *supra* at 84.

III.[24] Here the Post remained until its disappearance as a real town in the 1930s. The Post was never located at the mouth of the Arkansas as has been suggested.[25]

24. *See* text, *supra* at 90.

25. *See, e.g.*, Faye, *supra* note 10, at 640; Faye, *The Arkansas Post of Louisiana: Spanish Domination*, 27 LHQ 629, 641 (1944). In 1820 Thomas Nuttall passed the mouth of the Arkansas and in his book he wrote that a "house now . . . stands on the otherwise deserted spot where once was garrisoned the troops of France, at the terminating point of the river." T. NUTTALL, *supra* note 22, at 249. He was, in fact, right since this is where La Boulaye first camped in 1721 before removing upriver to Law's colony. *See* text, *supra* at 9. Tonti's post never had a garrison associated with it so this is hardly a reference to the 1686 post as Nuttall's editor has maintained. *See* T. NUTTALL *supra* note 22, at 249, n. 16. Tonti's post was nowhere near the mouth of the Arkansas. *See* Ford, *supra* note 1.

Appendix III

Judges of the Arkansas
1686–1808[1]

I. French Domination

1. 1686–1699   Henry de Tonti[2]

2. August, 1721 to   Jean-Baptiste Ménard,
   March, 1722   Martin Merrick, and
        Labro[3]

3. March, 1722 to   Bertrand Dufresne, Sieur
   1726   du Demaine[3]

4. 1726 to 1731   Unknown[4]

[Note: From Sept. 20, 1721 to March, 1725, Lieutenant La Boulaye was commandant of the French

1. This list draws on a very large number of sources for its content. Chief among them are Faye, *The Arkansas Post of Louisiana: French Domination*, 26 LHQ 633 (1943); Faye, *The Arkansas Post of Louisiana: Spanish Domination*, 27 LHQ 529 (1944); Thomas, "The Arkansas Post of Louisiana, 1683–1783" (M.A. Thesis, University of California, 1948); and Din, *Arkansas Post in the American Revolution*, 40 AHQ 3 (1981).

2. Tonti doubtless had judicial authority since he was the feudal lord of Arkansas, but there is no evidence that he ever held court there. *See* text, *supra* at 15–16.

3. In May of 1722 a provincial council was established in St. Louis, with jurisdiction over the Arkansas settlement. But it is doubtful that this council ever adjudicated Arkansas cases. It seems more likely that those in charge of Law's colony did so. *See* text, *supra* at 14–15.

4. Father Du Poisson, the Jesuit missionary resident from 1727 to 1729, no doubt did his best to mediate and settle disputes. *See* text, *su-*

garrison at Arkansas. It is not clear what part, if any, he played in the resolution of civil disputes. In 1731 civil and military authority were combined in the commandant of the garrison.]

5.	Late in 1731 to 1734	First Ensign De Coulange
6.	1734 to 1739	First Ensign Jean Ste. Thérèse de Langloiserie
7.	1739 to Autumn, 1748	Lieutenant Jean-François Tisserant de Montcharvaux
8.	Autumn, 1748 to 1751	First Ensign Louis-Xavier-Martin Delinó de Chalmette
9.	1751 to August, 1753	Lieutenant Paul Augustin le Pelletier de La Houssaye
10.	August, 1753 to 1757	Captain De Reggio
11.	1757 to 1763	Captain De Gamon de La Rochette
12.	1763 (temporary)	First Ensign De Brichet
13.	Sept. 27, 1763 to Spring, 1764	Captain Pierre Marie Caberet de Trépi
14.	Spring, 1764 to 1766	Ensign Le Gros de Grandcour

---

pra p. 15. There seems to have been no other civil government for Arkansas during this period except for what might have been provided by the Illinois provincial council.

II. Spanish Domination

1.	1766 to February, 1768	Ensign Le Gros de Grandcour
2.	February, 1768 to December 13, 1769	Captain Alexandre de Clouet
3.	December 13, 1769 to December 10, 1770	Captain François Demasellière
4.	December 10, 1770 to April 29, 1771	Lieutenant Josef Orieta
5.	April 29, 1771 to April 18, 1774	Captain Fernando de Leyba
6.	April 18, 1774 to June 16, 1776	Captain Josef Orieta
7.	June 16, 1776 to September 7, 1776	Sergeant Garcia (*ad interim*)
8.	September 7, 1776 to June 19, 1782	Captain Balthazar de Villiers
9.	June 19, 1782 to January 7, 1783	Lieutenant Luis de Villars
10.	January 7, 1783 to March, 1787	Captain Jacobo Dubreuil Saint-Cyr
11.	March, 1787 to July, 1790	Captain Josef Vallière
12.	July, 1790 to July 11, 1794	Captain Juan Ignace Delinó de Chalmette
13.	July 11, 1794 to Summer, 1802	Captain Carlos de Villemont
14.	Summer, 1802 to March 23, 1804	Captain Francisco Caso y Luengo

III. American Domination

1. March 23, 1804 to   Lieutenant James B.
   March, 1805   Many

2. March, 1805 to   Stephen Worrel
   June(?), 1805

3. June(?), 1805 to ?   Robert Weir Osborn

4. ? to November 15, 1808   Captain George
   Armistead

Appendix IV

Number of *Habitants* at Arkansas Post, 1686–1798, Free and Slave

(Numbers above bars refer to notes.)

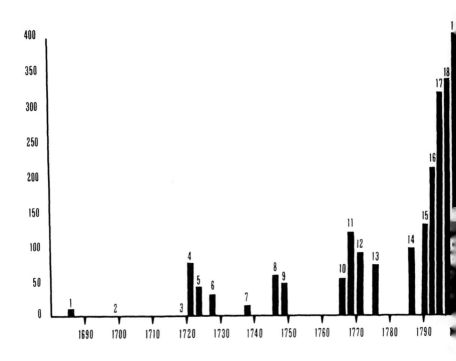

1. *1686.* Six Frenchmen first occupied Tonti's post in 1686; only two of them were left when Joutel visited there in 1687. Faye, *The Arkansas Post of Louisiana: French Domination*, 26 LHQ 633 at 635 (1943).

2. *1699.* Tonti's post was abandoned by 1699. *See* 18 COLLECTIONS OF THE WISCONSIN HISTORICAL SOCIETY 427, n. 37 (1908); 1 M. GIRAUD, HISTOIRE DE LA LOUISIANE FRANÇAISE 8 (J. LAMBERT trans., 1974).

3. *1721.* There were no French settlers in Arkansas in 1721 before the

arrival of Law's colonists in August of that year. *See* J. DELANGLEZ, THE FRENCH JESUITS IN LOWER LOUISIANA 434 (1935).

4. *1721*. There were about eighty Frenchmen in the party which landed at the Arkansas in August of 1721. ANC, G¹, 464. (Transcript in Little Rock Public Library.)

5. *Feb. 18, 1723*. Forty-one whites and six slaves occupied the Arkansas at this time. They were divided into two groups: Fifteen whites and six slaves at Law's Concession; twenty-six whites (including four bondsmen) two leagues up the river where the troops were. *Les Arkansas du 18. Fever 1723. Rescensement.*, Louisiana History Center, Louisiana State Museum, New Orleans; 4 M. GIRAUD, HISTOIRE DE LA LOUISIANE FRANÇAISE 274 (1974). The version of this census appearing in C. MADUELL, THE CENSUS TABLES FOR THE FRENCH COLONY OF LOUISIANA FROM 1688 THROUGH 1732 at 30 (1972) is misleading and contains erroneous information. A census of Jan. 1, 1726, reported only fifteen *habitants*, but this was probably just at Law's concession proper. The census included Le Sieur Dufresne and one Indian slave. *Rescencement, Les Arkansas, sur la droitte en descendant, Jan. 1, 1726.*, Louisiana History Center, Louisiana State Museum, New Orleans.

6. *1727*. In this year Father Du Poisson estimated the European population at the Arkansas at thirty. J. DELANGLEZ, *supra* note 3, at 436.

7. *1739*. There were said to be three *habitants* at Arkansas post at this time. Assuming that each had a family and that the average family size was four, there would have been only twelve white persons resident at the Arkansas. Governor Bienville wrote that "our fort of the Arkansas is falling in ruins; there are only a missionary and three *habitans* there who do nothing." *See Journal of Father Vitry of the Society of Jesus, Army Chaplain during the War Against the Chickasaw*, 28 MID-AMERICA 30 at 34, n. 25 (1941).

8. *1746*. In this year there were said to be a dozen male *habitants* and ten black slaves at the Post. Assuming an average family size of four, the total population at this time would have been fifty-eight. *See Mémoire sur l'État de la Colonie de la Louisiane en 1746*, ANC, C¹³ᴬ 30:242 at 249 (Transcript at Little Rock Public Library.)

9. *1749*. Arkansas Post contained at this time thirty-one whites, fourteen slaves, three horses, twenty-nine bulls and steers, sixty cows, and twenty-nine pigs. *See Resancement General des habitants, voyageurs, femmes, enfans, esclaves, chevaux, beufs, vaches, cochons, etc. de Poste des Akansa, 1749.* Vaudreuil Papers, Lo. 200, Huntington Library, San Marino, CA.

10. *May 22, 1766*. There were forty whites and ten slaves at the Arkansas at this time according to the census of May 22, 1766. See

J. VOORHIES, SOME LATE EIGHTEENTH-CENTURY LOUISIANIANS, CENSUS RECORDS OF THE COLONY, 1758–1796, 157 (1973). Captain Harry Gordon in October of 1766 remarked that "the few Banditti of Arkansas don't deserve the name of settlement"; and two months later George Morgan remarked of the Post as he passed through that it contained "about 10 Families in the neighborhood of the Indian Village, which has near 200 Families." THE NEW REGIME, 1765–1767, 11 ILLINOIS HISTORICAL COLLECTIONS 303, 442 (1916).

11. *December 2, 1768.* A census taken at this time claimed a population of eighty-nine whites and thirty-seven slaves for Arkansas Post. *Recensement des habitants, femmes, enfants, et esclaves du Poste des Arkansas,* AGI, PC, *leg.* 107. But this included a family of five which, the census said was "going to settle at the Arkansas," and the commandant's wife, five sons, and five slaves were reported to be in New Orleans; thus the actual number of residents was seventy-eight whites and thirty-two slaves. A census of Jan. 5, 1770, showed eighty-eight whites; the slave population was not given. *See Estada presente de todo los inhabitantes del puesto de los Arkancas . . .* AGI, PC, *leg.* 107.

12. *September 2, 1771.* The Louisiana census of this date showed sixty-two whites and eleven slaves at the Arkansas. 1 L. KINNAIRD, SPAIN IN THE MISSISSIPPI VALLEY, 1765–1794, 196 (1949).

13. *1777.* On August 3, 1777, De Villiers reported fifty whites and eleven slaves at Arkansas Post. *See Dénombremant du Poste des Arkansas et de la Nation Sauvage de ce Nom . . . ,* AGI, PC, *leg.* 190.

14. *1788.* The general Louisiana Census for this year gave Arkansas a population of seventy-five free persons and forty-four slaves.

15. *1791.* 107 free persons and thirty-six slaves were reported at the Post for this year. *Rescencement du Poste des Arkansas de l'Anée 1791,* AGI, PC, *leg.* 2365.

16. *1793.* There were 167 free persons and thirty-one slaves reported at Arkansas this year. *Padron del Puesto de Arkansas,* AGI, PC, *leg.* 123.

17. *1794.* A large jump in population occurred in the year 1794. At the end of that year there were 274 free persons and forty-four slaves listed in the census. *See Padron del Puesto de Arkanzas,* AGI, PC, *leg.* 2364.

18. *1796.* 282 free persons and forty-two slaves were reported resident at the Post in this year. *See Padron del Puesto de Arkanzas,* AGI, PC, *leg.* 2364.

19. *1798.* The last census surviving from the Spanish period gave Arkansas Post a free population of 344 and a slave population of fifty-six. *See Padron de Puesto de Arkancas,* AGI, PC, *leg.* 2365.

Appendix V

An Early Opinion of an Arkansas Trial Court

The opinion printed below merits notice because it is apparently the oldest surviving opinion of an Arkansas trial judge.[1] It was delivered in 1824 in a suit in equity, evidently an accounting between partners, which was brought by James Hamilton against William Montgomery in 1823.

Relatively little of relevance can be discovered about the plaintiff James Hamilton. He was a merchant in Arkansas Post at least as early as November of 1821 when he moved into the "[s]tore lately occupied by Messrs. Johnston [and] Armstrong."[2] Montgomery, on the other hand, is quite a well-known character. From 1819 until 1821 he operated a tavern at the Post which was an important gathering place:[3] A muster of the territorial militia was held there on November 25, 1820,[4] and the village trustees were elected

---

1. Some appellate opinions of the Superior Court of the Territory of Arkansas from 1819–1836 were published in 1856 and are called HEMP-STEAD'S REPORTS.

The opinion below appears to be in the hand of a clerk, whose punctuation, when there was any, was erratic. I have added punctuation and divided the opinion into paragraphs since this did not seem to be taking liberties with the work of the judge himself. Some of the words, after 160 years, are illegible, and I have indicated these with a question mark.

2. *Arkansas Gazette*, Nov. 3, 1821, at 3, col. 4.

3. *See generally*, E. BEARSS, MONTGOMERY'S TAVERN AND JOHNSTON AND ARMSTRONG'S STORE (1971); P. MARTIN, AN INQUIRY INTO THE LOCATIONS AND CHARACTERISTICS OF JACOB BRIGHT'S TRADING HOUSE AND WILLIAM MONTGOMERY'S TAVERN (1977).

4. *Arkansas Gazette*, Nov. 18, 1820, at 3, col. 4.

there in January of the following year.[5] The first regular legislative assembly for the Territory of Arkansas met in February of 1820 in two rooms furnished by Montgomery, perhaps at his tavern.[6]

Important people travelling through the territory often stopped at Montgomery's establishment. In 1820, the famous American ornithologist, John James Audubon, who stayed there two nights, said that it was "the Only Tavern in the Country."[7] Audubon does not mention Montgomery, but he found his wife "a handsome Woman of good Manners and rather superior to those in her rank of Life."[8] In 1821 Montgomery moved to the confluence of the White and Mississippi rivers, a place which was thereafter known as Montgomery's Point.[9] The Point became in time a famous steampoint landing. In 1828 General Andrew Jackson stopped there on his way to New Orleans and was entertained by Montgomery; the next year, President Andrew Jackson appointed him a Brigadier General in the militia.[10]

---

5. *Arkansas Gazette*, Jan. 20, 1821, at 3, col. 1.

6. E. BEARSS, *supra* note 3, at 21.

7. AUDUBON'S AMERICA 146 (D. PEATTIE ed., 1940).

8. *Id.*

9. P. MARTIN, *supra* note 3, at 5.

10. Herndon, *A Little of what Arkansas was like a Hundred Years Ago*, 3 AHQ 97, 123 (1944). The tavern at the Point was "built in the style of French houses, and was commonly thought of as a mansion for its day." *Id.* at 121. It is said to have been erected soon after the turn of the century by Francis D'Armand, a French trader who, it is claimed, settled at the point in 1766. Scully, *Across Arkansas in 1844*, 13 AHQ 31, 36 at n. 8 (1954). But I have seen no mention of D'Armand in the Spanish records and this seems altogether odd if he in fact had an establishment for so long at the point. In 1832 some of the old log cabins said to have been erected by D'Armand in 1766 were still standing. W. POPE, EARLY DAYS IN ARKANSAS 62 (1895).

Judge Thomas P. Eskridge, the author of the opinion, was a Virginian who had come to Arkansas in 1820.[11] He was appointed circuit court judge by Acting Governor Robert Crittenden shortly after his arrival, and in January of 1823 he announced his candidacy for territorial representative to Congress.[12] But the next week he withdrew, apparently as a favor to Crittenden, who had decided to support Henry W. Conway for the post.[13] Eskridge became a judge of the Superior Court of the Territory in 1827[14] where he served until shortly before his death in December of 1835. His obituary in the Arkansas Gazette contains very little information of interest,[15] and though a few orders relative to his estate were entered from 1837 to

11. M. Ross, Arkansas Gazette: The Early Years, 1819–1866, 51 (1969).

12. Id.

13. Id.

14. J. Shinn, Pioneers and Makers of Arkansas 201 (1908).

15. On December 15, 1835, the Arkansas Gazette ran the following obituary of Eskridge:

The painful duty devolves on us today, of announcing the death of another of our distinguished citizens. The Hon. Thomas P. Eskridge, late one of the Judges of the Superior Court of this Territory, and formerly a Judge of the Circuit Court, is no more. He died at his residence in Crittenden County, week before last, after a short illness, of cholera morbus—leaving an amiable and interesting family to mourn the loss of a most affectionate husband and father, and a numerous circle of friends and acquaintances, the loss of a sincere and devoted friend, and intelligent and enterprising citizen. Judge Eskridge was a native of the State of Virginia, (of Stanton, we believe), from whence he emigrated to Arkansas in 1821, since which time he has been a citizen of our Territory. He had been a member of the Presbyterian Church for several years, and sustained the character of a sincere christian and an exemplary and useful man.

Arkansas Gazette, Dec. 15, 1835, at 3, col. 1.

1839, no will was recorded and no inventory of his property was filed.[16] Eskridge was not among the most prominent of Arkansas's territorial judges. He passed virtually unnoticed and his background is thus obscure. Probably he had learned his law as a clerk to a Virginia lawyer, although even this is uncertain. He did not rank high in popular estimation, did not attract the attention of the press or the public, and later writers have all but ignored him. In fact, he is the only judge of the Superior Court of Arkansas who does not rate a full-fledged biography in any of the various Arkansas histories. He chose to live in Crittenden County, out of the limelight, evidently preferring to leave politics and matters of public visibility to others. But the opinion printed below reveals that he was a thoughtful craftsman, well-trained, and more than competent. The opinion is not brilliant, nor can it be called creative. Still less is it sprightly or animated. But it reveals an acquaintance with many of the best authorities, both English and American, and the quotation from Judge Roane (Eskridge's fellow Virginian) shows the judge's appreciation at least of the well-turned phrase. More importantly, it demonstrates that only five years after Arkansas had become a territory even a middling judge could be conscientious, well-educated, and workmanlike. It is more than we have the right to expect

16. Mary B. Eskridge, "widow and relict of Thomas P. Eskridge," qualified as executrix for him on January 7, 1837. WILL RECORD, VOLUME A, 1826–1852, CRITTENDEN COUNTY (on microfilm at Arkansas History Commission, Little Rock). In the 1837 April term of the County Court two claims were allowed against the estate. Another claim was allowed in January of 1839. In the July term of that year all claims were ordered to be paid out of Eskridge's personalty. Finally, on October 31, 1839 the court ordered the sureties on Mrs. Eskridge's bond to show cause why judgment should not be entered against them in the amount of the claims, as the order of payment had not been obeyed. No further proceedings in this estate have been discovered.

of such a time and place, and the judge's learning stands in strong contrast to the situation which prevailed in Arkansas only ten years before when the bench had been composed entirely of laymen totally unfamiliar with the form and substance of the law. This state of affairs had existed for more than 100 years, as a lawyer did not sit on an Arkansas bench until 1814.[17] Eskridge's opinion demonstrates a sophisticated knowledge of the recondite issues which plague the relationship between law and equity, difficulties which even today generate learned debate.

It is equally noteworthy that at the end of his opinion the good judge upbraids losing counsel for his lack of learning; and he opines in his last sentence that "most cases which are lost may be ascribed to the inattentions of the Bar." This view, and Eskridge's manner of expressing it, cannot have endeared him to all the members of the bar, and spreading it upon the public record was, at the least, somewhat impolite if not impolitic. But it is, in any case, indicative of the standards to which the members of the Arkansas bar were expected to adhere in 1824. Remarks of this sort are not uncommon in other parts of the country during this period, and they reflect a class war that was being waged at the time in an effort to make the law a learned

17. As we noted *supra* at p. 174–75, the first lawyer to sit on an Arkansas court was George C. Bullitt of Ste. Genevieve, Missouri who was appointed pursuant to an Act of Congress of January 17, 1814, creating "an additional judge for the Missouri Territory . . . who shall reside at or near the Village of Arkansas." Bullitt had been admitted by the General Court of the Territory of Indiana when it met in St. Louis on October 1, 1804. W. ENGLISH, THE PIONEER LAWYER AND JURIST IN MISSOURI 25 (1947). He served on the first board of the Ste. Genevieve Academy appointed in 1808 (*id.* at 128) and "was a successful politician but never a very active lawyer" in Ste. Genevieve (*id.* at 25–26). He was a member of the first House of Representatives of the Territory of Missouri. 3 L. HOUCK, A HISTORY OF MISSOURI 3 (1908). When Arkansas became a territory in 1819, Bullitt's court was abolished and he left soon thereafter.

profession. In an extremely short time the law in Arkansas was becoming professionalized.

Circuit Court Records of Arkansas County, 1824–1829 (January term, 1824) (On microfilm at Arkansas History Commission, Little Rock. Roll 59. p. 186)

James Hamilton
    vs.   }   Chancery
William Montgomery

A motion has been made by Mr. Sevier, counsel for the defendant, to dismiss the bill in this case, on the ground that an affidavit has not been annexed to it, or, in other words, because the truth of it has not been sworn to by the plaintiff.

This is a bill for discovery and relief. In some respects every bill may be said to be a bill of discovery, but there are bills purely so and known in practice by the denomination of bills of discovery, and in such bill a Court of Equity is only called upon to compel a discovery in order to enable the plaintiff to proceed at law; and having done so its power ceases. There are also bills for discovery & relief, and in such a Court of Equity is not only called upon for discovery but relief also. The bill under consideration is of that character & to such it has always been considered necessary to have an affidavit annexed. But independent of this there is a general rule in Court of Equity as to the affixture of an affidavit to a bill, and which rule it seems is applicable to the present case. The rule is this, that whenever the bill has a tendency to evoke the jurisdiction from a Court of Law to a Court of Equity it is necessary to have an affadivit annexed to it. See Mitford 52,[18] Barton's

18. J. Mitford, Treatise on the Pleadings in Suits in the Court of Chancery by English Bill 52 (1792).

Equity 53,[19] & 1 Equity Cases Abridged 13.[20] The Court should here stop as the point last decided is conclusive as to the [?] of the bill, & therefore an expression of an opinion on the other points suggested would be extra judicial, not being fairly before the court. However, as an opinion has been asked, and as such an opinion may operate in favor of the parties by exempting them from future costs and vexation, it cannot reasonably be withheld.

First it is contended that there is no equity in the bill, and secondly that there has been a trial at law upon the merits & that the same is conclusive against the plaintiff. The first point was certainly made under a total misapprehension of the jurisdiction of a Court of Chancery. The jurisdiction of a Court of Chancery is either assistant to, concurrent with, or exclusive of that of a Court of Law. It is assistant to by removing impediments to a fair decision at Law, as by compelling a discovery, by perpetuating testimony, etc. It is concurrent with in cases of fraud, accident, mistakes, account, partitions, and dower; and its jurisdiction is exclusive in most matters of trust, trusts being the mere creatures of Equity. The boundary between the two jurisdictions was at one time in greater uncertainty than any other legal subject. The line of demarcation is now however fixed and certain, & it may be remarked that in modern times there has been an infinitely greater conformity of decision in the Courts of Chancery than those of Law. But from the earliest period the Courts of Chancery have exercised concur-

19. C. Barton, History of a Suit in Equity from its Commencement to its Final Termination 53 (1796).

20. Eskridge is using the three-volume Dublin edition of Equity Cases Abridged which appeared in 1792. Since I do not have that edition ready to hand, it has not been possible to supply citations to it. The earlier two-volume edition is reproduced in volumes 21 and 22 of English Reports.

rent jurisdiction with Courts of Law in matters of account, & whenever a surety case has been made out for relief, relief has never been denied. See Ludlow vs. Simond, 2 Caines Cases in Equity.[21] It is there said that Equity has jurisdiction in all matters of account, notwithstanding there is relief also at law, & though the relief at law may be had, yet if it be doubtful or difficult Equity will interpose. See also—Russell vs. Kennedy & Bruce, 9 John. Reports 1170.[22] The Court of Chancery has [*i.e.*, having] concurrent jurisdiction with Courts of Law in all matters of account, there can be no doubt thus that the bill under consideration presents a fair and legitimate case for the interposition of a Court of Equity. It indeed makes one of the strongest cases within the recollection of the Court.

But admitting this, it is contended secondly that the Plaintiff by having made his election to proceed at law, & there having had a trial by jury upon the merits, has thereby precluded himself from coming into a Court of Equity. The Court feels no kind of difficulty in pronouncing that he has. Although it is abundantly manifest that the plaintiff might, in the first instance, have resorted to Equity, it is now too late after having made his election to take a trial at law. Why, it may be inquired, did not the plaintiff, as he undoubtedly had a right to do, in the Court of Law, when he discovered that the defendant was about to avail himself of all legal advantages, suffer a non suit & thereby reserve to himself the right of coming into a Court of Equity? Having failed to do so, he cannot, with any kind of plausibility, much less of right, avail himself of his own negligence and inattention as a ground of coming here. It is a rule of Equity, settled by a long & uniform succession of decisions, that where a defendant in a Court of Law through negligence and inattention fails to avail himself a [?] de-

21. Ludlow v. Simond, 2 Cai. Cas. (N.Y., 1805).
22. *See supra* note 20.

fense at law he cannot afterwards resort to Equity. This rule, it is apprehended, applies with equal, if not greater force to the case of plaintiffs. See Linply's Exect. v. Doby, 1 Wash. 185;[23] Atkyns 233, 215 referred to [in] Mitford, page 208, 9, 10;[24] 3 Equity Cases at 524, 5, 6;[25] 3 Call 351;[26] Cunnigham vs. Caldwell, Hardin 136;[27] Long vs. Colston, 1 Hening & Munford 110.[28] The case from Wash. is conclusive on the subject of election. The subject matter of controversy in the case from H & M was certain covenants between Long & Colston, which clearly furnished ground for the interposition of a Court of Equity, by way of decreeing a specific performance. Long, however, made his election to proceed at law in the action of covenant for damages & Colston, before the termination of the suit at law, filed his bill in the High Court of Chancery for an injunction and relief. The Court of Appeals decided that Long, having made his election to proceed at law for damages, could not be forced into Chancery unless upon strong & peculiar circumstances of equity; from which decision it would appear that it is only in extraordinary cases that a defendant in a Court of Law can force a plaintiff thence into a Court of Equity. With much less propriety, then, can the Plaintiff, after full trial there upon the merits by jury, come here. The celebrated Judge Roane in the course of his decision in the above case, speaking of the jurisdiction of a Court of Equity and the necessity of restricting it to its proper sphere, makes the following pointed remarks which may be considered as applicable to the case under consideration, as well as to all cases brought to a Court of Equity after a trial by jury upon the merits. "But," says he, "this

23. Tarpley's Administrator v. Dobyns, 1 Wash. 185 (Va. 1793).
24. Not identified.
25. See supra note 20.
26. Probably Terrell v. Dick, 1 Call 346 (Va. 1799) is meant.
27. Cunningham v. Caldwell, 3 Ky. 123 (1807).
28. Long v. Colston, 1 Hen. & M. 110 (Va. 1806).

jurisdiction must have its limits. It ought not to engulph and destroy the salutary jurisdiction of the Common Law. I wish not to see this small and precious germ, which within times not far remote took root and was with difficulty nourished as a wholesome & goodly plant yielding its friendly aid to the soil in which it grew, now outstrip its proper size, outrage its own nature, and like the famed Upas tree by its deleterious effluvia administer death and destruction round. I wish not to yield up everything to that encroaching jurisdiction, which knows not the inestimable trial by jury, and is blind to the incalculable superiority of viva voce testimony."[29] The circumstances of the plaintiff having evaded to mention in his bill the trial at law certainly cannot avail him any valuable purpose, for it is competent for the defendant to plead that fact, which would be conclusive. So, on the other hand, if the facts of the former trial appeared on the face of the bill, the defendant may demur which would be equally conclusive in his favor.

From the best consideration which the Court has been able to give this case, it is constrained, however reluctantly, to say that the Plaintiff is wholly without relief both at law and in equity. The Plaintiff's case may and probably does involve considerations of extreme hardship, but it is the duty of the court to administer the law as it exists. It cannot alter it, nor can it depart from it as evidenced by the decisions of the sages of the law, not only from England but our own country, without justly incurring the imputation not only of ignorance but of presumptuous stupidity. The court may be permitted to remark in conclusion that it hopes that this decision may operate as a salutary admonition to the gentlemen of the Bar. It is a fact too well attested to admit of doubt that most cases which are lost may be ascribed to the inattentions of the Bar.

Let the bill be dismissed at the cost of the plaintiff.

29. *Id.* at 130.

Index

CPSIA information can be obtained
at www.ICGtesting.com
Printed in the USA
FFOW02n2153271016
28820FF